IDENTITY DESIGNS

THE ARNOLD AND CAROLINE ROSE BOOK SERIES
OF THE AMERICAN SOCIOLOGICAL ASSOCIATION

IDENTITY DESIGNS

The Sights and Sounds of a Nation

KAREN A. CERULO

RUTGERS UNIVERSITY PRESS
New Brunswick, New Jersey

Library of Congress Cataloging-in-Publication Data

Cerulo, Karen A.
    Identity designs : the sights and sounds of a nation / Karen A.
Cerulo.
        p.   cm. — (Arnold and Caroline Rose book series of the
American Sociological Association)
    Includes bibliographical references and index.
    ISBN 0-8135-2211-0
    1. Emblems, National. 2. National characteristics. 3. Symbolism
in politics. I. Title. II. Series.
JC345.C45   1995
306.2—dc20   95-4326
                                                            CIP

British Cataloging-in-Publication information available

For Carmela Nicastro

CONTENTS

CONTENTS

FIGURES AND TABLES

Figures

Tables

ACKNOWLEDGMENTS

THIS BOOK REPRESENTS the culmination of a long, evolving research agenda. During that journey, the following people took time from their all-too-busy schedules to read my work and respond to it in a meaningful way: Sam Baily, Al Bergesen, Judith Blau, John Boli, Harry Bredemeier, Daniel Chirot, Randall Collins, Paul DiMaggio, Priscilla Ferguson, Judy Friedman, Larry Gross, Ellen Idler, Michèle Lamont, Tim Futing Liao, Carolin Marvin, John Meyer, Marty Oppenheimer, Pat Roos, Tom Rudel, Michael Schudson, Barry Schwartz, Randy Smith, Sheldon Stryker, Ann Swidler, Andrea Tyree, Susan Watkins, Richard Williams, and Charles Wright.

Among the many who have made an impact upon this work, four individuals deserve special mention for their long-term contributions to my intellectual development: Jim Beniger, who convinced me that symbolic communication deserved my most serious intellectual attention; Janet Ruane, who helped me recognize sociology in every part of the everyday; Bob Wuthnow, who encouraged me to be true to my intellectual interests and showed me how to link these interests to the mainstream discourse; and Eviatar Zerubavel, who softened and enriched my sociological gaze and always encourages my sociological imagination. Their wisdom and their friendship have been my blessing.

I am grateful for two Rutgers University Research Council Grants and a Douglass College Fellows Opportunity Grant that provided much-needed research funds for this project. Finally, many thanks go to Lisa Bonchek and Joan Manley for help with clerical tasks; Kate Harrie at Rutgers for her editorial advice; copyeditor Karin Kaufman for her fine work; Judy Gerson, Maureen and Francis Gorman, Sarah Hewins, Beth Kosiak, and Mary Ruane for brews, burgers, pep talks, and overall kindness; and to Judith Blau, whose excellence as an editor made my initiation to the world of book publishing a sheer pleasure.

INTRODUCTION

National Symbols

IN 1965, THE GOVERNMENT of Guyana initiated a special competition—a "search" for a new national flag. Anticipating independence in 1966, political leaders invited the public to submit original
designs intended to represent the new nation's identity. Response
was enthusiastic, and the national flag committee reviewed scores of
offerings. Ultimately, the committee was drawn to a green-yellow-
red flag design. Yet although that submission was favored over all
others, committee members were hesitant to finalize the selection.
Something about the flag seemed less than perfect. After some discussion, one member suggested that the colors of the flag be reversed
to a red-yellow-green ordering, with two borders of black and white
added to the design. Upon doing so, the committee found that the
flag suddenly took on a clear sense of correctness, and the amended
design was enthusiastically adopted as *the* fitting representation of
the nation's character.[1]

Communication by Design

What factors accounted for the choice of this red-yellow-green
design over all other alternatives? What was it about these colors,
and the order in which they were presented, that rendered the final
version of the Guyanese flag the one and only suitable representation

of the nation? In essence, these are the questions addressed by this book. Using national symbols (particularly anthems and flags) as a case study, my work highlights the social factors that guide the process of collective symbolization. In this book, I explore the elements that lead collectives to embrace certain symbols and eliminate others—an issue in keeping with concerns central to sociologists of culture (see, e.g., Beisel 1993, DeVault 1990, Griswold 1987, Lamont 1987, Schudson 1989, Sewell 1992). In addition, I chart the role of design in the selection of symbolic images. Building on a well-established semiotic tradition,[2] my research demonstrates that symbols are chosen not just for the messages they convey, but *how* they convey them.

The pages that follow reveal that the symbolic designs of a nation's identity are not simply the product of indigenous characteristics as conventional wisdom might suggest. Nor can these designs be solely credited to the specific, perhaps unique sociopolitical events that surround a symbol's adoption. Rather, this work moves beyond such considerations and demonstrates that the banners and songs by which nations represent themselves also are generated by broad social forces, forces that transcend the peculiarities of any one nation. In the pages that follow, I identify a set of social structural factors that delimit rules of symbolic expression within the global political community. In so doing, I illustrate patterns of design that emerge from adoption decisions waged in seemingly distinct historical moments. Further, this book suggests the benefits of adhering to these rules and explores the costs of violating them.

As we review the anthems and flags of the 180 nations in my sample, it will also become clear that the power of symbols is as much derived from their design as from their substance. Consider that every nation adopts national anthems and flags. The content of these symbols is necessarily similar, because anthems and flags are built from a limited vocabulary of colors, images, themes, and words.[3] Yet in perusing these symbols, it is the immense variation among them that continually strikes our eyes and ears. Clearly, these distinctions emerge not from the content of these symbols, but from the manner in which their content is combined. Because of this quality, national anthems and flags provide a site in which to study what I refer to as a symbol's *syntactic structure*—the design or configuration of a symbol's elements. In essence, a symbol's syntactic structure embodies the strategy by which its information is conveyed. With this premise in mind, I explore the factors that influence the selection of one strategy over another, and I examine the ways in which audiences respond to different configurations of their identity.

My emphasis on symbol syntax fills a gap in the literature. To date, most research on national symbols emphasizes their content. Such works isolate a symbol's elements, attempting to decipher the meaning of each component—that is, the red stripe of a flag symbolizes bloodshed, the upbeat anthem tempo depicts triumph over enemies, etc. To be sure, some studies have implicitly suggested the importance of attending to national symbol syntax (see, e.g., Eco 1985:173–74; Firth 1973:346; Nettl 1967:30), yet few have brought syntax to the foreground. This inattention to syntax is puzzling. Communication theorists, particularly semioticians, tell us that syntactic structure is just as important as content when it comes to communication effectiveness, as syntactic structure orders or organizes a symbol's various elements. Thus although the content of two symbols may be identical, repeating content elements, emphasizing one element over another, or altering the way in which the elements are combined can change both the meaning and the effectiveness of the symbol's message. Knowing this, a full understanding of any collective's symbolization process must include the study of their symbols' designs.

Why National Symbols?

Ostensibly, national symbols may seem little more than calling cards by which nations identify themselves. But on closer reflection, we must note that these symbols accomplish much more. National symbols objectify each nation's identity, making tangible that which might otherwise be impossible to meaningfully apprehend, and bringing a sense of concreteness to the highly abstract. As Michael Walzer writes, "[The nation] is invisible; it must be personified before it can be seen, symbolized before it can be loved, imagined before it can be conceived . . . these images [national symbols] provide a starting point for political thinking" (1967:194).[4] Thus, just as a weapon can objectify feelings of anger, or a romantic musical interlude can objectify feelings of love, national symbols codify the subjective nature of the nation: its moods, desires, and goals—its complexion. They function as modern totems that merge the mythical, sacred substance of the nation with a specified, manifest form, one that is grounded in the everyday experience of sight, sound, or touch. By blending subject and object,[5] national symbols move beyond simple representation of nation. In a very real sense, national symbols *become the nation.*

In the modern world, few other entities offer us the vantage point provided by national symbols. By studying them, we acquire sharp insight into the process of collective identity construction, and the tools and strategies by which that identity is communicated and sustained. Indeed, national symbols offer us a powerful case study in the symbolic communication of the collective self—a prototype illustrating the ways in which a collective, in a conscious and intentional way, chooses its voice.

Communicating Collective Identity

The development, adoption, and diffusion of national symbols follow a classic model of symbolic communication. Consider the elements of the process. Political elites constitute the *senders* of the communication. These senders formulate a specialized *message* and select the symbols that best embody the information. A nation's population, as well as the world community, represent the *targets* of the communication—audiences that senders hope to influence with their message. Finally, audience response to national symbols, the many purposes that the symbols serve, and the relative enthusiasm with which they are received, can be equated with communication *effects.*[6]

Traditional models of symbolic communication assume intention on the part of the sender. National symbol selection clearly exhibits this characteristic. National leaders purposely and meticulously select their message, emphasizing some information at the expense of other information. Indeed, every national symbol—anthems and flags as well as crests, currencies, monuments, mottoes, etc.—represents a carefully constructed, carefully projected image of identity that results from a conscious decision-making process. Of national anthems, for example, Joseph Zikmund writes, "We must recognize that in virtually all cases, it [constructing the message] *was done consciously* and that in the course of concentrating on some themes the country was generally de-emphasizing others" (1969:78, emphasis added). Sasha Weitman expresses similar sentiments with regard to flags: "The characteristics of the flag . . . are viewed as specific sign-vehicles through which the nation-state *communicates more or less specific messages about itself to others* (1973:335, emphasis added). Specific moments in history document the intentions of which these social scientists speak. When adopting coats of arms, for example, records show that rulers frequently alter these emblems so as to reflect significant changes within the nation. Note that after World War II, the Austrian government added a broken chain to the feet of its traditional eagle, signifying the nation's regained freedom. Similarly, when the Philippines moved from Spanish to American domination, they added the American eagle to their state arms (Talocci 1977:43, 107). National monuments, too, are frequently redefined according to the intentions of those in power. Consider that in 1830, citizenship was sufficient qualification for heroes included in the Walhalla, a monument dedicated to famous and patriotic Germans. In 1920 these criteria were explicitly restated, excluding all candidates of less than pure German extraction (Mosse 1975:55). Intention permeates the history of national flags as well. For example, the stars of the United States' "stars and stripes" were intentionally chosen so that growth of the new nation could be signified by the addition of starlike ornaments (Gordon 1915:192). These examples, and countless others, underscore the consciousness and purpose that drive the symbol selection process.

It is this communication model, one encompassing sender, message, target, and assumed intention, that informs the organization of this book. Indeed, each chapter addresses a portion of the process. Part 1 deals with the message itself. Specifically, chapter 1 charts the history of national symbols, explores the scope of their power, and suggests the many social functions they serve in the modern world. In so doing, the significance of symbols is substantiated and the breadth of their reach is itemized.

Chapter 2 explores the communicative power of symbol syntax. I begin by unfolding the literature on "structure as message," reviewing the importance of symbol design to effective communication and exploring the ways in which syntactic-level information is processed. The chapter then offers a distinct conceptualization of anthem and flag structure, one based on a continuum of basic versus embellished design. The basic-embellished continuum addresses the density, detail, and flexibility of a symbol's syntactic structure, elements that characterize the very nature of musical and graphic communication.

In Appendix A, I introduce a set of specially formulated indicators allowing researchers to systematically classify the relative embellishment of musical and graphic symbols. Thus, this section lays the groundwork for a combined qualitative/quantitative analysis of national anthems and flags. While some frown on the quantitative analysis of cultural objects, I urge readers to remain open-minded. My training in the arts enabled me to design measures of musical and graphic structure that accurately capture the very special nature of these "data." Using these indicators, it becomes possible to specify the syntactic alternatives available to those constructing national anthems and flags. Further, the measures enable us to pinpoint the precise range of variation among these symbol designs. Consequently, while this study provides in-depth information via specific historical examples, it also provides the breadth offered by aggregate comparative analysis.

Part 2 redirects our attention to senders. Here I explore both the intranational and international factors that guide political leaders in symbol selection. My argument suggests that the referents of a nation's identity delimit the strategies by which that identity is symbolized. As such, chapter 3 highlights several indigenous national traits—colonial history, historical point of emergence, the dominant ideological tradition, and regional location—and charts the impact of such traits on symbolic representation. For example, I consider the symbols of a nation's colonial power, determining if a nation's political leaders mirror the syntactic structures used by their former rulers. The chapter also explores a nation's temporal referents, ascertaining if the syntactic variation among anthems and flags is systematically related to the historical period in which the symbols are adopted. I approach concurrently established nations as cohorts with the potential to share forms of expression—designs that can bind nations within a cohort together while simultaneously distinguishing cohorts from one another. The chapter classifies each nation's ideological stance, exploring whether such philosophies influence a nation's symbolic representation of self. Finally, I consider the symbol structures of a nation's "neighbors" and explore the ways in which the designs of a particular region influence each nation's symbolic voice.

While chapter 3 reviews the role of a nation's "personal history" in symbol selection, chapter 4 directs us to the influence of broader social forces. Here, I explore the ways in which certain external stimulants of a nation's identity—specifically, a nation's socioeconomic position in the world—delimit the strategies by which national identity is symbolized. Using world-systems theory as a guide, I identify the various economic strata within the world community and explore the syntactic strategies favored within each location. The chapter compares the symbolic designs adopted by structurally equivalent nations and contrasts the designs selected by structurally disparate nations.

Chapter 5 connects sender and target, as it explores the ways in which political leaders tailor their symbol selections with reference to the condition of the nation's population. Specifically, I attend to a condition called *intranational focus*. Intranational focus refers to the point or points of attention to which a collective body is directed; it reflects the nature of the collective conscience. I argue that intranational focus is a by-product of social structural factors, and it is ultimately related to a population's form of social solidarity. So, for example, high intranational focus is associated with mechanical solidarity, with decreasing focus linked to organic solidarity, or in more severe cases, conditions of anomie. The communication literature clearly demonstrates that differentially focused audiences, those manifesting varying levels of cohesion, call for different communication strategies.[7] Building on that premise, chapter 5 specifies the conditions that lead to divergent levels of intranational focus and examines the national symbol structures that emerge from these variant conditions.

Part 3 brings the audience to the foreground, examining the ways in which collectives respond to differentially structured symbols. This section relies heavily on historical reports documenting audience reactions to national symbols, and personal testimony derived from more than 120 interviews with citizens of various nations. The data direct us to two specific dimensions of audience response. In chapter 6, I classify national symbol designs as normal or deviant, exploring the differential reception of each genre. Specifically, I trace the reaction of national audiences toward anthems and flags whose syntactic structures are "inappropriate" or deviant within the social contexts of their adoption. On the basis of this analysis, I detail the pros and cons of adopting symbols that contradict accepted norms of communication.

Chapter 7 addresses the rare phenomenon of symbol change. Although national symbols fall in and out of sync with the social conditions of their referents, few are ever changed. Indeed, less than 15 percent of the nations currently in existence have replaced their anthems and/or flags. I highlight the factors that instigate this unusual action; specifically, the conditions that can sever the link between a symbol and that which it signifies, leaving the symbol vulnerable to change.

In speaking of national symbols, Napoleon I once commented: "It is by such baubles that men are led" (Smith 1975:7). History testifies to the truth of this claim. For more than four hundred years, we have watched aggressors, protesters, and celebrants alike proclaim their causes amidst the aura of their nations' symbols. And in a world that some would argue is increasingly anomic and void of deep personal commitment, it is interesting to note that national symbols, modern totems with ancient roots, remain one of the few entities for which men and women continue to march, debate, fight, and die. Modern political leaders still drape their campaigns in such symbols, modern revolutionaries still defile the symbols of those they overthrow, protesters still argue their causes on symbolically charged sites. This book is devoted to understanding the source of this long-standing power—the ways in which national symbols are selected, the manner in which their meaning is conveyed, their potential effects, and the sustenance of their power.

How to Use This Book

This book employs a variety of styles in the study of national symbols, ranging from the in-depth analysis of historical documents and secondary sources, to detailed interviews, to structural measurement and statistical analysis—primarily multiple regression. Although the subject matter of this inquiry will appeal to a those from wide variety of intellectual traditions, the "comfort level" of readers, no doubt, will vary with regard to these methodological techniques.

Because statistical analysis generally proves most problematic for readers, this section serves to "flag" areas of the book that the non-quantitatively inclined may wish to avoid. For example, while the bulk of chapters 3 to 5 are qualitative in flavor, each chapter ends with reports of the statistical analyses used to test the premises forwarded in the study. Readers can garner the "bottom line" of these results by turning to the summary paragraphs of each section of the analysis. There, findings are italicized and stated in nontechnical terms. Further, I have summarized significant findings in each chapter's conclusion.

To enhance the book's readability, I frequently relegated methodological comments and elaborations, as well as certain statistical findings, to the endnotes. The mathematically minded will want to take the time to peruse these notes, but the qualitatively minded can choose to avoid them without seriously threatening the impact of the findings.

Finally, those interested in issues of measurement will find Appendix A a "must read" section. It is not, however, essential to the full understanding of the analyses. Again, the nonquantitatively oriented may wish to avoid this material.

1

WE PLEDGE ALLEGIANCE

WITH THE FALL of the monarchy in 1848, French revolutionaries proposed replacing the French tricolor with a plain red flag. The plan sparked bitter debate nationwide, culminating in a fight on the floor of the French parliament. But the flag controversy came to a grinding halt when met with the stirring words of poet Alphonse de Lamartine, then the French minister of Foreign Affairs: "The Tricolor has made a tour of the world with the name, the glory, and the liberty of the fatherland! If you take away from me the tricolor flag, you take away from me half the force of France, both here and abroad!" (quoted in Smith 1975:137).[1]

The Power of National Symbols

The passionate support invoked by Lamartine's use of the French flag exemplifies a much wider phenomenon. For the power of national symbols has repeatedly stirred and guided social action, even when other tools of motivation have failed. This chapter traces the history of that power, beginning with the totemic roots from which national symbols emerged. Further, I underscore the centrality of these symbols by exploring the many social functions they serve in the modern world. Finally, the pages that follow evidence the intention that underpins the construction and the projection of national symbols.

The Roots of National Symbols

National symbols represent a recent chapter in the long history of collective symbolism. Well before the emergence of nations, primitive tribes and clans searched for distinguishing, novel signs that would characterize each group exclusively. Thus, every clan developed *totems,* unique signifiers of the tribe that served as visible, material markers of the group's personality. Whatever their form—images of plants or animals, signs of nature—totems marked all that was a part of the clan: its possessions, sacred areas, and people. For primitive tribes, totems were a personification of the clan itself and they were viewed as a communal possession.

The royal families and ruling houses of the ancient and medieval periods promoted the practice of totemism as well. During these periods, however, the rules guiding the production and reception of these signs stood in contrast to those guiding the primitives.[2] While primitive clans merged with their totems, symbols of the ancient, classic, and medieval periods became the logos of the powerful, imposing the identity of the ruling class upon those they controlled. So, for example, ancient Egyptian leaders imposed emblems of the gods or insignia of the pharaohs on the citizen subjects they hoped to rally. Similarly, ancient Romans rulers maintained sole control over the civilization's glittering standards, symbols considered so sacred that they were guarded in temples when not in use. The powerful used such symbols to stimulate awe and terror, especially in those the Romans set out to conquer and amalgamate. During the medieval period, totems were so closely associated with a ruler's legitimacy that to capture the banner of an army or noble house was equated with stripping the ruler of his power. Captured banners were commonly displayed on the tombs of victorious generals or in the homes of those who had won them, serving as cues of the victor's dominion. All in all, the ancient, classic, and medieval periods represent a tenure of elitism in the history of collective symbolism. During these eras, a collective's leadership defined its symbolization.[3]

The birth of organized nations signified a new phase in totemic representation. During the nationalist period, initiated in the eighteenth century, every national government adopted its own special set of symbols—anthems, capital cities, crests, coins and currencies, flags, heroes, holidays, icons, monuments, mottoes, shrines, etc. From the onset, national symbols presented a synthesis of the totemic symbols that preceded them, for they *combined* the popularism of tribal totems with the elitism of ancient and medieval emblems. In this way, national symbols redemocratized collective symbolism.

On one hand, national symbols identify political leadership. When heads of state visit a foreign country, they are greeted with their national anthem. A nation announces its ambassador's presence by draping the embassy and its official vehicles with national flags and crests. National currencies both extol rulers to citizens and present leaders to those beyond national boundaries. In this way, national symbols mirror their ancient and medieval counterparts. Like their primitive predecessors, however, national symbols are wide-reaching, and hence, more democratic than ancient and medieval emblems—a critical distinction. The symbols of the nation are not the sole property of rulers and elites, but belong to all the people. They are designed to reflect general ideals rather than the lineage of monarchies and regimes; they refer to the unification of a people and the statement of their goals. These words, taken from publications of the Indian government, highlight the premise: "The National Flag, National Anthem, and National Emblem are the three symbols through which an independent country proclaims its identity and sovereignty . . . Yet, in themselves, they reflect *the entire background, thought, and culture of a nation*" (quoted in Firth 1973:341, emphasis added).

Various histories of national symbols illustrate their inclusive thrust. For example, experts contend that the American flag transformed the essence of its genre. Rather than representing a monarch or regime, the American flag was consciously designed as a graphic manifestation of a new political program. Born of the American Revolution (1775–83), the flag outlined the new structure of the governed—stripes and stars representing the distinctiveness, yet unity, of the states. All citizens were encouraged to display the American flag, making it a living symbol of the masses as opposed to a relic of rulers. Further, these features reportedly encouraged the popularization of many other national flags (Smith 1975:55). Similarly, early national anthems have been characterized by their mass appeal.[4] While enthusiastically embraced by rulers, the songs were often written or officially adopted because of their ability to capture and inspire the hearts of citizens. For example: "When Haydn visited England, he was so much interested in the effects of "God Save the Queen" on the public on solemn occasions, he resolved, after his return to Vienna, to present his fellow countrymen with a similar composition" (Sousa 1890:89). Unlike many of his other works, Haydn viewed the anthem as a "popular" song that would appeal to and move all citizens.

The democratic foundations of national symbols go well beyond flags and anthems. National monuments, for example, are often realized only through broad-based popular support. Such public support brought Germany's Hermannsdenkmal to completion. In 1863, Ernst Bandel (the monument's architect) wrote to the best pupils in every German high school, urging them to collect money for the monument's construction. The generous response of the students motivated Bandel to describe the Hermannsdenkmal as "the first national monument erected by the entire German people" (Mosse 1975:60–61). National icons, too, are usually chosen to represent the common citizen rather than the political elite. America's Uncle Sam, a case in point, emerged in response to a "public hunger for an earthy, paternal figure" (Zelinsky 1988:25). Uncle Sam was deemed a more accurate signifier of the American collective than the relatively ethereal and virginal Miss Liberty. Similarly, Maurice Agulhon (1981:115–21) tells us that female symbols of the French Republic were dubbed Marianne, as it was a common name meant to represent the common people.

Taken together, these examples underscore the relative inclusiveness of national symbols. Although created and adopted by an elite, these symbols appeal to the common characteristics, the shared history, and the passions and loyalties of the collective. Because of this wide embrace, national symbols come to serve a variety of important functions in the daily existence of the nation.

National Symbols in Action

The power of national symbols is illuminated by the important functions they serve. In this section, I highlight those functions, noting that their purpose remains remarkably stationary from nation to nation.

First and foremost, national symbols *crystallize the national identity.* They tell citizens "who they are, by demarcating what is authentically theirs from what is alien" (Smith 1986:202). In this regard, Anthony Giddens speaks of national symbols as the content of nationalism. A nation's symbols establish the cultural autonomy of its population, thus becoming the basis of a unique conceptual community (1985:216–19).[5] National symbols enable a unique collective "self," distinct from any other entity in the international arena. Via these symbols, political leaders inject the essence of the nation into every citizen. As these "identity injections" take hold, citizens become filled, not with a mere representation, but with the reality that these symbols represent. Recall Durkheim's observations on the process: "The soldier who dies for his flag, dies for his country; but as a matter of fact, in his own consciousness, it is the flag that has the first place" (1915:251; see also Balibar 1988:98–99).

To accomplish crystallization, political leaders give national symbols high exposure. Governments equip official institutions with national flags and emblems. Anthems, mottoes, and pledges of allegiance are inculcated early, as they are taught in the primary grades and recited daily through the completion of secondary education. These symbols can permeate leisure settings as well; in many nations, citizens sing the anthem or salute the flag at the onset of concerts, sporting events, and other public assemblies. Beyond anthems, flags, and pledges, political leaders support the erection of monuments and historical sites throughout a nation. Citizens are encouraged to visit such sites and share in the sacred ideals they enshrine. Such monuments collectively commemorate the past strengths or sufferings of the national body, and by so doing, rejuvenate that body for future challenges. Often, national leaders create special holidays that revolve around these shrines. For example, each April, the Japanese celebrate Yasukuni Matsuri, a holiday during which citizens are encouraged to visit Tokyo's Yasukuni shrine and honor Japanese soldiers who died for their country (Gregory 1975:153). On Memorial Day in the United States, flowers and flags decorate the grave sites of military casualties, with citizens engaged in parades or memorial services designed to honor the dead. The interjection of such national occasions into the routine calendar of events is meant to disrupt citizens' individualistic activities and refocus the population on collective national issues (Zerubavel 1985:46). Through these ritualistic exposures, citizens are directed to their shared national membership and national identity is continually reenforced.

Crystallization is so crucial to defining and sustaining a nation that political leaders spare no expense in connecting citizens to their nation's symbols. Knowing this, it should not surprise us that more than $230 million were collected for the one-hundredth "birthday" renovation of the Statue of Liberty. In addition, more than $30 million were spent on the 1986 weekend celebration commemorating the statue's unveiling—a celebration complete with hundreds of tall ships from around the world and more than ten tons of fireworks (Collins 1986:82–83; Martz, Kasindorf, and McKillop 1986:14–18; McFadden 1986:1; Quindlen 1986:58). Note that these combined costs exceed the annual budgets of many long-standing federal programs; the costs were sixteen times greater than the 1986 federal budget for the School Milk Program, twice the 1986 budget for the Nutrition for the Elderly Program, and 68 percent of the 1986 federal budget for Medical Research (*Statistical Abstracts* 1988:88, 90, 120). Similarly, the United States spends thousands of dollars annually to supply national flags for the funerals of American veterans. The justification of this enormous expense was articulated during a Senate debate: "It is a patriotic thing to provide that the symbol of the unity of our country, the national flag, should be placed upon the casket of every deceased man who has served. . . . *The expense involved would be an investment in patriotism which will bring back huge dividends to our beloved Nation in the future"* (*Hearings of Committee* 1937, emphasis added). Clearly, this logic supports the notion that an investment in national symbols is an investment in the nation.[6]

National symbols also function to *create bonds* between citizens. This bonding power emerges from the unique, sacred nature of these symbols—one distinct from that of any individual who apprehends the symbol, and one that becomes the object of intense collective reverence. In this way, national symbols exert a moral authority that renders individual interests secondary to the collective attributes the symbols represent. Moreover, the symbols bring individuals out of themselves and into contact and communication with others. They represent a power that binds citizens in a shared consciousness, linking them despite differences in wealth, social standing, power, or age: "By uttering the same cry, pronouncing the same word, or performing the same gestures in regard to these [symbolic] objects, individuals become and feel themselves to be in unison" (Durkheim 1915:262).[7]

National anthems, for example, unite citizens every time they are performed, bringing citizens together (albeit mentally in many cases) in patriotic communion. During World War II, the BBC used these symbols for just such a purpose, airing weekly broadcasts of the Allies' national anthems. Ruth Mead (1980:46) notes that European listeners (numbering in the millions) reported a strengthened resolve and increased feelings of camaraderie after hearing such broadcasts. In essence, the broadcasts created a nationalistic "community of the mind—a unity based on a spiritual bond and the cooperation in a common task" (Tonnies [1887] 1957:42–43; see also Cooley [1909] 1962:54). A similar phenomenon can be witnessed when national anthems are sung at the onset of sporting events or international competitions. By singing the national anthem, a seemingly disconnected crowd is momentarily united as they collectively applaud and celebrate their national identity.

Just as anthems bind via performance, flags unify via usage. In many nations, schoolchildren pledge their allegiance to the flag before starting the day's activities. Similarly, adults often join in such pledges during festivals, public meetings, and theatrical events. On national holidays, flag displays at home or business can link private citizens in common adoration. At times, such displays take on a sacred aura. A colleague of mine, for example, recalled the morning hoistings of the American flag at the military bases on which she spent her childhood. She described this daily ritual as a moment of intense reverence. No matter the task in which individuals were engaged, the raising of the flag halted all activity; it focused the eyes of the community on a tangible expression of their collective self.

National heroes, too, function to bond citizens. These figures become civil deities with the power to both draw the collective to them and bring members closer to one another. For decades, Vladimir Lenin served such a purpose in the Soviet Union. Ironically, his death best marks the initiation of this power, for as a man Lenin was admired, but as a symbol he became the heartbeat of a national movement. A posthumous tribute in the Soviet newspaper *Pravda* highlights the point: "Lenin lives in the hearts of every member of our party. Every member of our party is a small part of Lenin. Our whole Communist family is a collective embodiment of Lenin" (*Pravda,* 23 January 1924, quoted in Lane 1981:216). In passing from life to death, Lenin transcended the rigidity of observable human behavior. Thus in death, his image could be freely molded to suit the evolution of the national cause. As such, many Soviet citizens were joined in a moral unity that was contingent not on a leader's real actions, but rather on a collective agenda.

Barry Schwartz documents a similar phenomenon in his study of George Washington, arguing that the social construction of this hero has been a basis of American community for more than two centuries: "It [Washington's image] has been evoked and reinforced by periodic commentaries in schools and in the mass media, and by the material signs of the Washington cult—its icons, shrines, place names, and observances. *By their common exposure to these media, millions of people are drawn into a moral communion*" (1987:205, emphasis added). Commemorating a figure such as Washington does not necessarily celebrate the man; it defines and personifies the national character. Because they were once living beings, such heroes give citizens a seemingly tangible example of the values around which they are unified. In the moral communion of which Schwartz speaks, heroes like Washington or Lenin become the common food, the mystic substance that creates every national member's being.

The bonding function of national symbols often goes beyond the intranational experience. Some symbols are designed to express unity between nations. Consider the case of Thailand. Because the flags of its World War I allies contained red, white, and blue, the nation added a blue stripe to its red and white flag. This inclusion effectively expressed Thailand's solidarity with its allies. Similarly, when designing their national flags, many Arab and African nations made a concerted effort to include common colors. Such "overlap" conveyed the ideological unity of the nations involved. Coats of arms, too, often are amended to indicate international unity. In 1258, following the marriage of Alfonso III and Princess Beatriz of Castille, the Portuguese arms were redesigned to include a red border with seven golden Castillian castles. By intentionally merging Portuguese and Castillian signs, Portuguese leaders effectively projected the union of territories and peoples (Mucha 1985:90, 47). In a similar way, national monuments sometimes are erected with international unity in mind. The French monument to John F. Kennedy (which stands in Paris) and the American monument to Winston Churchill (located in Fulton, Missouri) underscore the solidarity of longtime allies.

It is important to note that the bonding power of national symbols is sometimes invoked with instrumental ends in mind. Political leaders can use this bonding power to further their own agendas. For example, King George II adopted the British anthem "God Save the King" as a tool for retaining loyalty to the crown during the Jacobite threat. And indeed, as the anthem spread through London and the surrounding areas, it was thought to "encourage strong support for the Monarch" (Griffith 1952:26). Similarly, Icelandic officials commissioned the nation's current anthem (adopted on the one-thousandth anniversary of the country's settlement) in an effort to rally public support for the nation's new constitution (Cartledge et al. 1978:208).

Certain national flags were designed with specific political bonds in mind. In such instances, leaders attempted to structure real social relations by imposing symbols depicting desired relations. Such flags became a blueprint for that which leaders thought *should* be. Consider the design of the United Kingdom's Union flag. Officially adopted in 1801, the flag symbolically merged three distinct political groups. By combining the red cross of England's patron St. George, the white saltire of Scotland's patron St. Andrew, and the red cross of Ireland's patron St. Patrick, the flag graphically outlined a new political union (Mucha 1985:51–52). Similarly, the Irish national flag symbolically merged the country's religious groups. The flag's green field represented Catholics, while its orange field represented Protestants. The flag also included a white field meant to indicate the peaceful coexistence of the two groups. And note the Soviet flag's imagery. The five-point star symbolized the unity of the peoples of the five continents; the hammer and sickle represented the bond between workers and peasants. With this design, Soviet leaders attempted to unify the populous behind the ideas of the October revolution (Talocci 1977:22, 19).

Such "instrumental" bonding persists in the present era. During the 1988 U.S. presidential campaign, for example, both George Bush and Michael Dukakis readily employed the flag as a tool for solidifying campaign support. Indeed, proprietors of The Flag Store in San Francisco note that the 1988 campaign was the busiest in the store's history. During that period, the store provided more U.S. flag displays than for any other presidential campaign during its existence. Some contend that in the final analysis, Bush's superior ability to "successfully wrap himself in the American flag" aided his victory (Garbus 1989:369). By more effectively pairing himself with this unifying symbol, Bush was better able to bind voters to his cause. Christel Lane (1981:153) offers similar observations in discussing the modern symbols and rituals of the Soviet Union. She contends that Soviet elites devised such tools not only to commemorate people or events but also to unify the population behind the leadership's causes. In this way, national symbols and rituals explicated leaders' characteristic values and modeled their ideal relationships. Events such as the familial life-cycle rights, the holiday of hammer and sickle, or the passport ritual helped leaders direct unity, foster strength, and inspire future collective efforts toward the leadership's ends.

To be sure, there are isolated instances in which national symbols divide rather than bond. In such cases, national symbols destroy cohesion in a nation by illuminating the differences between dominant and subordinate groups (see, e.g., Dubin 1987). When symbols create a context of "them" versus "us," they motivate separatism rather than unity, operating according to what Leach calls a "binary code" (1976:55). During the 1930s and 1940s the swastika flag functioned in this way. Defined as an exclusive sign of "true Aryans," the flag placed that group in opposition to all others. Non-Aryans, especially Germany's Jews, were forbidden to fly the flag. Such restrictions created two independent and adversarial symbolic vocabularies in Germany: the Aryan and the non-Aryan. To be restricted from using dominant Aryan symbols was to be delineated as not only separate but also inferior.

The black liberation flag of the 1960s also carried divisive consequences. In establishing their own national flag, black activist groups visibly broke from the national body and united around a new and separate set of themes. To be sure, such actions helped clarify the goals of the black liberation movement and increase solidarity within this subculture. But the creation of a secondary symbol system—one that stood in clear contrast to the dominant system already in place— also illustrated the separate existence, the divisions, between blacks and whites in the United States (Firth 1973:348; Palmer 1970).

National symbols can also engage and propel a collective, serving to *motivate patriotic action*. Because the ties that bond members of the collective to the symbol and to each other are emotionally charged, national symbols become what Durkheim called a "rallying center" for the group. The group fights to protect their symbols as they would fight to protect themselves. The symbols spur groups to victory and celebration and comfort the group in defeat. The group creates rituals to honor national symbols, just as they would for living beings. And as statements of purpose and justification, the symbols can trigger group resistance. All of these actions bring the sentiment of the symbol to life. By merging action and symbol, a national collective creates and re-creates the ideals embodied by the symbol.[8]

Political leaders clearly recognize the motivational power of national symbols and often adopt such symbols with this specific purpose in mind. Mayor Dietrich of Strasbourg, for example, is said to have directed Claude-Joseph Rouget de Lisle, the composer of "La Marseillaise," to "produce one of those hymns which convey to the soul of the people the enthusiasm which it [the music] suggests" (Sousa 1890:99). And indeed, when the tune made its way to France, it garnered credit for motivating a battalion of volunteers assembled in Marseilles as they prepared to descend on Paris. Paul Nettl (1967:69) tells us: "When they [the volunteers] joined the storming of the Tuileries on August 10, they sang and roared their favorite song in a frenzy of enthusiasm which imparted itself forthwith to the inflammable Paris mob."[9] Years later, the French experience was repeated in the Philippines. General Emilio Aguinaldo implored native musician Julian Felipe to write a piece of music that would rally his fellow countrymen against the forces of Spain. After the "fight," the general also contended that such an anthem would solidify the new regime, as it would rekindle feelings of patriotism and loyalty each time it was heard (Nettl 1967:168). Note also that motivational power became central to debates surrounding the adoption of the "Star-Spangled Banner" as the U.S. national anthem. In support of the anthem, the following arguments were offered on the floor of the Senate: "The veterans of all wars are calling to the Senate now to put its official stamp upon this sacred song which *inspired them to do or die* for the 'land of the free and the home of the brave'" (*Congressional Record* 1931:6231, emphasis added) and "This song of Key's aroused the dormant patriotism of the nation. It lifted the national spirit from the vale of gloom and despair. It heralded the dawn of a new day to our government. In moral value, it was worth 10,000 bayonets" (*Congressional Record* 1930:2322). Implicit in these statements is the notion that symbols with the power to motivate can save, sustain, or bring a nation to life.

In this regard, David Brinkley discusses the motivational power of the U.S. flag. During a key congressional vote aimed at extending the military draft, the symbol became a tool used to win the endorsement of "isolationist" voters. After countless futile attempts, the power of the flag is credited with swaying the vote:

> Rayburn and Johnson called secretary Hull and asked for a letter in support of extending the draft . . . Rayburn sent a messenger to the State Department to pick up Hull's letter, and he read it on the floor. Its message was that whatever happened in Europe, the great and glorious American republic must be ready to defend itself, and that—a clause that caught them emotionally—"the American flag is too precious to endanger." (Brinkley 1988:31)

Brinkley's story suggests how easily a national flag can trigger the call to patriotic action. And other national symbols display a similar power. Political leaders often declare national holidays, for example, to motivate citizen action. Consider the case of Japan. When Japanese leaders wished to stimulate a greater interest in traditional Japanese culture, they established Culture Day (November 3). The government hoped that the holiday's focus would motivate citizens—particularly the youth—to delve further into Japanese history and culture, thus creating a greater commitment to the country. Similarly, U.S. leaders reconstructed the Memorial Day holiday (May 30) so as to stimulate patriotic reflection among citizens. Note that private citizens first initiated the holiday in 1868 as a day of mourning for soldiers lost during the Civil War. Eventually, however, legislatures in each of the fifty states federalized the holiday, deeming it a day to honor the *ideals* for which soldiers die and urging the citizenry to reflect on the victories achieved by the tragic wars involving the United States (Gregory 1975:126, 68).

In much the same way, national martyrs can spark collective action. Such individuals, clearly prominent when alive, become inspirational, almost godlike, after death. As such, national martyrs gain a sacred influence over the collective. They acquire the ability to stimulate deep emotional commitments—ones superseding those that they, as living human beings, were capable of generating. These commitments often lead to extraordinary action. Consider Filipino activist Benigno Aquino. While living, Aquino and his followers energetically opposed the Marcos regime. Yet only after his assassination (August 1983) were Aquino's followers able to effectively unite and oust Marcos from power. Similarly, Father Miguel Hidalgo y Costilla preached revolution to the Indian peasants in Mexico for years. Yet only with his execution in 1811 did his words gain the power to trigger the insurrection of 1814. Martyrs, like other symbols, become the spark that ignites nationalistic fervor, serving to turn sentiment into action.

National symbols also function to *honor the efforts of a nation's citizens.* When nations link their sacred symbols to the efforts of citizens, they not only credit the citizen but also enhance the tangibility of the symbol. Here lies the significance of the honoring function. The process creates a symbiotic relationship between the living nation and the symbolic nation. On one hand, valorous citizens breathe life into the symbol by providing concrete examples of that for which the symbol stands. At the same time, the efforts of individuals become basked in the symbol's sacred aura. During the moments in which citizen and symbol are linked, the nation becomes "real" and the citizen becomes consecrated.

Nations honor citizens in a wide variety of arenas. In world competitions such as the Olympics or the World Cup, we honor winning athletes by playing their national anthem and hoisting their national flag. Similarly, we welcome military victors against the backdrop of their national anthem and flag. To commemorate their bravery, we decorate military heroes with medals that display their nation's symbols. When citizens die in service of their country, we drape the national flag over their coffins to signify their heroism. We memorialize patriotic sacrifice with national monuments: L'Arc de Triomphe[10] in France, the Volkerschlachtdenkmal in Germany, the Lenin Mausoleum in Russia, and the Vietnam Veterans Memorial in the United States. In all of these examples, we honor the nation, making the best and strongest of its people a representation of the collective body. Honored individuals become material extensions of all that the nation claims to be.

National holidays also serve the honoring function. José Martí Day in Cuba honors the famous patriot and his struggles (January 28). Tomb-Sweeping Day in Taiwan honors the nation's dead (April 5). Matilda Newport Day honors the Liberian patriot and the ideals for which she fought (December 1). These holidays, and others like them, relocate private activity to the public domain. As such, the individual actions referenced by the symbols become the possession of the collective.

The honoring function so strongly links symbol to populous that when individuals defile national symbols, the action is often equated with insulting the national body. Such actions are shunned as they bring profanity to the sacred realm. This fact explains the intense displeasure directed at Roseanne Barr after her cavalier rendition of the "Star-Spangled Banner" at a July 25, 1990, baseball game.[11] President Bush denounced Barr's actions as "disgraceful" (O'Connor 1991:1), and popular public opinion followed suit. Readers may recall the hundreds of polls run by local newspapers indicating the public's horror over the incident. In an interview with Barbara Walters, Barr reported receiving thousands of angry letters accusing her of flagrant disrespect for the nation. Clearly, Barr's attempts at being comedic were misplaced in the realm of the sacred. National citizens took Barr's disrespect toward the anthem as an act of disrespect toward the American people.

The dangers of defiling the sacred also explain violent reactions toward Scott Tyler's 1989 art work *What Is the Proper Way to Display the American Flag* (presented at the Art Institute of Chicago). In Tyler's exhibit, the U.S. flag was spread on the museum floor. Beyond the flag were two diaries in which spectators could record their reactions. However, the flag was so positioned that those wishing to access the diaries were forced to walk on the flag. The exhibit triggered multiple demonstrations fraught with angry words and near blows. While some argued for the legitimacy of the artist's use of the flag, most demanded the removal of the piece. Disagreements became so severe that the issue made its way to the judicial system, with veterans petitioning the courts to shut down the museum. Although Tyler's use of the flag could be rationally defined as an act of free speech, at an emotional level it was perceived as a desecration of the flag, and thus, a violent affront to the ideals and people that the flag represents.

Negative reactions to symbol defilement are not confined to the United States. In 1958, for example, when a Japanese student tore down the flag of the People's Republic of China, diplomatic relations between the two countries were severed for several years (Smith 1975:104). Disrespect toward the symbol of another country is generally interpreted as an act of overt hostility.

Note that the honoring function carries an important corollary. Collectives can direct shame and *dis*honor toward individuals by *withholding their access* to national symbols. Recall that during Benedict Arnold's isolation for treason, he was forbidden to set eyes on the American flag. In Nazi Germany, the official *swastika* flag was withheld from Jews as a method of dishonoring them. In a related vein, note that only those businesses and corporations approved by the British monarch gain the honor of displaying the royal coat of arms in their business logos, thus creating a distinction between nationally endorsed and non-endorsed endeavors. American advertisers attempt to create a similar illusion when they market their goods as the "official" product of the nation's Olympic team. Such products enjoy a prestige that is withheld from items that fail to win this nationalistic endorsement.

The *legitimation of authority* represents another function of national symbols, a process by which a symbol's sacred aura is transposed to a nation's formal authority structure. This phenomenon occurs at multiple levels. First, at the establishment level, the projection and recognition of new symbols legitimates an entity's new nation status. Thus, the inclusion of a nation's flag at the United Nations is significant as it serves to mark the acceptance of a new, full-fledged member in the "national club." Similarly, when more than one hundred nations celebrate an Independence Day, they institutionalize the birth of a national entity. Many nations commend certain military victories to holiday status: Cuba's Day of Revolution (January 20) commemorating Fidel Castro's 1959 victory, Bolivian National Day (April 9) commemorating the 1952 uprising, Yemen National Day (October 14) honoring the 1962 revolts, and Bangladesh Victory Day (December 16) commemorating the end of the 1971 conflict with Pakistan (Gregory 1975). By highlighting these triumphs and the subsequent establishment of beginnings, boundaries, and independent control, such holidays liken the nation to other "authorized" sovereign powers.

Note that although the introduction of national symbols can legitimate new national authority structures, the dissolution of these symbols can concretize the demise of old structures and political orders. For example, more than treaties and agreements, it was the fall of the Berlin Wall in 1989 that signaled German reunification and the end of communist rule. Similarly, despite weeks of political votes, speeches, and formal resignations, some consider the lowering of the Soviet flag on December 25, 1991, the most decisive sign of the death of the Soviet Union.[12] Because symbols become a nation rather than merely represent it, their fate becomes tangible evidence of the stream of national events.

At another level, symbols can legitimate changes to a nation's internal authority structure. During such transitions, symbols are often re-created or altered so as to embody the shift in the power structure. In Bolivia, for example, the coat of arms currently contains nine stars, each representing one of the country's departments. Each star appeared on the arms as a new province emerged. In this way, symbolic alterations helped integrate new Bolivian departments into the traditional conception of authority. Similarly, upon declaring independence, Venezuela added the phrase "19 de Abril de 1810—Independencia; 20 de Febrero de 1859—Federación Republica de Venezuela" to its coat of arms. By linking the independence move-

ment to the past history of the arms, the new Venezuelan government was more easily woven into the existing national identity
(Mucha 1985:38, 176, 181).

At a third level, national symbols help legitimate the extension of a
nation's authority over new territories or over other nations.[13] Recall
that Buzz Aldrin's first task when arriving on the moon was to post
the American flag, claiming the territory for the United States. Similarly, nations often impose their own currency systems on countries
they acquire or dominate. British currency, for example, was used
exclusively in Australia, the Bahamas Islands, Belize, Bermuda, the
British Caribbean territories, British Honduras, British West Africa,
Canada, the Cayman Islands, Ceylon, the Cook Islands, Cyprus, Fiji,
Gambia, Hong Kong, Jamaica, Mauritius, and New Zealand. Similarly, under the reign of the Soviet Union, Czechoslovakia and the
Baltic states pictured Lenin, and, later, Joseph Stalin on their currency
(Yeoman 1974). Enforcing the use of the controller's symbols within
acquired territories both indicates and legitimates the central seat of
authority in these areas.

In the same vein, invading forces traditionally flaunt their national
symbols during the forced occupation of other nations or the re-
claiming of territory. Radio broadcast stations, for example, become
the immediate targets of invaders. By flooding the airways with the
nationalistic music of the new regime, the former order is symbolically dissolved and the power of new authorities imposed. Flags
and banners, too, often legitimate forced take-overs. It would be hard
to dismiss history's memory of the Soviet flag being draped on the
buildings of Berlin as the Soviet army took control of that city in 1945.
And recently, the Iraqis signified their 1990 domination of Kuwait by
replacing Kuwaiti currency with that of Iraq and forbidding the
display of the Kuwaiti flag or pictures of the emir. By accompanying
invasions with national symbols, invaders attempt to justify their
actions in the name of their own belief systems. More importantly,
the replacement of the symbols of the conquered with the symbols of
the invader provides a powerful statement of domination and of a
new political order.

At a fourth level, national leaders often use symbols to legitimate
their personal authority. Knowing that national symbols are sacred to
citizens and thus exercise a moral authority over a collective, political

leaders often attempt to merge their persona with these symbols. By doing so, the power invested in the symbol is subliminally transferred to the leader. It is not surprising, then, that when rulers address their nations, national symbols are often central to the setting. The U.S. president frames his public addresses with the national flag and our national emblem, the eagle. For nearly five decades, the Soviet premiere spoke to the Politburo against the backdrop of a larger than life picture of Lenin. Heads of state often have a song, seal, or flag that becomes a permanent accompaniment to their presence—"Hail to the Chief" in the United States, "The Royal Fanfare" in Iraq, or the president's flag in Gabon, Korea, Liberia, Peru, and so on. And national rulers often are honored on the country's postage stamps or national currency. Leopold III, for example, was commemorated on Belgium coins. The accession of Jigme Wangchuk was depicted on Bhutan's currency. Jawaharlal Nehru could be found on certain Indian coins. Francisco Franco was pictured on Spanish currency (Yeoman 1974). Combining leader with symbol renders the leader the standard-bearer of all that the nation's citizens value and believe. Leaders, like symbols, become revered, respected, and empowered.

It is important to emphasize the conscious efforts that link symbol and ruler. Leaders intentionally exploit the legitimating function of national symbols in an effort to solidify their control. For example, in attempts to promote Russian independence and sovereignty, Boris Yeltsin resurrected the pre-1917 Russian flag. During 1991, the white, blue, and red striped flag became an obvious accouterment to Yeltsin-sponsored rallies and functions. Merging the Yeltsin persona with the Russian flag of old not only served to demarcate his policy from that of Gorbachev but also invested him with the power and greatness of pre–civil war Russia and legitimated his notion of an independent Russia. In the same way, national leaders consciously choose verbal symbols that will legitimate their personal authority, developing mottoes, slogans, titles, or quoting national heroes. In her discussion of modern Soviet society, for example, Lane contends that by selecting certain quotes from famous recorded speeches by Lenin, Soviet national leaders "combined with the preeminence of the speaker to evoke pride in, and reverence for, the revolutionary past, adulation for Lenin, and fresh enthusiasm for the political tasks of the present" (1981:201–2). National constitutions, too, are frequently used by leaders attempting to legitimate their personal authority. The prime purpose of such documents is to define the boundaries of a government's power, making these points clear to a nation's citizens and to those beyond the nation's borders. But because constitutions are symbolic instruments, they enjoy the sacred, moral character of other national symbols. Thus constitutional statements become more than common directives; they take on the aura of divine dictates. When a leader's authority is questioned, he or she will often appeal to this sacred document as a way of justifying his or her actions. Before the December 8, 1991, vote that formed the New Commonwealth of Independent States, for example, Yeltsin had staff members clearly document the constitutionality of the government change, thus legitimating his power from the onset. Yeltsin's strategy was hardly novel. Before being proclaimed Consul for Life, Napoleon Bonaparte insisted upon the drafting of a new constitution that would confer unlimited power to his hands. Understanding the impact of symbols, he saw such a constitution as a key legitimator of his extended authority.

In contrast to legitimating authority, national symbols can also be used to challenge authority, functioning as *tools of popular political protest*. This function differs significantly from those cited thus far. When symbols are used to crystallize identity, motivate bonds or action, honor, or legitimate, their ability to control social behaviors and define social settings travels downward through the social system; such social control is directed from those that govern to the governed. Conversely, when symbols become tools of protest, the public takes command of them, using the symbols to convey their discontent with national leadership. This phenomenon emphasizes the popularistic nature of national symbols. By making ruling elites the receivers rather than the transmitters of the symbol, protesters inject their group with the national symbol's power. That power can help to elevate the protesters' cause, putting the public in a position to challenge ruling authorities. In another context, M. P. Baumgartner refers to such a strategy as *social control from below*—a method by which the less powerful pursue grievances against the more powerful (1984:305).

The protest function of national symbols is most evident when leaders and their constituents become glaringly divided. Under such conditions, leaders are defined as violators of the public trust, forcing protesters to reclaim the sacred symbols of the people and return them to the hands of the "virtuous." During the Second Empire, for example, French resisters called on this strategy. When Napoleon III outlawed "La Marseillaise," deeming it too dangerous for public consumption, resisters chose the anthem as a tool of dissent, resolving to use "La Marseillaise" as a reminder of revolutionary ideals. These citizens sang "La Marseillaise" at both "underground" settings and public displays of unrest. In this way, the anthem became an expression of the collective will and a direct challenge to formal authority (Mead 1980:54). Now recall the Bonus March of 1932. Throughout this protest, American veterans consciously cloaked their grievances in the American flag, carrying it during rallies and posting it on their temporary settlements. The flag became aligned with the veterans' fight and equated with the veterans' spirit. By taking command of the flag, the veterans placed the leaders of formal government in opposition to the will of the people. Needless to say, when President Hoover ordered federal troops to forcibly evacuate the veterans, millions of Americans were aghast. Physical attacks on the veterans became attacks on the flag, and thus, symbolically charged attacks on the collective body.

The instances described above pertain to temporary divisions between rulers and those they govern. However, one can imagine situations in which such divisions become long-term periods of alienation. In such cases, the general population may define national symbols as "public property" now lost to ruling elites. When disconnected from their popularistic roots, the role of national symbols in protest takes on a different character. The symbols, like those who control them, become the target of protest. Under these conditions, popular protest can involve some form of attack on national symbols.

Attacks on national symbols can be implicit or explicit. Implicit attacks occur in the form of *manipulation* and *juxtapositioning*.[14] Manipulation involves the altering of a symbol's content or form such that it conveys a message different from the one with which it is normally associated. In general, this "new" message is antagonistic to the policies of ruling elites. Student protesters of the 1960s and 1970s often manipulated the U.S. flag. The most common manipulation replaced the fifty stars with a peace symbol. This alteration conveyed the students' displeasure toward the government's formal policies, while simultaneously promoting an alternate plan of peaceful inter-national coexistence. Similarly, rock guitarist Jimi Hendrix expressed his opposition to government policy when he manipulated the "Star-Spangled Banner" at the Woodstock Music Festival. The "new" an-them contained abundant musical distortion, symbolizing, according to Hendrix, the government's perversion of traditional American values such as freedom of expression and equality.

Juxtapositioning contrasts a new symbol with a traditional one, or a popular symbol with one strongly promoted by ruling elites. In this way, the protesters force a confrontation between what "is" and what "should be." Citizens of the Soviet republics frequently used this technique in their initial bids for independence from the central gov-ernment. Rallies in Estonia, Latvia, and Lithuania often included the singing of pre-Soviet national anthems and the flying of pre-Soviet national flags. By contrasting the old order with the present one, the people conveyed to the formal leadership their desired direction of political development. In much the same way, Chinese students in Beijing's Tiananmen Square used the Goddess of Democracy (a thirty-five-foot sculpture modeled after the Statue of Liberty) as a powerful tool of defiance toward the government. The statue, erec-ted in the square, sat in opposition to a massive portrait of Mao Zedung. In essence, this juxtapositioning of statue and portrait em-bodied the challenge of democracy against communism.

Explicit attacks involve the *defacing* of national symbols and illus-trate the most direct and radical side of the protest function. These assaults occur under conditions in which the population is most severed from power. Because national symbols are embodiments rather than mere representations, marring or defacing them serves as a direct denunciation of both the leaders who control these symbols and the ideals those leaders have attached to the symbols. History is rich with examples of defacing. During the 1960s, flag burning and the burning in effigy of national leaders—most notably Richard Nixon—enjoyed some popularity in the United States.[15] Those op-posed to U.S. involvement in Indochina and domestic policies on crime and economics used this form of explicit attack to express both unequivocal disapproval of government positions and their per-ceived lack of power. Similarly, Romanian protesters regularly defaced the national flag during the 1989 revolution. Cutting the communist ornament from the center of the flag was said to signify the public's desire to eradicate communist rule. In the words of Andrei Codrescu, a journalist and Romanian exile, "It is through that hole that I am returning to my birthplace" (1991:67). And in 1990–91, the independence movements in the Baltic republics saw the defacing of communism's most sacred symbols. In Lithuania, citizens danced on a toppled statue of Lenin. In Russia, plans were made to dismantle Lenin's burial shrine. These symbols were central to the identity of the Soviet Union. Thus, their defilement crystallized the people's rejection of the standing political structure. Indeed, the ease with which citizens brought profanity to these sacred national symbols highlights the sense of alienation experienced by those the symbols were originally meant to represent.

Note that the protest function is often exercised in the international arena. When a colonial government overpowers its colonies, when core powers restrict the economic growth of semiperipheral and peripheral nations, or when political superpowers attempt to restrict or silence less influential nations, subordinate national players often resort to both implicit and explicit attacks on the symbols of the dominant power. For example, upon independence, Barbados made implicit attacks on the symbols of its mother country. When controlled by the British, the Barbados coat of arms included a trident. Upon declaring independence, the new government immediately removed the shaft in order to signify a clean break from both the nation's colonial past and the symbols developed by its former British rulers (Mucha 1985:154). Similarly, during the 1979 revolution Iranians waged explicit attacks on American symbols. They frequently burned American symbols and images of American leaders in effigy. Imposing profanity on these sacred American symbols dramatically indicated Iran's strong disapproval of U.S. involvement in the Arab world.

Conclusion

Crystallizing the national identity, creating bonds among citizens, motivating patriotic action, conferring honor, legitimating authority, and aiding popular political protest—all are key functions of national symbols. Each area plays a role in empowering modern totems; each task has been universally practiced and sustained throughout the history of nations. But note that these functions are successfully executed only through the careful selection, and proper projection and reception, of these symbols. In essence, *the functions of national symbols are accomplished only through the successful communication of their message.* Therefore, any examination of national symbols must thoughtfully attend to the cognitive processes by which they are constructed and diffused. Chapter 2 directs us to this task.

2

SYNTACTIC STRUCTURE

AT ONE TIME or another, we have all heard the adage, "It's not what you say that counts, but how you say it." The lesson is simple: effective communication occurs when senders attend not only to the content of their message but also to the way in which that content is put together or designed.

Meaning from Design

In this chapter, I apply the familiar adage to the study of anthems and flags, shifting our attentions away from symbol content and encouraging us to consider the relationships between the elements that constitute a symbol. Earlier, I referred to these relationships as the syntactic structure of a symbol—the design or configuration of a symbol's elements. Now, we consider syntactic structure in greater detail, assessing variations in it, and exploring the importance of such variations to the process of symbolic communication.

The Importance of Syntactic Structure

Ferdinand de Saussure was among the first to intently consider syntactic structure. He promoted the semiotic study of communication, an approach that analyzes the symbolic "pieces" of a message and examines them as part of a unified system ([1915] 1959:16).[1] "Each linguistic term," he argued, "derives its value from its opposition to all other terms. . . . Whatever distinguishes one term from another constitutes it" (ibid.:88, 121). From Saussure's perspective, a message is best understood by attending to the connections and distinctions between its independent elements.[2] Communication revolves around the relations between message "parts." In this way, syntactic structure becomes as important as content to a message's meaning.

While Saussure articulated the role of structure in the creation of meaning, others before him implied its importance. For centuries, artists have underscored the centrality of syntactic structure in the successful communication of their messages. Henri Matisse noted, for example: "What I am after, above all, is expression. But expression does not consist of the passion mirrored upon a human face. It is the whole *arrangement* of my picture that is expressive" (quoted in Janson and Kerman 1968:184, emphasis added). Here, Matisse clearly argues that content, though undoubtedly important, is secondary to the communicative power of each painting's very design. Indeed, he suggests that each painting's syntactic structure represents a strategy by which an artist can convey meaning. Years earlier, Vincent van Gogh made a similar point in a letter to his brother, Theo: "I am always in hope of making a discovery in the study of color, to express the love of two lovers by a marriage of two complimentary colors, *their mingling and their opposition, the mysterious vibrations of kindred tones*" (quoted in Goldwater 1953:24, emphasis added). Van Gogh, too, focuses our attentions on message organization. Like Matisse, he discusses syntactic structure as a method of presentation, and he implies that certain methods are more appropriate than others in conveying particular ideas.

Musicians, too, frequently note syntactic structure's importance to communication. In 1780, for example, Jean Benjamin de LaBorde cited two key aspects of a musical message: "The first is the *ordering or disposing* of several sounds in such a manner that their succession pleases the ear. The second is the rendering audible of two or more simultaneous sounds in such a manner that their *combination* is pleasant" (quoted in Forte 1979:1, emphasis added). For LaBorde, the effectiveness of a musical work is completely contingent on the work's design. The message emerges from the way in which particular notes or patterns of sound are transformed into a whole, a single unit consisting of interrelated parts. Composer Arnold Schoenberg offered a similar argument when describing his "twelve-tone" works.[3] To fully understand his music, Schoenberg instructed listeners not to focus on the independence of notes, or on their distance from a tonal center, but on their *"relationship to one another"* (quoted in Dallin 1977:301, emphasis added).

Saussure's "discovery" of what many communicators implicitly knew triggered a flurry of scholarly research on the syntactic structure of symbols. Study upon study demonstrate structure's centrality to the communication process, as it *orders* or *organizes* the various components of symbols.[4] Thus, the syntactic *combination* of a symbol's components conveys a meaning that differs from that of any single component of the symbol. So, although the elements—the content—of two symbols may be identical, repeating those elements, emphasizing one element over another, or altering the way in which the elements are combined can change both the interpretation and the effectiveness of the symbol's message.

Language offers the most accessible example of syntactic structure's importance. Consider the statement: I love you. As written, it clearly conveys affection. However, we can change the syntactic structure of the elements "I," "love," and "you," thus producing an entirely different message. We can, for example, repeat one or more of the elements, saying: I, I, . . . I love you. Through repetition, nervousness or anxiousness is conveyed in addition to affection. In another instance, we might alter syntactic structure by changing the emphasis placed on these elements, saying: *I* love you, or I love *you.* Each example uses emphasis to clarify meaning. In the first statement, emphasis clarifies the source of the affection; in the second example, emphasis underscores the target of the affection. In addition to changes in emphasis, we can alter this statement's meaning by changing the form of the sentence from declarative to interrogative: *I love you?* Such a change transforms an expression of affection to a incredulous query. Finally, we can change the grammatical ordering of the elements: *Love* you, . . . *I?* This example changes the standard subject-predicate-object format to a less conventional predicate-object-subject format. Such a change conveys confusion rather than a firm declaration of affection.

In reviewing all the verbal statements of love just cited, we cannot help but note that their content is identical. Yet each statement displays a different syntactic structure. Thus, *by varying the syntactic structure, we effectively vary the statement's meaning.*

Musical messages, too, can be altered by varying their syntactic design. Melodies offer a clear example of the phenomenon. Consider the traditional Christmas carol "Here We Come A-Wassailing":

By shifting the position of these melody notes, making no changes in content, I can change a holiday wish to a comical nursery rhyme:

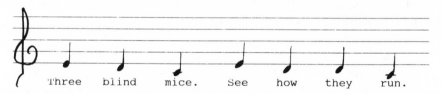

Similarly, consider the buoyant melody from the "Beer Barrel Polka":

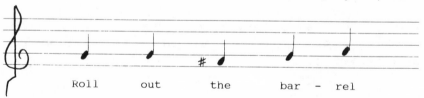

Reordering these notes changes a declaration of fun to a painful realization of time's fleeting quality:

Harnick/Bock

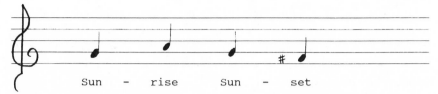

In these examples, *the ordering of content rather than content itself determines the musical message.* As such, each melody's syntactic structure is integral to its meaning.

The role of syntactic design is central to the study of national symbols. Indeed, the pages that follow demonstrate that the way in which the words, sounds, colors, or images of these symbols are combined plays a major role in determining their meaning. In the symbolic communication of a nation's identity, the existence of differentiating features equals the importance of symbol content.[5]

The Syntactic Structure of Anthems and Flags

To date, most research on national anthems and flags addresses their content; symbol syntax receives little attention in this literature. This is puzzling, because experts in the area have repeatedly implied the importance of syntactic structure. In his book on national anthems, for example, music historian Paul Nettl clearly suggests that the content of an anthem is secondary to its structure: "The full patriotic appeal of an anthem is determined by *the association and relationship between its parts*" (1967:30, emphasis added). Similarly, in writing of flags, Umberto Eco emphasizes the importance of syntactic structure: "In national flags, categorization overwhelms discrimination . . . Certain colors form a clear-cut system of oppositional units which are, in turn, clearly correlated with another system concerning values or abstract ideas. The nature of these values (hope, peace, etc.) is irrelevant. *What counts is the structural architecture of their basic oppositions*" (1985:173–74). Raymond Firth makes a similar point, noting, "It is not simply the content of flags that is important, *but their form and the combination of their elements*" (1973:46, emphasis added).

A review of the anthems and flags in my sample offers good

reason to question our neglect of national symbol structure. Case after case suggests that in deciphering the meaning of these symbols, structure clearly matters. Consider, for example, two familiar anthems, "God Save the Queen" and "La Marseillaise." A moment's reflection reminds us of the drastically different messages the songs convey. The former is a stately hymn of honor, the latter a rousing call to arms. Careful examination of the anthems' musical characteristics reveals that their divergent meanings emerge from structural rather than content differences. For instance, both anthems are written in the same key—the key of G. As such, music theory requires that both anthems use the same content, the same "vocabulary" of notes: G, A, B, C, D, E, F#, G—the G scale.

Figure 2.1A illustrates the melodic content of these anthems, graphing the distribution of the notes used in each song. Note that the correlation between these two distributions is quite high (r = .77), indicating great similarity of content. Hence, we can conclude that content cannot account for the overall differences between the anthems. Now consider the syntactic structure of the anthems. Figure 2.1B aids us by presenting each melody on a pitch-time plot. Pitch-time plots are constructed using two pieces of information: the point in musical time at which each pitch is sounded (measured in single beats and plotted on the X axis), and the location of the pitch—that is, its numerical ranking on the musical scale (measured in half-steps and plotted on the Y axis). Pitch-time plots allow us to focus on the relationship between notes as they combine to form a complete melody.

In comparing the two graphs, it becomes clear that the syntactic differences between the anthem melodies distinguish the messages they convey. The structure of "God Save the Queen" renders movement from note to note slow and gradual; the musical distance between each note (each note's relative position on the musical scale) is small; the melody is smooth and continuous and contains little or no ornamentation. The opposite is true for "La Marseillaise." Here, movement is quick, jagged, and the distance between notes is often considerable. Hence, the juxtapositioning of each anthem's notes renders similar content into vastly different messages. "God Save the Queen" conveys a noble, somber message, whereas "La Marseillaise" is invigorating and dynamic.

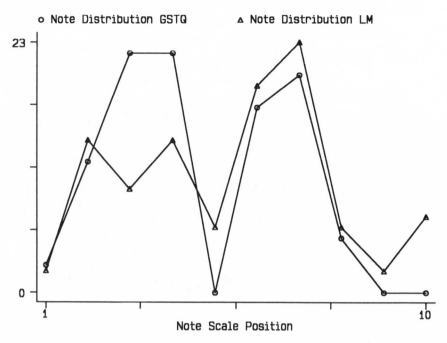

Figure 2.1a. Melodic content of "God Save the Queen" and "La Marseillaise"

In turning to national flags, we find additional links between structure and meaning. Consider the history of the French flag. With the revolution of 1848, leaders redesigned the national flag, hoping to symbolically capture the tenor of the times. Change was instigated not by altering the existing flag's content, but by changing its syntactic structure. The blue-white-red tricolor flag was changed to a blue-red-white flag, placing the two primary colors adjacent to each other as opposed to separating them with a white bar (Smith 1975:135–38). The new flag took on higher contrast, conveying more activity and movement than its predecessor.[6] In this way, a simple alteration to the flag's design effected the desired change in its message.

The national flag of Mozambique underwent a similar reconstruction. The flag change embodied one of the government's many coping strategies invoked in response to threats by the RENAMO in Angola and the ANC in South Africa. The content of the new flag

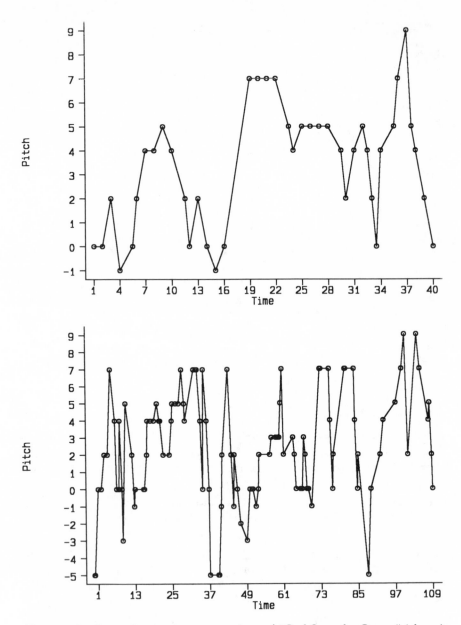

Figure 2.1b. Syntactic structure comparison of "God Save the Queen" (above) and "La Marseillaise" (below)

(adopted in 1983) was identical to its predecessor: four sections of color—green, red, black, and yellow, and an emblem taken from the national coat of arms. However, the syntactic structures of the two flags were dramatically different. In the original symbol, stripes of color radiate from the flag's upper hoist with the emblem superimposed upon them. The new flag is a horizontal tricolor—green, black, and yellow—with a red triangle and the emblem superimposed on the left half of the symbol (Crampton 1990:71–72). This case, like the French example, suggests that structure was employed to delineate a message. Structure, not content, provided Mozambique with a new signature of identity.

Several key issues arise when we acknowledge structure's role in the symbolization of nations. Knowing that national leaders clearly prefer some syntactic designs over others, it becomes important to determine the source of such design choices. Is structure selection a random process? Is the decision motivated by characteristics peculiar to each nation's unique history? Are decisions systematically linked to broader social forces? Further, we must explore the consequences of the design decisions executed in the adoption of anthems and flags. Are some syntactic structures more readily embraced, respected, or utilized by their targets than others?

To fully address these issues, we must be able to accurately characterize the structural nature of each nation's anthem and flag. Only then will we gain the ability to systematically group and compare symbol designs. With this agenda in mind, I have devised a set of quantitative indicators that allow researchers to precisely classify anthem and flag structure. These measures were constructed by carefully considering the core characteristics of the musical and graphic systems upon which these symbols are built.

Conceptualizing and Measuring Syntactic Structure

Music

Music is a form of communication, and like other forms of communication—language, numbers, pictures—it is a symbol system by

which senders convey thoughts, emotions, and information to receivers. The musical symbol system is built from notes—neutral objects that have come to be linked with particular sound qualities. Just
as letters of an alphabet are arbitrary symbols representing certain
vocalizations, or integers of a number system are neutral symbols
representing certain quantities, every note is an arbitrary symbol that
represents a particular sound frequency. Notes are purely representational and possess no inherent meaning.[7]

But although independent notes bear no inherent meaning, they
can derive meaning when combined with other notes. So, for example, middle C, sounded in isolation, has no significance for a
listener. In fact, a listener (unless possessing perfect pitch) may be
unable to identify that note if heard as an independent unit. It is only
when the listener hears middle C with reference to the melody of
which it is a part, or with reference to its chordal accompaniment,
that the pitch takes on meaning.[8]

In every musical composition, notes are consciously patterned to
convey a specific idea; they form a message with a discernible syntactic structure. To properly analyze such a message, we must acknowledge the following points. First, *musical messages are multidimensional*. Any piece of music is patterned at several levels: melody,
phrasing, harmonics, form, dynamics, rhythm, and orchestration.
Thus, in analyzing a musical message, we must consider each dimension's syntactic structure—that is, melodic structure, phrase structure, and so forth.

Second, *the syntactic structure of each musical dimension can vary
across a wide variety of characteristics*. This work attends to the most
central of those qualities, interrelated characteristics identified by
music theorists as key to the nature of a composition. Specifically, I
consider factors such as the way in which movement from note to
note is generated, the range of musical sound encompassed by a
work, the density of notes in a piece, the complexity of a composition's note combinations (melodically, harmonically, and rhyth-
mically), and the relative presence of ornamentation, distortion, or
manipulation of conventional musical patterns. (For literature validating the centrality of these factors, see, e.g., Apel 1974, Benward
and Jackson 1975, Kerman and Kerman 1970, Meyer 1967, Moles
1966, Ringer 1980, Siegmeister 1965, or Youngblood 1958.)

I consider the central aspects of music as they exist on a continuum of basic to embellished design. *Basic syntactic structure* is characterized by limited musical motion. In this design, movement from one central note to another occurs via the most direct route. There is little ornamentation of simple musical patterns and minimal informational input. Rather, this design unfolds in a stable, gradual manner. Because of these properties, basic musical structure exhibits modest numbers of musical note combinations and a restricted range of musical sounds. All in all, basic syntactic structure represents adherence to the foundational elements or building blocks of music composition. It offers the most concise, direct method of fulfilling the rules upon which Western tonal music is based.[9]

Embellished syntactic structure embodies opposite qualities. It is highly detailed and represents a decoration or distortion of basic syntactic design. Embellished structure is characterized by erratic, wandering motion. This design permits broad alternatives for movement as the music proceeds from one central note to the next. Thus, embellished structure supports maximum informational input and high levels of ornamentation; it is necessarily flexible, appealing to a wide range of musical sounds and combinations. Unlike basic syntactic structure, embellished structure elaborates, manipulates, and sometimes disrupts the central elements of Western tonal music.[10]

Finally, *every musical message also contains a syntactic metastructure designed to organize or coordinate its seven major dimensions:* melody, phrasing, harmony, form, dynamics, rhythm, and orchestration. Analyzing this metastructure provides important information on the composite nature of a musical work. The metastructure characterizes a whole work rather than its constituent parts. And like the structure of the independent elements of music, syntactic metastructure can be analyzed on a continuum of basic to embellished design.

Identifying the foundations of music structure enables us to operationalize and measure it. Appendix A of this book offers a detailed description of this measurement process. There, interested readers can follow both a step-by-step account of the ways in which I capture the basic-embellished nature of music's various dimensions (melody, phrasing, etc.) as well as the method by which I classify music's syntactic metastructure. It is important to reiterate that these methods are derived from the central principles of music theory. As such, they allow us to quantitatively analyze music structure while remaining true to the essence of this art form.

In this study, I employ my measures of music structure to systematically compare the key aspects of anthem design as we move from nation to nation. The findings reported in the body of the book will refer to the summary measure described in Appendix A, *music's syntactic metastructure*. Using this indicator, we will asses the relative embellishment of national anthems' overall or composite structures. (Note: syntactic metastructure, a continuous measure, ranges from −3.105 to +2.948, with a mean of −.015 and a standard deviation of 1.303. Negative numbers on this continuum represent basic structure. The movement to positive numbers corresponds to increasingly embellished structure.)

Attaching syntactic metastructure scores to specific anthems will give readers a more tangible notion of the distinctions in anthem design. Consider, for example, the scores for "God Save the Queen" versus "La Marseillaise." Using my measures, the British anthem (syntactic metastructure = −2.267) appears considerably more basic than the French anthem (syntactic metastructure = +.625). These scores illustrate the construct validity of my indicator.[11] Listeners can easily detect the comparatively basic nature of "God Save the Queen" in relation to its French counterpart. The British anthem displays slow, gradual, and direct motion; its note density is low, and it contains little ornamentation or distortion. The anthem's phrasing and dynamics are stable and its rhythmic structure is highly regular. "La Marseillaise," in contrast, ranks higher along each of these dimensions. The French anthem is audibly more embellished.

In Appendix B, readers will find the syntactic metastructure score for all the anthems analyzed in this book: 161 anthems representing 161 nations (descriptive statistics also are included). Reed and Bristow (1987), Mead (1980), and Cartledge et al. (1978) provided the primary data sources. These volumes represent the most exhaustive collections of national anthems in print.[12] By referring to these scores, interested readers can gauge the relative embellishment of any single anthem with reference to the entire sample or with reference to other specific entries.

Graphics

Like music, graphics represent a form of communication. The graphic system consists of geometric shapes and colors, elements which combine to convey thoughts, emotions, and information to receivers. Like notes, the shapes and colors of the graphic symbol system are purely representational. Shapes are linked to specific areas corresponding to mathematically determined borders and angles; colors correspond to particular light waves and frequencies. Hence, shapes and colors hold no inherent meaning. Rather, meaning is culturally injected into these entities.

A single shape or color may be injected with cultural meaning, but that meaning can change when the item is combined with other shapes or colors and becomes part of a message. A common American road symbol, the children crossing sign, illustrates the point. This graphic message combines two colored shapes: a black silhouette depicting two children walking and a yellow, diamond-shaped backdrop. Viewed individually, each of these colored shapes could convey a variety of meanings. However, when the elements are combined, the sign's meaning becomes unmistakable: Exercise care! There are children in the area. Thus, the meaning of the graphic message supersedes the content of a single shape or color. Rather, its meaning rests in the interdependency of the image's shapes and colors—the connections and juxtapositionings of the image's parts.

Every graphic message has a discernible syntactic structure. Its shapes and colors are consciously combined to convey a particular idea. To properly analyze this structure, we must consider those features that, according to experts in cognition, graphic design, and color theory, are key to the nature of a graphic message. Specifically, we must attend to the information density of the message, including the number of items contained in the image as well as the way in which the image is partitioned. We must consider the visual stability of the image, examining the contrasts and distinctions (both geometric and color) between sections of the message. Finally, we must consider the image's levels of distortion, including the ornamentation or manipulation of the message's focal points. (For literature validating the centrality of these factors, see, e.g., Barthes 1985:chap. 1;

Bergesen 1984; Cerulo 1988a, 1995; Cowen et al. 1987; Eco 1976; Ellis 1950:88; Gombrich 1981; Koffka 1935:184; Kohler 1947:202; Latner 1973:26–32; Lotman 1977; Morgan and Welton 1992; Stockton 1983.)

As with music, I examine the aspects of graphic structure as they exist on a basic-embellished continuum. In the graphic realm, *basic syntactic structure* presents minimal informational input. Basic symbols display few color distinctions and contain modest numbers of fields or sections. In addition, such symbols favor primary colors (blue, red, or yellow) or white (the absence of color) over secondary colors. This is because secondary colors emerge from two or more hues, thus representing greater information density. Basic syntactic structure also is visually stable. Thus, basic symbols contain few color contrasts; when contrast does occur, the adjoining points of color generally combine hues of similar intensity. As such, basic structure precludes the stark meetings that can be jarring to the eye and thus more difficult to process (see, e.g., Munsell 1946:37–40; Stockton 1983:6–8). Finally, basic graphic structure displays little distortion. If a symbol's structure is comprised of horizontal fields, for example, fields of opposing shapes will not be overlaid upon the symbol. In addition, basic structure utilizes little ornamentation. Such symbols include few emblems or decorations. By limiting inconsistencies and ornaments, basic graphic structure restricts information to the foundational elements of graphic design. Thus, it offers the most concise, economical method of conveying a graphic message.

Embellished syntactic structure displays opposite qualities. It contains great detail, often decorating, distorting, or, in some cases, manipulating basic graphic patterns. (For additional support of the basic-embellished continuum for graphic symbols, or for more information on the characteristics upon which this continuum is based, see, e.g., Bergesen 1984:191–95; Cowen 1987; Eco 1985; Gombrich 1981; Guiraud 1975:31; Leach 1976:58; Lévi-Strauss 1969:20; Lotman 1977; Marcus and Zajonc 1985:137–230; Munsell 1946:13–16, 42–47; Stockton 1983:4–8.)

This conceptualization of graphic structure provides a viable basis for operationalization and measurement. In Appendix A, I detail the process for interested readers. As I did for music structure, I describe the ways in which each dimension of a graphic symbol—its density, stability, and level of distortion—can be measured. In addition, I develop a composite measure that taps the ways in which these qualities combine to form a graphic symbol's syntactic metastructure. Here too, it is important to reiterate that these measures were constructed with a watchful eye toward the essential elements of graphic design. Thus, the measures allow for meaningful comparisons of graphic design rather than empty empirical counts.

In the present study, I use measures of graphic structure as a means to systematically compare the flag designs of the world's nations. My sample consists of 180 flags representing as many nations. Smith (1975), Crampton (1990), and Devereux (1992) provided the primary data sources. These volumes represent the most exhaustive collections of national flags in print. The findings that follow will refer to the composite measure of graphic structure—*graphic syntactic metastructure.* (Note: This indicator is a continuous measure, ranging from −4.271 to +3.449, with a mean of −.016 and standard deviation of 1.377. Negative numbers correspond to basic structure. The movement toward positive numbers indicates increasing embellishment. See Appendix A.)

To fully understand the properties tapped by my measures, readers may find it useful to visualize two national flags. First, consider the national flag of Libya, a plain green banner. It contains no sections, no points of contrast, no ornaments or distortions. Those viewing the flag receive one piece of visual information: a dark shade of the secondary color green. The syntactic metastructure score for the flag is −4.271, a low score that aptly captures the flag's very basic nature. Now consider the flag of the United States. This flag utilizes three colors, two of which are primary colors; it also contains fourteen sections (thirteen stripes and a single canton). Further, the flag displays multiple points of contrast, many of which juxtapose primary colors. Finally, the flag contains fifty ornamental stars. The flag's characteristics bespeak a highly embellished design. My measures accurately reflect that design, as the syntactic metastructure score for the flag is +3.449. (Interested readers can turn to Appendix B and peruse and compare the syntactic metastructure scores for all flags in the sample.)

The measures presented in this chapter address many of the central elements to which music theorists, students of visual design, and specialized cognitive theorists attend when qualitatively analyzing musical or graphic symbols. Yet my measures allow musical and graphic specialists and nonspecialists alike to perform systematic analyses of symbol structure. Any researcher can analyze musical and graphic symbols using these indicators, and can do so knowing that they are being true to the essential characteristics of each genre. In this way, my measures render musical and graphic symbols extremely accessible sources of social science data, amenable to all of the rigorous methods that are central to the social science tradition. In addition, these new indicators allow dichotomous categories like basic versus embellished syntax to be analyzed on a continuous scale, making any comparison of symbol structures richer and more precise. In short, this new system of measurement opens the door to both fresh research questions as well as the reexploration of standing issues in the areas of communication and cognition.

To be sure, my approach to symbol analysis is not exhaustive. My measures tap the foundational elements of music and graphic structure but admittedly leave other important dimensions unaddressed, most notably the relative aesthetic qualities of various designs (Cerulo 1994). Knowing this, I offer my approach as a starting point from which to gather much-needed information on the selection and projection of nonverbal messages. Like any new method, my system is not flawless. But through application and feedback, improvements to these measures will ensue, as we build on current strengths and identify and correct existing flaws.

With a method of measurement in hand, we begin a scientific excursion aimed at better understanding the selection of symbol designs. Our first stop sets a nation's symbols side by side, comparing the syntactic structure of anthems and flags. In so doing, we can determine if political elites select these very different statements of identity with a unified design format in mind.

The Comparative Structure of National Anthems and Flags

Every national symbol is only one member of a national symbol set— a "cluster" that contains a nation's anthem, crest, flag, motto, etc.

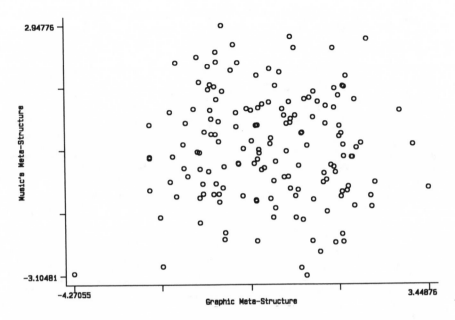

Figure 2.2a. Comparison of anthem and flag syntactic metastructure for 163 nations

Knowing this, we must consider the possibility that those selecting any particular national symbol may be sensitive to the structure of other cluster members. A desire for consistency within a symbol set may drive the adoption of one symbol design over another. If such is the case, we would expect the syntactic metastructure of anthems and flags to be highly similar. Because anthems and flags are members of the same symbol cluster, they may display like designs.[13]

We can explore this hypothesis by plotting the syntactic metastructure of national anthems versus flags, checking for the strength of the relationship between their designs. Figure 2.2A presents such a plot, displaying data on the 163 nations for which both anthem and flag scores were available. This plot suggests little correspondence between anthem and flag designs. We see no linear pattern in the

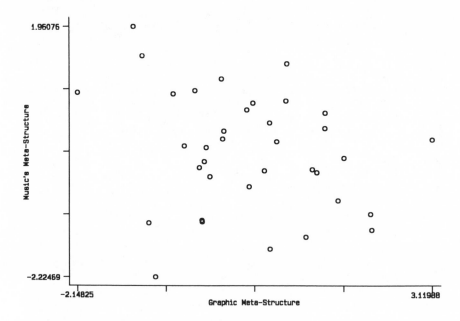

Figure 2.2b. Comparison of anthem and flag syntactic metastructure for nations that adopted anthem and flag concurrently

plot, but rather, a cloud of data. (Note that a weak correlation coefficient confirms the visual impression: r = −.009; p = .85.)

The weak association between anthem and flag syntax occurs even when the symbols are simultaneously adopted. Figure 2.2B displays the anthem and flag metastructures for the thirty-eight nations that adopted these symbols concurrently. (See Appendix B for the adoption years of all anthems and flags.) Here too, the data suggest little similarity between symbol designs (r = −.123; p = .27). Consequently, the analysis offers insufficient support for the notion of symbol sameness. Although joint members of a national symbol set, anthems and flags are often differentially structured by genre.

Differences in anthem and flag structure may stem from variations in the cognitive processing of aural and visual stimuli. Communication theorists tell us that we differentially processes information depending on the genre of the input. Visual information, for example, can be more emotionally stimulating than verbal or aural messages; visual information is often better recalled than aural speech or verbal text. In contrast, aural or verbal messages are usually more effective than visual ones in communicating detail or particulars, and so forth.[14] Such divergent reactions to stimuli may necessitate the differential structuring of musical and graphic symbols, despite their joint membership in a symbol set.

Conclusion

"The art of making art," wrote Stephen Sondheim, "is putting it together."[15] But Sondheim's claim need not be restricted to art. Indeed, I have argued that we derive meaning from *any* symbol—artistic, religious, or in the present case, political—by reviewing not only the symbol's content but also the way in which that content is configured or designed.

In this chapter, I have highlighted the importance of structural variation, arguing that such variations represent different communication strategies—strategies that are consciously selected and manipulated by those projecting a message. I have also presented a method by which symbol structures can be quantified and systematically examined and compared. With this method in hand, we began a detailed inquiry into the forces that determine the syntactic structure of national anthems and flags.

Thus far, we have explored the influence of one symbol's structure on another's. The data suggested that a nation's symbols are not uniformly formatted; rather, structures differ by genre. I suggested that distinctions in the cognitive processing of aural and graphic stimuli may help to explain this finding. Yet that factor provides only a partial explanation of the phenomenon. Note that anthems are not systematically more embellished than flags; anthems and flags do not consistently exhibit opposing syntactic structures. Thus, factors beyond known processing trends are influencing the selection of symbol designs.

In searching for these factors, we must remain mindful that the cognitive aspects of symbol projection and reception are socially and culturally situated (see, e.g., Beisel 1993, DeVault 1990, Griswold 1987, Katz 1986, Lamont 1987, Schudson 1989, Sewell 1992). Certain dimensions of both the sender's and the audience's environment will effect the strategies that the sender perceives as appropriate to her/his target. The next three chapters are devoted to identifying and exploring such dimensions.

3

"EDITORS" OF NATIONAL SYMBOL STRUCTURES

THE BIRTH OF a nation is the birth of a new social arrangement. At its inception, a nation reorders those it engulfs, for it takes groups of people previously bound by virtue of region or communal republic and merges them into a single, distinct political entity. With the formation of a nation, a fragmented people are united under a central authority. A population is redefined in terms of shared similarities rather than distinctions. A people are encouraged to internalize a new affiliation, a newly forged cultural homogeneity, and a newly created collective history.

The "Lumping" and "Splitting" of Designs

The reorientation of which I speak rests largely on the process of identity construction. Much like a human infant, a new nation embarks on a journey of identity development. Just as the infant looks inside and outside itself in an effort to define its own integrity, a nation's leaders look both within and beyond the nation's borders, assessing the new entity's place in the world. In this way, national leaders gradually build an image, a national "self" that, like its individualistic counterpart, is dualistic. It combines a national "self-consciousness"—one built upon selected indigenous strong suits,

55

with a national "social consciousness"—one that reflects the reactions of the nation's "significant others," the members of the world community. As such, a nation's identity falls subject to cognitive strategies of impression management—here, the leadership's ways of seeing and thinking about the national self.

Because the formation of national identity parallels processes typically confined to discussions of individual development, there is much to be gained by applying traditional theories of identity construction to the macro level. Further, such theories also provide a basis for understanding the formation of national symbols. As this chapter will demonstrate, national symbols develop in conjunction and in support of each phase of identity construction. Because these symbols objectify the national identity, the referents that mold a nation's identity also edit its symbolic expression. More specifically, the referents of each nation's self-image denote and limit the parameters by which that image can be symbolized.

Phases of Identity Construction

Identity construction begins when individuals conceive of themselves as insular entities, persons separate and distinct from their surroundings. In forming an identity, individuals must experience themselves as both subjects and objects, players that can both form and be formed by social encounters (see, e.g., Allport 1961:112–13; Cooley [1902] 1964:210; Erikson [1950] 1963:235; Mead 1934:138; Stein 1987:109, 117; Wiley 1979:96; Zerubavel 1991:22, 41).

A nation undergoes much the same process of cognitive *insulation* when building its national identity. It becomes self-conscious, defining itself as an independent entity, distinct within the world community. The nation reflects on itself as a viable player on the world stage, one that can both act and be reacted to. In essence, the nation perceives itself as a discrete "figure," distinct from the background in which it is embedded.[1]

Nations develop a variety of symbols to underscore this insular character. Constitutions or declarations of independence, for example, articulate separateness and unique integrity. Consider the opening paragraph of the U.S. Declaration of Independence: "When in the Course of human events, it becomes necessary for one people to *dissolve the political bands which have connected them with another,* and to assume among the Powers of the earth, the separate and equal station to which the Laws of Nature and of Nature's God entitle them" (emphasis added). Similarly, the preamble of Mauritania's constitution states: "The people of Mauritania hereby proclaim their will to safeguard the *integrity of their territory* and to ensure their free political, economic, and social evolution" (emphasis added). These documents initiate a nation; they reference a new entity's origins, and help identify its parameters. As such, constitutions and declarations of independence serve to set a nation apart from others.

In much the same way, nations adopt holidays such as independence days or national days to delimit their unique identity. By defining a nation's beginning, such holidays temporally insulate the entity. When U.S. citizens observe the Fourth of July, the French celebrate Bastille Day (July 14), or Argentinians commemorate National Day (May 25), they acknowledge a figurative "starting line" that separates each nation's history from that of all others. Such symbols enforce a sense of inclusion and exclusion, a boundedness that is vital to every nation's identity.

National border rituals and the symbols they include provide another common tool of insulation. Ritualizing the processes of entry and exit demarcates both a nation's physical and identity boundaries. So, for example, when leaving one nation and entering another, we use passports to clarify citizenship, we change currencies, and often, we adopt new languages.[2] The objects and actions involved in crossing national borders provide a physical "lining" that protects each nation's unique integrity and flags the transition from one entity to another.

At the level of the individual, insulation represents the self-conscious phase of identity construction. The process emphasizes discovery. The same can be said for the nation. Insulation allows a nation to articulate its own special presence and character. Via insulation, the nation configures its indigenous traits into a unique self-image.

In human development, *integration* represents the next phase of identity formation. During this period, individuals come to see themselves in relation to the other objects in their environment. They learn their position relative to a set of significant others, and later, "generalized others." As individuals internalize the reactions of their audience, and the overall configuration of the arenas in which these reactions occur, identity is formed (see, e.g., Cooley [1902] 1964:152; Elkin and Handel 1984:54; Erikson 1968:22; Hunt et al. 1994; McCall and Simmons 1966:54; Mead 1925:269; Mead 1934:154–63; Stryker 1987).

A nation's integration experience is similar. For once defined, a nation must learn its position in the world community. It must apprehend the interrelations between itself and other nations; it must master its role in community interaction and exchange. For each developing nation, the world community becomes a generalized other. As a nation presents its self, the nation reflects upon the generalized other's organized reactions and incorporates those reactions into an evolving national identity. In this way, the world community helps to form the "me" of the national self.

National symbols reflect a nation's integration experience. Their creation, modes of projection, and the reactions they receive tell us much about the way in which a nation perceives its position on the world stage. Consider diplomats, living symbols of the nations they represent. Their placement and patterns of action provide a grid of a nation's community of reference. A nation, for instance, exchanges diplomats with allies and severs diplomatic ties with enemies. It places heavy resources in embassies of nations important to its economic and political well-being, while making only minimal investments in nations with which it has no significant interactions. Similarly, the world community's treatment of a nation's diplomats gauge that nation's station in the international arena. The location of the nation's embassy, its ambassador's protocol rank at official gatherings—all of these factors reflect the external perceptions of the nation's stature.

National flags also can illuminate a nation's integration experience. For example, a nation that perceives strong bonds to its colonizer may include portions of that country's flag in its own. So, for instance, the flags of Australia, Fiji, and New Zealand bear the Union Jack. Similarly, Chad, the Ivory Coast, and Mali adopted the French tricolor design. Tunisia mirrored the design of the Turkish flag. By embracing its colonizer's symbols, each nation exposed its sense of historical place.

Some developing nations use flags to indicate anticipatory integration. In such instances, nations copy the flag design of an established power, thus indicating a desire to bond with or model that power. For example, in their bids for independence, Belgium and Italy adopted the French tricolor design. Similarly, during its fight for independence from Spain, Honduras mirrored the flag of Argentina, a nation that had successfully rebelled against Spain. And upon declaring independence, Iceland linked itself to other Scandinavian nations by including the Scandinavian cross in its flag. In each of these cases, national flags charted international alliances. As such, they shed light on nations' perceived sociopolitical locations.

At the level of the individual, integration emphasizes self-comparison, relative assessment, and the internalization of perceived external evaluations. The same can be said for the nation's integration experience. Integration involves nations in a "compare and contrast" exercise. It adjusts a nation's self-image on the basis of the nation's relative social placement.

Two additional cognitive processes emerge from insulation and integration: *lumping* and *splitting*. Lumping defines or classifies an image with reference to other like entities. With lumping, we construct identities by attending to similarities. Splitting, on the other hand, specifies an image by distinguishing it from other entities. The process builds identities with reference to contrast (Zerubavel 1991:16–17; also see Bruner et al. 1956:2–4; Cohen 1969:109–11; Johnson 1967:242; Smith and Medin 1981:110–11; Sokal 1977:7).

Lumping and splitting are simultaneous practices, helping us to concurrently perceive what an image, object, or person is and is not. These processes occur across numerous dimensions. For example, when we classify groups with reference to custom or tradition, we engage in *lineal* lumping and splitting. Identifying individuals as students of the impressionist painters or graduates of Ballanchine's ballet program lumps them within one artistic school while splitting them from others. *Temporal* lumping and splitting occur when we construct identities on the basis of certain time periods or eras. Defining a group as "baby boomers," for example, links them to other children born during the forties and fifties, while simultaneously distancing them from the "beatniks" who came of age in the fifties. Frequently, we lump and split on the basis of *ideology*. Lumping ourselves with liberals links us to a particular political agenda and splits us from the policies of moderates and conservatives. And when we refer to American "East Coasters" or the "north wingers" of our office building, we engage in *spatial* lumping and splitting. We identify a group in terms of physical location, while distinguishing the group from those outside the confines of that space.

When constructing national identities, lumping and splitting occur as well, as nations focus on their ancestries, traditions, and immediate environments—what we might think of as nations' indigenous characteristics. Lineal lumping and splitting occurs, for example, when nations link their identities to those of their colonizers, while separating their images from other colonial traditions. In this way, Spanish customs greatly influence the identities of Spain's colonies; English traditions help to mold the identities of British colonies, and so forth. Further, any one power's colonies are linked via their connection to the same colonizer—for example, every Spanish colony is lumped with other Spanish dependencies. At the same time, colonial lumps draw our attentions to the cultural differences existing between colony groups, thus splitting Spanish colonies from French, Portuguese, or Japanese possessions.

Temporal lumping and splitting influence national identity construction as well, as nations construct their histories via consecutive yet discrete blocks of time. Greece, for example, refers to its Golden Age. The United States makes reference to the Reconstruction period. The People's Republic of China speaks of the Cultural Revolution. In so doing, each nation lumps together certain events in its past, while distinguishing those events from other occurrences. Upon these temporal blocks, with all their similarities and differences, national identities unfold.

Temporal lumping and splitting hold additional implications for national identity. For a nation's "birth date" locates it among a cohort of others who experienced the same thing at the same time. Therefore, we view Mexico's independence as part of a larger Latin American movement. We use Ghana's independence in 1957 to mark the establishment of other independent African nations. In this way, temporal lumping merges one nation's character with those that developed simultaneous to it. At the same time, temporal splitting limits the periods from which each nation selects the foundations of its identity. This explains, for example, that despite great similarities surrounding America's rebellion against England and Brazil's revolt against Portugal, both incidents are seen as products of distinctly different eras, and thus, two independence movements with drastically different flavors.

A nation's identity is also guided by ideological lumping and splitting, with the processes creating distinct ingroups and outgroups. Ingroup members become connected through systems of belief, even though they may exhibit vastly different ethnic, historical, or regional traditions. In this way, communist ideology links nations as different as China, Cuba, and Congo. Similarly, Islamic ideologies bind Middle Eastern nations together, even though they may be political or economical rivals. Such ideological lumping simultaneously distances ingroup members from nations with opposing beliefs: communist nations distinguish their sentiments from capitalist nations; Islamic nations differentiate their beliefs from those of their Christian neighbors.

Finally, nations' assessments of their indigenous traits include careful reflections on immediate environments. Nations lump themselves with their geographic neighbors, while simultaneously splitting themselves from more distant lands. Such spatial categories incorporate region into the construction of national identities. Thus, when we speak of the Baltic states or the United Arab Emirates, we stress each group member's similarities to others nations in the regional lump. At the same time, we use "place" to distinguish each group member from nations that are geographically removed.

Lumping, Splitting, and Symbolic Expression

The influence of lumping and splitting transcends the formation of national identities. I argue that the two processes also delimit the symbolization of identities. National symbols emerge from a standardized symbolic system, one consciously designed to ensure clear communication between world community members. This symbol system specifies a bounded vocabulary and grammar from which expressions of a nation's identity can be built. However, the international subgroups formed by lumping and splitting serve to segment the broader symbol system. When lumping subdivides the community into smaller, more cohesive groups, the process simultaneously sequesters certain parts of the symbol system. When splitting underscores the distinctions between subgroups, the process apportions the symbol system, making some sections available to certain nations and unavailable to others. In this way, a nation's symbols can be limited by those of their ancestors, their contemporaries, their ideological affiliates, and their regional neighbors.[3]

Consider the ways in which lineal lumping and splitting can influence a nation's symbolic voice. As a colony, a country is weaned on the culture and practices of its colonial power. Thus in many ways, it is through the eyes of the colonizer that a colony comes to see the world. This guided exposure is especially true with regard to the world symbol system, for the symbols of the colonial power serve as the colony's template of expression. When independence ensues, a former colony must add its own unique symbols to the world "pool." As such, the colonial power's symbols serve as the primary window through which the colony views its expressive options.

Temporal lumping and splitting exerts a similar influence on symbolic expression. Consider that each new cohort of nations marks a distinct phase of growth in the world community. I argue that each such era develops a unique "signature." Nations entering the community adopt symbols that distinguish them from their predecessors, while simultaneously bonding them to their fellow initiates. In this way, the symbols of a nation's forerunners serve as reference points for expressive splitting, whereas those of contemporaries become references for expressive lumping.

Ideological lumping and splitting subdivide the world symbol system on the basis of belief. Certain vocabularies and designs become associated with specific points of view or particular philosophical movements. In this case, national leaders invoke certain symbolic images as a mode of affiliating with other ideological group members, while avoiding the images of ideological opponents.

Lastly, consider the impact of spatial lumping and splitting on symbolic expression. Spatial classifications can "regionalize" the world symbol system. In adopting national symbols, then, leaders of a nation attend to the symbols that dominate their region, using them as a point of reference for the symbolic expression of self. At the same time, the images of other regions are rejected and defined as appropriate to other locations.

The content of national symbols confirms the influence of lumping and splitting processes. Several examples suggest that lineal, temporal, ideological, and spatial referents delimit a nation's symbol vocabulary. Consider the lineal dimension. Nations lumped by colonial tradition frequently display currency systems with uniform content. Australia, Ireland, and Jamaica, among others, maintained shilling coins after independence. Algeria, Belgium, and Monaco kept a franc system in their postcolonial eras. Similarly, nations lumped by colonial tradition exhibit overlapping content in their cuisines. Both Laotian and Vietnamese cuisines, for example, use French ingredients. Elements of Japanese cooking are sprinkled throughout Korean and Taiwanese cuisines. Spanish and Portuguese foods are central to many South American cuisines.

The lineal aspects of content are especially visible in anthems and flags. For example, the lyrics of Burundi's, Rwanda's, and Zaire's national anthems mirror the devotional theme of their colonizer's anthem, that of Belgium. Similarly, the Finnish anthem echoes the pastoral strains of the Swedish anthem. In the realm of flags, note that Liberia and Panama modeled their flag colors after those of the United States. Similarly, Iceland's flag reflects the Dannebrog, the emblem of its referent, Denmark. With regard to content, imitation often permeates the relationship between colonial power and former colony.

Evidence also suggests the temporal lumping and splitting of national symbol content. National icons offer a case in point. Icons popularized during the same time period frequently share content characteristics. This is true despite the cultural differences in the nations or events the icons represent. Consider the similarities between two dominant images of eighteenth-century nationalism: Miss Liberty of the United States and France's Marianne. Although the social movements represented by these two symbols were quite different in substance, the iconic images were nearly identical in content. Both symbols portrayed a pastoral, female image, one possessing an ethereal aura. Now consider two key nineteenth-century icons, Uncle Sam of the United States and the British Bulldog. Despite the cultural differences in the nations they represent, both symbols promoted a rugged, earthy tone, one that championed the notion of the "common man." Finally, note that whereas iconic contemporaries share content, icons emerging from different temporal periods often present opposing images. Thus, the earthy Uncle Sam stands in direct contrast to the ethereal Miss Liberty, the Bulldog in contradiction of Marianne.

A perusal of anthem and flag content offers further evidence of temporal lumping and splitting. For example, note that the first cohort of nations to adopt national anthems—the Netherlands, Great Britain, and Spain—all chose hymns whose lyrics edified the nations' rulers. The next cohort—France, Argentina, and Peru—divorced themselves from this theme, opting for rousing songs bespeaking triumph over oppression. These content distinctions lump the nations within each cohort together and split the two cohorts from each other. Now consider the content of flags adopted during the first and second quintiles of the time period spanned by this study, 1785–1993. Table 3.1 illustrates that content distinguished the products of the two periods. First, note that the number of flag colors increases from four in the first period to five in the second. In addition, the table shows that the predominance of each color changes significantly from quintile to quintile.

History reveals substantial ideological lumping and splitting of symbol content. Note that the hammer and sickle, the five-point star, the color red, and Marx and Lenin constitute the content of most communist national symbols. The crescent and five-point star, the color green, and the scimitar are all part of the Islamic symbolic tradition. Such ideological content serves as a reference points for nations guided by each specific set of beliefs. So, for example, the symbols conventionally associated with democracy serve as models for emerging democratic nations. The images of pan-Africanism influence the symbols of nations seeking membership in that community.

The ideological lumping and splitting of anthem content is quite visible. For example, South American "revolutionary" anthems all boast lyrics that call citizens to arms. Similarly, the anthems of Islamic nations utilize majestic marchlike rhythms. Flag content, too, reflects ideological lumping and splitting. Pan-African nations, for example, use the same colors in their flags: black, green, red, and yellow.

Table 3.1. Content of Flags, Period 1 (1785–1825) versus Period 2 (1826–1866)

Period 1 Nations: Spain, France, San Marino, United Kingdom, Argentina, Chile, Norway, and Peru

Color	Proportion of Flags Using Color
Blue	.625
Red	.750
White	.875
Yellow	.125

Period 2 Nations: Belgium, Uruguay, Tunisia, Paraguay, Dominican Republic, Liberia, Denmark, Japan, Colombia, and Andorra

Color	Proportion of Flags Using Color
Black	.100
Blue	.500
Red	1.000
White	.700
Yellow	.400

Nations bound by the Islamic tradition use the color green in their flags. Those sympathetic to the causes of the French revolution built their national flags around the colors red, white, and blue. In all of these examples, shared ideologies resulted in shared symbol content.

Spatial lumping clearly influences national symbol content. Consider, for instance, the blending of national cuisines. The Tex-Mex items of the U.S. Southwest, the immense overlap in English, Irish, Scottish, and Welsh menus, or the "French" nature of northern Italian cuisines—all of these edible hybrids constitute a regional subset within a larger world vocabulary of nationalistic foods. Further, such subsets simultaneously contrast one region's vocabulary from others within the world community.

The spatial categorization of anthem and flag content is easy to document. The national anthems of Middle Eastern nations, for example, are uniform in their lauding of national rulers. Similarly, the anthems of northern Europe share slow, majestic rhythms. Crosses dominate the content of northern European national flags. And the color blue plays a major role in the flags of Central America. Such examples attest to the influence of region in a nation's selection of its symbolic vocabulary.

All of these examples suggest a segmenting of the broader world vocabulary of symbols—segments created along lineal, temporal, ideological, and regional lines. And as lumping and splitting influence symbol content, I suggest that the processes influence the selection of symbol design as well. Specifically, I argue that *the structure of a nation's symbols is contingent on those nations with whom they are lumped and split.* In the next section, we systematically explore this hypothesis. Using the data detailing the syntactic structure of national anthems and flags, we explore the ways in which cognitive processes can influence strategies of collective expression.

Lineal Lumping and Splitting of Structure

Evidence suggests that colonial powers influence *what* appears in their former colonies' symbols. Do colonizers influence *how* that content is conveyed? Such an inquiry begins by matching colonial powers with their colonies.

Seventeen nations in my sample functioned as colonial powers. However, only ten such nations possessed more than one colony; my analysis is restricted to those ten colonizers. (Appendix B lists each nation's colonial power.)[4] Note that France, Great Britain, and Spain controlled the largest number of colonies, followed by Portugal, Turkey, and the Soviet Union,[5] each possessing five colonies or more.

In my analysis, I compared the syntax score of each colonial power's anthem with the mean score of its former colonies.[6] I used t-tests to distinguish significant differences from nonnotable discrepancies.[7] The findings show that the anthem scores of Belgium, France, Great Britain, Italy, Spain, and Turkey are significantly different from the mean scores of their respective colony clusters.[8] Note that although these nations represent only six of the ten mother countries, their colonies account for 88 percent of all those considered. Thus, the findings substantiate the influence of lineal classifications in the symbol selection process. But, counter to trends surrounding the selection of symbol content, *these findings suggest a tendency for former colonies to differentiate their anthems from those of their mother countries.*

I also compared anthem scores within colony groups. These comparisons helped to determine if the possessions of any single colonial power shared their syntactic strategies. Such lumping characterizes colonies of Belgium, Germany, Italy, the Netherlands, and the United States, as the anthem scores for these colony clusters all fall within 1.5 standard deviations of their respective group means. But the anthem scores for French, British, Portuguese, Spanish, and Turkish colony clusters show much greater diversity, with some scores falling 3 standard deviations beyond their group mean. On the basis of these observations, we must conclude that *nations are not necessarily apt to lump their anthem structures with those of fellow former colonies.* Shared former-colony status does not appear to be a powerful influence in the symbolic designs of identity.

The results for national flags are identical. The mean graphic scores for the colony groups of Belgium, France, Germany, Great Britain, Japan, Spain, and the United States (79 percent of all colonies) are significantly different from the scores of their colonizers.[9] Thus with regard to flags, nations break from the design traditions of their colonial powers. Further, no clear trend in the lumping or splitting of flag structures appears within colony clusters. Although the flag structures of Belgian, German, Italian, Japanese, Dutch, and U.S. colony clusters display some resemblance, scores within the remaining colony groups display significant variation.

When considering the analyses in total, the effects of lineal classifications on the adoption of symbol designs is clear. *At the syntactic level, a nation's anthem and flag stand in contrast to the symbols of its colonial power.* Any discussion of national symbol design must take this tendency into account. For while nations use symbol content to bind themselves with their colonial pasts, they use symbol structure to differentiate themselves from their symbolic roots. The syntax differences in the anthems and flags of colonial powers and their former colonies represent the enactment of distinctive communication strategies—attempts on the part of new nations to develop a different voice. Therefore, content may indicate a nation's past tradition, but syntax appears to illustrate its future.

Temporal Lumping and Splitting of Structure

The content of anthems and flags varies with time. Plotting a symbol's year of adoption against its syntax score helps to illustrate the temporal lumps and splits of symbol structures. (The adoption year for each anthem studied is listed in Appendix B.) Figure 3.1A shows the data for anthems. The plot, coupled with relevant statistics, indicate significant temporal influence; the data suggest an inverse relationship between time and syntactic embellishment. Early adopters tend toward highly embellished structures; anthems adopted in subsequent periods display increasingly basic designs ($r = -.344$; $p = .02$).[10]

Temporal lumping and splitting also have an impact on flag design. Yet the nature of that impact proves opposite to time's influence on anthems. Figure 3.1B reveals a positive association between adoption year and embellished graphic structure. The plot reveals that early adopters share basic graphic structure. Flags adopted during subsequent eras become increasingly embellished in design ($r = .347$; $p = .02$).

These findings crystallize two important points. First, *nations tend to lump their symbol structures with those of their contemporaries and split them from those of other eras.* Knowing this, we must consider a symbol's year of adoption when exploring the determinants of its design. Second, the data suggest that *temporal lumping and splitting patterns differ by symbol genre.* Although anthem structure becomes more basic over time, flag structure becomes more embellished. This result supports the notion that different media may call for different communication strategies.

Ideological Lumping and Splitting of Structure

Nations often use symbol content to underscore ideological bonds and rifts. I classified each of the nations in my sample according to five dominant ideologies: communism, democracy, Islam, pan-Africanism, and socialism. Nations not formally articulating one of these stances formed a residual sixth category.[11] Classifications were made with reference to two time periods: the year in which a nation

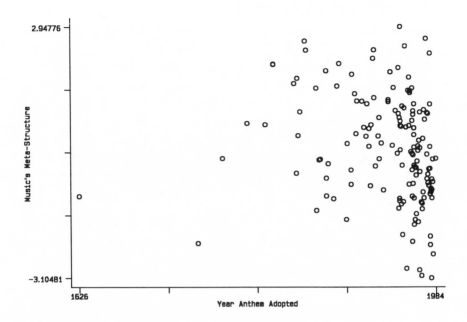

Figure 3.1a. Correlation between music structure and adoption year

adopted its anthem and the year of flag adoption. (Appendix B lists these data.)

In analyzing anthems, I searched for significant syntax differences among the six ideological nation groups. A one-way analysis of variance revealed no such distinctions. Between groups, variation in anthem structure was not statistically significant (F = 1.08; p = .382). I also compared the mean syntax score of each ideological lump with that of the world community at large. T-tests indicated only one significant comparison. *Islamic nations adopt more basic anthems than other nations of the world community* (t = 2.35; p = .021). Overall, then, *these findings suggest only a minimal impact of ideology on anthem structure.*

Ideology demonstrates no impact on the syntactic structure of flags. A one-way analysis of variance revealed no significant differences between the flag structures of the six ideological groups (F = 1.25; p =

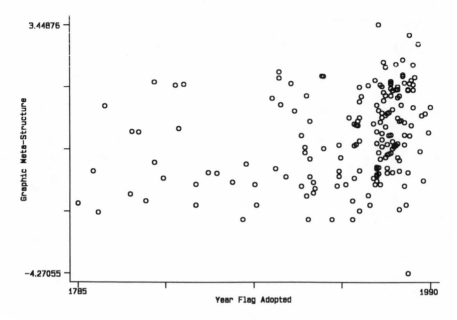

Figure 3.1b. Correlation between graphic structure and adoption year

.270). Similarly, t-tests failed to yield significance when contrasting the flag structures of each ideological lump with those of the world community at large.

On the basis of these findings, we must conclude that *ideological lumping and splitting play little or no role in the selection of symbol syntax.* Although ideology may guide symbol content, nations bound by belief share few similarities in their strategies of symbolic expression.

Spatial Lumping and Splitting of Structure

Does region have an impact on symbol design? To pursue the issue, I located each nation within a specific geographic "neighborhood," defining neighbors as those countries directly bordering on the nation in question. For example, Ecuador's neighbors are Colombia and Peru. Angola's neighbors are Namibia, Zambia, Zaire, and Congo. In the case of islands, nations in the immediate periphery became neighbors. Thus, Japan's neighbors are Taiwan, China, South Korea, North Korea, and Russia.

I first compared the syntax score of each nation's anthem to the mean score of its geographic neighborhood. T-tests indicate that nations tend to lump their anthem designs with those of their immediate neighbors. Indeed, 65 percent of the nations in my sample adopted anthems similar in structure to those of their neighbors. The results for flags are similar. T-tests show that 63 percent of the nations in my sample lumped their flag designs with those of their geographic neighbors. Knowing this, the study of symbol design must consider regional influences. For in the symbolic expression of national identity, *communication strategies of spatial immediates appear to limit the strategies of the "speaker."*

Before leaving the data on regional lumping and splitting, note that these *spatial classification patterns frequently vary by genre.* While 47 percent of the nations analyzed here lump both their anthem and flag designs with those of their geographic neighbors, 34 percent of the nations lump either their anthem or flag design, and 19 percent of the sampled nations lump neither of the symbol designs (chi^2 = 9.714; p = .002; Cramer's V = .246. Appendix B locates each nation according to these four categories). These differences in regional classification again suggest that different media may call for different strategies of expression.

The Relative Impact of Lumping and Splitting

We have explored the independent effects of lineage, time, ideology, and space on the lumping and splitting of symbol systems. Equally important are the relative effects of these four dimensions. Beginning with anthems, I constructed a regression model that would address the relative effect of the four processes in question. Before performing the regression, I checked the appropriate levels of association between the variables contained in the model. Two indicators, year of adoption and neighborhood syntax score, were correlated at −.361. Because I saw indications of multicollinearity, I chose a conservative analytic design. Specifically, I constructed two regression models, alternating the inclusion of the two problematic variables (see models 1 and 2 in table 3.2).[12]

Table 3.2. Regression Analysis of Symbol Structure on Indicators of Lineage, Time, Ideology, and Space

Independent Variables	Model 1 Music (B/Beta)	Model 2 Music (B/Beta)	Model 3 Flags (B/Beta)	Model 4 Flags (B/Beta)
Colonial power's syntax	.25/.29[a]	.25/.29[a]	.37/.35[a]	.37/.35[a]
Adoption year	—	.01/−.06	—	.01/.07[a]
Presence of Islamic ideology	−.45/−.12	−.45/−.12	—	—
Neighboring	.26/.19[a]	—	.22/.15[a]	—
R²	.11	.06	.16	.16
F	8.47[a]	6.43[a]	11.00[a]	11.34[a]
N	149	149	161	161

[a]Indicates that coefficients are significant at the .05 level or lower.

Table 3.2 lists the regression results. *In this controlled analysis, only the syntax scores of a nation's colonial power and its neighborhood significantly influence anthem structure.*[13] These two variables overpower the effects of adoption year or Islamic ideology. As the table shows, the two significant variables account for 11 percent of the variation in national anthem structures. As such, considering the syntax of neighboring nations' anthems as well as that of a nation's colonizer represents the first step in understanding the most powerful determinants of anthem design.

In models devoted to flag structure, again, indicators representing adoption year and neighborhood syntax score were correlated (r = .383), and preliminary analysis suggested multicollinearity. Therefore, I repeated the strategy of running two regression models, alternating the inclusion of the two problematic variables (see models 3 and 4 in table 3.2).[14] The findings show that *the syntax scores of a nation's mother country and its neighborhood significantly influence a nation's flag syntax.* In addition, *a nation's flag syntax is associated with its year of adoption.* In the case of flags, then, lineage, time, and space are all important determinants of graphic syntax. Together, these variables account for 16 percent of the variation found in flag structure.[15]

Conclusion

The ways in which we cut up the world, drawing lines of inclusion and exclusion, clearly affects our perceptions of who we are, who we are not, and the appropriate ways in which to express those distinctions. The lumping and splitting of the social world creates distinct pockets of reference, pockets that give rise to discrete voices of expression.

In this chapter, we explored the lines that demarcate several reference groups within the world community, and we charted the shared communication strategies that reside within each group's borders. By examining the various ways in which nations classify themselves, lumping themselves to some groups and splitting themselves from others, we gained some insight regarding the preliminary forces that shape a nation's mode of symbolic expression.

We have discovered that a nation's colonial tradition influences its symbols. Former colonies tend to develop symbol designs that are significantly different from those of their colonial "parents." These syntax distinctions represent a new voice through which a nation's identity can be expressed. We have also seen that bonds of space breed similarity. National leaders use their immediate regional counterparts as reference groups from which to build strategies of communication. In this arena, spatial affiliations give rise to a unified voice. Finally, we have discovered that time can be a basis for the lumping and splitting of certain symbols. Cohorts of nations tend to develop similar strategies of graphic expression.

The role of lineal, temporal, ideological, and spatial categorization in the structuring of anthems and flags represents just the beginning of a long and complicated journey. The first stage of this analysis leaves abundant variation in symbol structure yet to be explained. Therefore, in the next chapter, we extend our focus, reviewing the selection of syntactic strategies in light of additional reference groups.

4

SOCIOECONOMIC POCKETS AND THE STRUCTURE OF NATIONAL SYMBOLS

"THE PRODUCTION OF ideas, of conceptions, of consciousness," wrote Karl Marx, "is at first directly interwoven with the material activity and the material intercourse of men" (1978:154). With this passage, Marx introduced a socioeconomic theory of cognition. He framed human cognition as a "transitory product," one whose essence is externally driven (Marx 1910:chap. 2, p. 1; Marx 1904:8). From the Marxian perspective, the mentality of any entity emerges from the social relations in which that entity exists.[1]

The social relations to which Marx refers differ significantly from the more traditional relational referents: lineage, time, ideology, and space. For Marx, social relations are the links that individuals establish as they participate in economic life.[2] These links forge economic categories that organize the arena in which identity is realized. Thus, social relations represent a critical addition to the study of identity construction. Such economy-based ties generate additional groups of reference. Like the traditional editors of identity heretofore explored, the relative location of an entity within the broader economic structure—its "class affiliation"—can contribute significantly to identity development.

The concept of social relations is generally applied to the study of individuals and the social classes they form. Yet the notion easily extends to the nation. Within the international community, social relations are defined by each nation's relationship to the world supply of raw materials, its links to established and emergent technologies, and its position within the transnational market. Nations exhibiting similar patterns in these regards form clusters, socioeconomic pockets characterized by differential power to move or control the larger global system. Thus, socioeconomic pockets both differentiate groups of nations and illuminate a vertical ranking of nations. Lumping and splitting nations with reference to social relations forms the equivalent of a stratified class system within the world community.

By charting the social relations within the international arena, this chapter identifies various economy-based clusters of nations and outlines the properties each cluster displays. Once doing so, I explore the ways in which these socioeconomic pockets of reference influence national self-perception, identification, and, ultimately, the strategies by which national identity is expressed.

Defining Socioeconomic Pockets: The World-System Approach

For many years, sociologists studied the nation solely in terms of its internal workings. Nations were viewed, in large part, as independently emerging entities developing according to general evolutionary patterns.[3] But in the 1970s, an alternate approach to national development emerged. Combining concepts and premises from Marxism, Lenin's work on imperialism, the Annales school,[4] and the Dependency approach,[5] *world-systems theory* was developed. The theory offered a historical and international model of national development, one far more broad than any of the theory's predecessors, and one that transported the concept of social relations to the macro level.

World-systems theory considers the location of all nations with regard to social, economic, historical, and political conditions.[6] But more important, the theory looks at the interrelations between nations, viewing all societies as an *ensemble des ensembles*—a set of components that form an organized whole.[7] In this way, the social structure of individual societies is viewed in terms of the context created by the larger system. Each nation is one facet of a larger global community, a single cog in a larger machine, one necessarily responsive to the actions of the parts to which it is linked.

Typically, the world-system is divided into three sectors: core, semiperiphery, and periphery. Nations located in the core enjoy economic and political dominance. Core nations maintain highly efficient agro-industrial production. They produce the system's most advanced goods, use the system's most sophisticated technologies, and possess the system's most highly mechanized means of production. Core nations also boast the greatest level of capital accumulation and the greatest military power of any world-system sector. In addition, they displays the greatest administrative organization in the system, making core nations highly centralized. Nations located in the periphery display opposite characteristics. These nations are labor intensive, their contributions to the system resting most heavily on raw materials and agricultural commodities.[8] The semiperiphery is an intermediary sector, one that often helps to bridge the core and periphery. Because of this role, semiperiphery nations display some core-like and some periphery-like qualities.

As this summary clearly illustrates, the *nature* of each sector's contributions to the world economy—the social relations of the system—are fundamentally asymmetrical and exploiting. The core, for example, produces capital-intensive, high-technology goods, some of which it exports to the periphery and semiperiphery, some of which it retains. The periphery, in contrast, produces labor-intensive, low-technology goods that are desired and freely utilized by the core and semiperiphery. And, of course, most of the surplus value in the system flows to the core.

World-systems theory alerts us to the importance of economic reference groups, as each of the system's sectors mandates a particular relationship between a nation and its global counterparts. Yet for all of the theory's insight, the approach is not without flaws. Note that most world-systems theorists discuss the system's economic relationships solely in terms of their economic consequences.[9] However, there is good reason to believe that these economic relationships carry cultural consequences as well. Cultural products and processes, like their economic counterparts, are commodities that can be shaped and molded by the system. Hence, the relative location in which such products are created, as well as the characteristics of the total system at the time in which these cultural products emerge, should influence both their content and form.[10]

A small number of studies have successfully highlighted the link between world-system structure and cultural products and processes. Studying the seventeenth-century scientific community, for example, Robert Wuthnow found that periods of increased scientific discovery were spurred by elevations in the interstate competition that characterized the core of the world-system (1980a:51). As a related point, he noted that structurally equivalent societies generated similar levels of scientific activity, producing comparable rates of scientists and scientific discoveries (ibid.:46–50). In another work, Wuthnow demonstrated that the development of certain religious movements was better explained by the world order than by elements internal to societies from which the movements emerged. A population's place in the world community strongly affected the manner in which that society defined the major problems of its existence and, therefore, the nature of its religious orientation (1980b:60). In the artistic realm, Albert Bergesen studied the diffusion of art styles, showing that the successful spread of any single style is largely a function of the world-system position held by the nation from which the style emanates. Using the rise of abstract art as a test case, Bergesen linked the supremacy of the style to American hegemony, arguing that the spread of abstract art was, in essence, a form of cultural imperialism by which a powerful nation imposed its cultural ideas upon the less powerful (1987:226–33).

Taken together, these studies suggest that the structure of the world-system may, in part, determine the ways in which culture is conceived, produced, and expressed. Spurred by that suggestion, we turn our attentions to the ways in which the strata of the world-system can form a critical backdrop to national identity construction and its symbolic expression.

System Position, Identity, and Symbolic Expression

Like each nation's memberships in lineal, temporal, ideological, and spatial clusters, a nation's ranking in the world-system provides a reference point for leaders as they craft and refine a nation's image.

Core, semiperiphery, and periphery locations form categories that force the comparison of the national self with others. These comparisons move nations beyond considerations of their real wealth and power, and focus nations on their wealth and power relative to their counterparts. Thus, economic reference groups—lumps and splits of nations—force a national definition that is based not just on what the nation is, but on what it is not as well.[11]

History documents the role of economic referencing in national identity construction. Consider, for example, work on American identity formation. Richard Merritt (1966:175–79) suggests that American national identity was successfully crystallized only when the colonies began to consider their power and status relative to Great Britain and the larger world order. In an earlier work, Merle Curti made a similar argument, writing: "When the shoe began to pinch, *the conviction that British and American interests differed became an important fact in the growth of American self-consciousness*" (1946:10, emphasis added; see also Greene 1993). Relative economic status also is said to have influenced the construction of modern Italian national identity. For at the turn of the twentieth century, many suggest that Italy's image was based on the nation's relationship to the world's great powers. Paul Kennedy, for instance, argues that Italians perceived their nation as economically, militarily, and technologically inferior to Austria-Hungary, Britain, France, Germany, and the United States. Such perceptions hindered passions for Italian nationalism and enthusiasm for Italian unification (1987:204–5). In Sri Lanka, too, the development of national identity fell subject to the influence of economic referencing. During the process of national definition, S. J. Tambiah posits that Sri Lankans looked not just inward but also outward, below, and above their place on the economic hierarchy: "The Sri Lankans feel *superior* to the Indians, the Malays, the Chinese, perhaps even the Japanese. For their *eyes are set on the West*, particularly Great Britain, which was their colonial ruler from the early nineteenth century until 1948" (1986:1–2, emphasis added). Each of these cases illustrates that a nation's identity is often solidified via cross-national economic contrasts. Nations reflect on their placement relative to others before defining who they are.[12] Relative material existence establishes a view of self that locates the nation among a larger world set of economic players.

Socioeconomic reference groups influence not only national identity construction, but its symbolic expression as well. I draw this claim from the massive literature linking socioeconomic class to systematic variations in symbolic communication. To date, most of that research focuses on interpersonal communication styles. But in that arena, scholars have convincingly demonstrated that certain socioeconomic class locations carry with them certain ways of seeing, and hence, certain messages and certain modes of expression.[13]

It seems reasonable to expect such links at the macro social level. A nation's relative economic status bespeaks its wealth or its poverty, its ability to influence or be influenced, control or be controlled. Just as different messages and forms of expression befit the rich man and the poor man, the mistress and the servant, so too should domination and subordination at the international level carry with them a different vision and a different voice. Put more succinctly, nations with structurally disparate positions in the world-system—core, semiperiphery, and periphery—will select different symbolic designs of their identities. Conversely, structurally equivalent nations will display common communication strategies.

In addition to hypothesizing differences in core, semiperiphery, and periphery symbols, we can speculate on the nature of those differences. In this regard, I argue that core nations will favor symbols with limited content and basic structure. Increasingly peripheral locations will tend toward more detailed and embellished forms of expression. These hypotheses are grounded in the mechanics of the status competition that occurs among world-system strata.

Status competition is an inherent characteristic of the world-system. It permeates not just the system's economic activity, but its cultural activity as well. As one moves from the core to the periphery, the implementation of both economic power and cultural power diminish. This means that core nations largely determine the unfolding of world culture. Using their immense economic resources, core nations shape social and cultural institutions[14] so as to reflect their own interests. By doing so, core nations continually reify their power, saturating the world-system with cultural products and practices that reaffirm the core's dominance. Further, the cultural products and practices emanating from the core become the markers by which less powerful nations of the world measure and alter their own objects and modes of expression. In essence, the core establishes the norms that guide the content and form of communication. Core communication forms the baseline for messages projected in the system at large.

When noncore nations communicate at the global level, they can either conform to the norms established by the core, break them, or manipulate them in some way. With regard to national symbols, I argue that noncore nations will choose manipulation. This contention stems from the delicate nature of the symbol adoption process. When adopting national symbols, leaders must remain ever mindful that the symbols will be projected to both those within the nation and those beyond the nation's borders. This presents leaders with a dual task. On one hand, they must choose symbols that make unique, individualistic statements; selections must be sufficiently different from those of other nations, thus making a novel statement regarding what the nation is and is not. Yet national leaders must take care to choose symbols that conform to world standards. A nation's symbols must reflect established modes of expression so as to avoid any hint of exclusionary sentiments. In striking this delicate balance between symbol "uniqueness" and "sameness," manipulation of core communication strategies presents the most viable alternative. Nations using normative manipulation can gain the attention inherent in disruption while avoiding both the stigma attached to norm breaking and the nondistinctiveness of total conformity.[15]

In manipulating established communication norms, noncore nations will enhance established structures rather than restrict them. Embellishment provides a method by which noncore nations can overcompensate for their weak implementation of power. By adopting dense, information-ladened identity signs, noncore nations can project, in great detail, all of the virtues and qualities that, as yet, these nations have been unable to demonstrate within the asymmetrical world-system. Whereas simplifying established communication norms would force the consolidation of information, embellishment provides the opportunity for elaboration in word where none may exist in deed.[16]

We find support for my hypotheses in perusing the content of national symbols. In his study of national constitutions, for example, John Boli notes that periphery nations adopt more expansive identity descriptions than their semiperiphery and core counterparts. He argues that such elaborations serve as cultural tools with which periphery nations attempt to gain power and status.[17] Via highly detailed constitutional statements, periphery nations create an image based upon "what is *believed* about what they (the nations) do, not simply what they do per se. . . . (In this way) what cannot be done in practice, tends to be more expansively described in ideology" (Boli-Bennett 1979:232–33). In a core-dominated world, periphery nations attempt to augment their position by augmenting the symbolic representations of that position.[18]

National anthem content provides additional support for my argument. Recall that anthem lyrics display a rather restricted set of themes: pastoral beauty, call to arms, edification of leader, patriotism, peace, or the struggle for independence (Mead 1980:46–47). These themes appear with similar frequency in the anthems of both core and periphery nations. However, identical themes are quite differently expressed depending upon the world-system position of the nation from which the anthem emanates. In core nations, for example, topics are generally expressed in abstract, concise, and referential ways. Conversely, anthems of peripheral nations detail and elaborate their topics. Compare, for example, two "call to arms" anthems: Italy's "Inno di Mameli" and the anthem of Kampuchea:

Inno di Mameli
Italian Brothers, Italy has awakened.
She has wreathed her head with the helmet of Scipio.
Where is Victory? She bows her head to you,
You whom God created as the slave of Rome.
Let us band together. We are ready to die.
Italy has called us.

Kampuchea's Anthem
The bright red blood was spilled over the towns
And over the plains of Kampuchea, our motherland,
The blood of our good workers and farmers and of
Our revolutionary combatants, both men and women.
Their blood produced a great anger and the courage
To contend with heroism. On the 17th of April,
Under the revolutionary banner their blood freed
Us from the state of slavery.

Hurrah for the 17th of April!
That wonderful victory had greater significance
Than the Angkor period!
We are united to construct a Kampuchea with a
New and better society, democratic, egalitarian,
And just. We follow the road to a firmly based
Independence. We absolutely guarantee to defend
Our motherland, our fine territory, our
Magnificent revolution!
Hurrah for the new Kampuchea, a splendid
Democratic land of plenty! We guarantee to raise
Aloft and wave the red banner of the revolution.
We shall make our motherland prosperous beyond
All others, magnificent and wonderful!

In Italy's core anthem, the lyrics are general rather than particular, amorphous rather than concrete. The words do not detail a battle, but paint an emotional rendering of war and its glory. In contrast, Kampuchea's periphery anthem offers particularized, concrete references, citing dates, battles, specific periods, and groups. The words provide factual description rather than poetic characterization. As such, this periphery anthem is ladened with details that "tell the news" as opposed to creating a mood.[19]

These core/periphery contrasts are present in other themes as well. Consider Sweden's "pastoral" anthem:

Thou ancient, thou freeborn, thou mountainous North,
In beauty and peace our hearts beguiling!
I greet thee, thou loveliest land on the earth,
Thy sun, thy skies, thou verdant meadows smiling.

Here, pastoral characterizations are broad and sweeping. The pictures painted by the lyrics are impressionistic rather than explicit. Compare this to the itemization of Bangladesh's pastoral anthem:

My Bengal of gold, I love you.
Forever your skies, your air set my heart in tune
As if it were a flute.
In spring O mother mine, the fragrance from your mango groves
Makes me wild with joy—Ah, what a thrill!
In autumn, O mother mine, In the full-blossomed paddy fields

CHAPTER FOUR

> I have seen spread all over—sweet smiles.
> Ah, what a beauty, what shades, what an affection
> And what a tenderness.
> What a quilt have you spread at the feet of banyan trees
> And along the banks of rivers!
> O mother mine, words from your lips
> Are like nectar to my ears.
> Ah, what a thrill!
> If sadness, O mother mine, casts a gloom on your face,
> My eyes are filled with tears.

These words enumerate the beautiful aspects of the nation, season by season and setting by setting. The lyrics do not imply beauty, they inventory it.

In addition to differences in the mode of theme expression, core and periphery nations differ with regard to the number of themes they include. Core anthems tend to be pointed, dealing with a singular theme. Consider, for example, Canada's sole theme of loyalty:

> O Canada! Our Home and Native Land!
> True patriot love in all thy sons command.
> With glowing hearts we see thee rise,
> The true North strong and free.
> From far and wide O Canada!
> We stand on guard for thee.
> God keep our land glorious and free!
> O Canada we stand on guard for thee!

In contrast, Swaziland's peripheral anthem deals with multiple topics. Issues of land and battle, unity and leadership are all packed into one exposition:

> O God, bestower of the blessings of the Swazi;
> We are thankful for all our good fortune,
> We give praise and thanks for our King
> And for our country, its hills and rivers.
> Bless those in authority in Swaziland,
> Thou alone art our Almighty One.
> Give us wisdom without guile,
> Establish us and strengthen us,
> Thou Everlasting One.

This comparison suggests that periphery anthems are not only more detailed than their core counterparts but also frequently broader in scope.

Flag content presents a similar story. Core flags utilize minimal content. The majority of these flags rely almost solely on two to three planes of color to convey their meaning. When ornaments appear, they are always sparse and abstract in nature—that is, the Canadian maple leaf or the Danish cross. In contrast, semiperiphery and periphery flags can become quite detailed, using elaborate ornaments, and frequently, verbal text as a supplement to graphic information. The flags of Brazil and Equatorial Guinea, for example, contain the national motto. The flags of Paraguay and Nicaragua display the nation's name. And Iran's flag repeats the date of the 1979 revolution twenty-two times! Overall, the increased detail of semiperiphery and periphery flags suggests an expansiveness in content, one absent from the banners of the core.

The government-generated narratives that describe each nation's flag underscore the links between system position and symbol content. Descriptions developed in core nations offer minimal information; they rarely detail the meaning of a flag or elaborate the source of its content. Consider, for example, this sparse description of the Canadian national flag: "Red and white are the heraldic colors of Canada. The maple leaf has been an emblem of Canada for more than a century" (as reported in Talocci 1977:174). Switzerland's narrative is similarly brief: "The arms and flag of Switzerland are derived from the symbol used by the canton of Schwyz, a white cross on red" (as reported in Crampton 1990:94). Core narratives often ground each flag's content in nothing more concrete than tradition.

In contrast, the narratives of periphery nations are much more explicit; they are dense with information and highly elaborate. Consider the detail of The Gambia's flag narrative: "The blue stripe running through the center of the flag represents the Gambia River, which flows through the center of the country. The agricultural resources of the Gambia are represented by the green stripe, while the red stripe symbolizes the sun; white stands for unity and peace" (as reported in Smith 1975:234). Similarly, Guyana's narrative is laden with information: "The green background symbolizes the agricultural and forested nature of Guyana. The white border symbolizes its waters and river potential. The golden arrow symbolizes Guyana's mineral wealth and its forward thrust. The black border, the endurance that will sustain the golden arrows forward thrust into the future. The red triangle symbolizes the zeal and the dynamic task of nation building which lies before our young and independent country."[20]

These contrasts in core and periphery narratives further illustrate the relationship between world-system position and cultural expression. At the level of content, nations lacking economic and political centrality project highly ornate expressions of self. Just as socioeconomic categories influence symbol content, I suggest that these reference groups will influence symbol structure as well. In the section to follow, I use my data on anthems and flags to explore the relationship between world-system position and syntactic structure of national symbols.

World-System Location and Symbol Syntax

This analysis requires that each nation in the sample be classified according to a core, semiperiphery, or periphery status. Furthermore, these locations must be recorded with regard to two distinct time periods: the year in which each nation adopted its anthem and the year of flag adoption. These criteria spread the analysis across a broad historical period, making it necessary to tap several sources for each nation's world-system rank (Bollen 1983; Chirot 1977; Shannon 1989; Snyder and Kick 1979; Wallerstein 1974, 1975, 1979, 1980). Appendix B lists these ranks.

I began the analysis with anthems, calculating the mean music syntax score for each strata in the world-system. Comparing the means highlights significant differences in each sector's communication style. Anthem structures of periphery nations are significantly more embellished than those emerging from the core and semiperiphery. As hypothesized, increased distance from the center of economic and political power is associated with embellished modes of self expression (t = −1.96; d.f. = 142; p = .05).[21]

Using regression analysis, we can explore the relative effect a nation's world-system location as compared to indicators of lineage,

Table 4.1. Regression Analysis of Syntactic Metastructure on Indicators of World-Systems Location, Lineage, Space

Independent Variables	Model 1 Anthems (B/Beta)	Model 2 Flags (B/Beta)
World-system location (periphery)	.367/.148[a]	.625/.123[a]
Colonial power's syntax	.257/.292[a]	.397/.376[a]
Space-Time Instruction[b]	—	.100/.140[a]
Neighboring natons' syntax	.238/.172[a]	—
R^2	.16	.21
F	8.47[a]	15.56[a]
N	156	177

[a]Indicates that coefficients are significant at the .05 level or lower.
[b]When entered separately, the figures on neighboring nation flag syntax were B = .193/Beta = .140, p = .05. The figures for time of adoption were B = .004/Beta = .124, p = .05.

time, ideology, and space. Recall that we were able to account for 11 percent of the variation in anthem structure by referring to a nation's lineage and region. By adding a nation's world-system location to the equation, we increase our predictive power considerably.[22] The new model accounts for 16 percent of the variation in anthem syntax (see table 4.1). Furthermore, the effect of world-system location holds true when controlling for the influence of both colonial power and neighboring nations.[23] *With regard to music structure, then, the final analysis suggests that economic reference groups are important editors of the methods by which nations express their identities. Periphery anthems are significantly more embellished than their core and semiperiphery counterparts.*

The analysis of flags yields similar results. In comparing the mean graphic syntax scores for flags from each world-system sector, we find that periphery flags are more embellished than their core and semiperiphery counterparts (t = −1.97; d.f. = 176; p = .05).[24] The regression coefficients substantiate this pattern; further, the model shows that the effect of world-system rank[25] remains significant when controlling for the influence of neighboring nations, time period,[26] and colonial power (see table 4.1).[27] The addition of world-system rank to the equation produces a model accounting for 21 percent of the variation in flag structure, an increase of 5 percent over previous models. Based on these findings, we can conclude that *socioeconomic pockets of reference influence the selection of graphic communication strategies. The more peripheral a nation within the system, the more embellished the structure of its flags.*

Note that some would disagree with the notion that a nation's economic reference groups lie beyond its borders. Modernization theorists, for example, contend that a nation's sense of economic place is contingent on important industrial and technological evolutions occurring within the nation. These theorists argue that national identity construction is an intranational process; it is tied to the specific characteristics of a society and hence unfolds quite distinctly in every developing nation. For modernization theorists, a nation's past and its targeted future serve as its significant economic points of reference. Thus, national "biography" is much more central to identity formation and expression than a nation's international ties (see, e.g., Black 1966, Plascov 1982, and Smelser 1966).

The modernization argument cannot be taken lightly. And indeed elsewhere (Cerulo 1993), I have explored the effect of modernization on the selection of national symbol designs. That work indicates that the impact of modernization is overshadowed by the effects of a nation's world-system location. A nation's place in the world economic network appears more influential to communication strategy selection than the unfolding of its personal economic history.

Conclusion

This chapter encourages us to view the world-system through new eyes. I suggest that we consider the system as more than just a pathway of economic exchange: it is an editor of cultural exchange as well. With reference to national symbols, I argue that the members of each world-system stratum form socioeconomic pockets to which differentially positioned nations compare and contrast themselves. In this way, the cognitive processes of lumping and splitting are extended to the economic realm. Nations react to the similarities they share with their economic equivalents, and they react to the differences that set them apart from those outside their "class." These reactions not only form the building blocks of a nation's identity but also delimit the structure of the voice by which identity is expressed.

When we couple these findings with those generated in chapter 3, we cannot help but be struck by the influence of reference groups on the symbolization of a nation's identity. Socioeconomic position, lineal, temporal, and spatial referents become information centers for emerging nations, providing comparative data on what a nation is and is not. These referents represent vital stops for national leaders on the road to constructing and projecting the national self. But although reference groups surely play an important role in national identity expression, these groups explain only a portion of the variation in the syntactic structure of national symbols. Clearly, additional factors are acting to modify communication strategies.

In forming a message, astute communicators must anticipate their targets. In this way, the structure of a message is contingent not only on the referents of the sender but also on the message's destination. In chapter 5, we direct our analytical eye to the national symbol's prime destination—the national audience.

5

OF THE PEOPLE, FOR THE PEOPLE

Lucy Van Pelt:	If you use your imagination, you can see lots of things in cloud formations. What do you think you see, Linus?
Linus Van Pelt:	Well, those clouds up there look to me like the map of the British Honduras in the Caribbean. That cloud up there looks a little like the profile of Thomas Eakins, the famous painter and sculptor. And that group of clouds over there gives me the impression of the stoning of Stephen. I can see the Apostle Paul standing there to one side.
Lucy Van Pelt:	Uh huh—that's very good. What do *you* see in the clouds, Charlie Brown?
Charlie Brown:	Well, I was going to say I saw a ducky and a horsie, but I changed my mind.

Intranational Focus and Symbol Design

What we say and how we say it is, in large part, a function of our audience. Although a sender may approach the communication act with one message in mind, audience composition or feedback can serve to alter that mindset. And so, much like Charlie Brown, all senders necessarily restructure, manipulate, or even discard messages according to the conditions of their targets. Truly effective[1] senders "give expression to their recipients' own concerns, tensions, aspirations, and hopes . . . they deny all distance between themselves and the audience" (Kecskemeti 1973:264).[2]

Symbolic expressions of a nation's identity follow the rules of sender-receiver interplay. In selecting symbols, national leaders target their citizen populations, hoping to solidify, motivate, and mobilize them. But to effectively accomplish these tasks, leaders must carefully tailor their messages to the circumstances of the intranational audience. In this way, we can say that the structure of a nation's population comes to play a major role in determining the content and form of national symbols. Certain symbolic designs of identity are rooted in specific audience configurations.

Central to the configuration of every national audience is its *intranational focus*. By intranational focus, I refer to the points of reference to which the collective body is directed—the range of issues considered by the citizen body as well as the depth of that concern. In essence, intranational focus reflects the nature of the collective conscience; it provides a gauge of a national population's macro-cognitive solidarity. By attending to it, we can determine if the collective conscience is unified and singular in its attention, or highly fragmented, attending to multiple concerns. As such, intranational focus represents a critical factor to which any sender must attend. For as I will argue, certain focus levels will demand specific symbolic designs.

The Collective Conscience and Intranational Focus

Since the writings of Auguste Comte, a distinct theoretical voice has urged us to study that which binds the parts of a social entity as opposed to that which segments those parts. This tradition directs us to the invisible currents that connect and energize members of a society. Through such currents, it is argued, a collection of individuals with varied personal histories and different social responsibilities and tasks come to function as a single social unit.

The currents that unite the members of a society operate in cognitive rather than physical space. Social actors may never physically see or touch those to whom they are bound by responsibility, task, or persuasion. Nevertheless, actors come to learn their position within a larger framework. Each individual learns the workings and goals of the larger social body; each hears the collective statement of the common good. As Anderson describes it, "In the minds of each lives the image of their communion" (1983:6; also see Calhoun 1991, Schlesinger 1993, Spillman 1994).

Durkheim termed the knowledge of which I speak the *collective conscience:*[3]

> The totality of beliefs and sentiments common to average citizens of the same society forms a determinant system which has its own life. One may call it the collective or common conscience. . . . it is, by definition, diffuse in every reach of society . . . It is, in effect, independent of the particular conditions in which individuals are placed; they pass it on and it remains. . . . (it) designates the totality of social similitudes. (1933:79–80)

With this definition, Durkheim alerts us to a place in which individual minds meet, merge, and form an entity that surpasses the reality of any one individual. The collective conscience embodies a sphere of common thought and knowledge. There, collective rules are stated, collective sentiments expressed, and collective lore constructed. Via the cognitive currents that bind social members, each individual is able to inculcate those dictums into their own unique existence.

The collective conscience spans the full array of issues and dilemmas facing every society. It defines the parameters of deviance and crime. It outlines the functions of social institutions. It prescribes religious doctrine and family values. It sets the boundaries of moral action. In essence, the collective conscience is a multiplex entity, omnipresent in all areas of social life. But in citing the enormous scope of this entity, note that certain cultural configurations, political arrangements, or particular social events can serve to direct and redirect that to which the collective conscience attends. (Calhoun 1993) So while the collective conscience is inherently multidimensional, the focus within it—the issues, places, or values to which the collective attends—can vary greatly in terms of scope, pointedness, and degree of concentration.

Consider, for example, the links between a collective's *cultural configuration* and the cohesiveness of its focus. Societies built on homogeneous ethnic, linguistic, or religious traditions necessarily display a more pointed collective focus than their heterogeneous counterparts. This is because the collective conscience of homogeneous societies emerges from a single cultural stream. This cultural "sameness" directs social members toward an identical history of development. Such social members reference one universally shared set of customs and converge on a common cultural tradition. By virtue of cultural homogeneity, collective focus is narrowed and concentrated.[4]

Nations such as France, Japan, or Poland epitomize culturally homogeneous societies. Because of their cultural "oneness," these populations enjoy moments of shared intranational focus that are less common to more heterogeneous nations. For example, the ethnic and religious homogeneity of France allows the nation to become nearly totally absorbed in the celebration of holidays such as Christmas or Easter. Similarly, Japanese ethnic and linguistic homogeneity promotes a uniform focus on form and order, as exemplified via widely embraced cultural products such as Japanese calligraphy, flower arrangements, or haiku poetry. And the ethnic and religious homogeneity of post–World War II Poland stimulates an intense nationalistic focus, evidenced in part by massive annual pilgrimages to Czestochowa, Kalwaria, Lanckorona, and Piekary Slaskie.

In contrast, culturally heterogeneous societies, those with multiple ethnic, linguistic, and religious groups, display a dispersed collective focus. Citizens of culturally heterogeneous nations refer to varying customs and traditions. They are directed to numerous ethnic and religious histories. In essence, these heterogeneous populations often operate as coexisting subgroups, groups that adopt a relative rather than a unified outlook. Consequently, cultural heterogeneity scatters a collective's attention. Such diversity necessarily broadens the focus of the group.

Northern Ireland, Lebanon, and pre–1991 Yugoslavia characterize culturally heterogeneous collectives. Because religious, ethnic, and linguistic divisions fragment these populations, intranational focus is consistently divided across divergent fronts. In Northern Ireland, for example, varying ethnic and religious loyalties act to split the collective's attention in two. In Lebanon, too, religious factionalism creates multiple groups with multiple goals. And although united in name in 1918, Yugoslavia's fragmented ethnic, linguistic, and religious groups focused the population in conflicting directions and eventually led to that collective's demise.

A collective's *political arrangement*—its form of government—also can influence the sharpness of its focus. Governments differentially direct population attention by framing domains of cognition for their citizens; they define the arenas that are open for public consideration. As such, governments set the public agenda; they point collectives to particular issues and values while steering populations away from others.[5]

Consider the varying impact of authoritarian versus democratic arrangements. Authoritarian regimes can concentrate collective focus by strictly limiting the public agenda. For example, Hitler employed such a strategy during his first four years in power. The führer banned concerns for the individual from the public discourse, directing the intranational focus solely toward the Fatherland. Best expressed through national slogans such as "Thy people is everything; thou art nothing," thoughts of the individual German were sacrificed for the "spirit of the total state." By singularizing the collective mindset, Hitler achieved a sweeping public unity (Toland 1976:254). Some contend that government activities in the Soviet Union created a similar condition. The nation's authoritarian regime continuously directed the population to a narrow and explicitly defined ideology. In so doing, leaders eliminated from public discourse all but those ideas approved by the ruling regime. Robert Kaiser writes: "All ideas in the USSR must be tested against an official ideology; any idea thought to contradict the ideology is unacceptable. An enormous police force, much of it operating secretly, enforces the decisions made in Moscow" (1976:112).

Frequently, authoritarian regimes maintain rigid classification systems in an effort to constrict intranational focus. In writing of the Mao regime, for example, Simon Leys notes: "The Maoist bureaucracy has thirty hierarchical classes, each with specific privileges and prerogatives. . . . In all of their contacts with foreigners, the Maoist civil servants insist on being given the exact titles, functions, and positions of each person, so as to be able to gauge precisely the length of red carpet each should have: any uncertainty about this makes them uneasy to the point of anxiety" (1978:113–14). The Chinese example illustrates the ways in which strictness of form reifies the narrow authoritarian message. Such rigidity deflects the collective view from creative possibilities. In this way, authoritarian governments limit the cognitive territory in which citizen minds can legitimately meet.

In contrast, democratic governments generally allow the influx of profuse and diverse information. Rather than advocating mental confinement, democracies tolerate the variety and debate that can stem from multiplex thought. But although this strategy may empower the individual, it simultaneously fragments collective focus. Democracy can subdivide the collective into competing factions, each with their own focal points of attention.

Consider the practice of "initiative" in modern Switzerland. Initiative allows citizens to add their own specialized items to government assembly agendas, giving individuals significant voice in their government. Yet as initiative celebrates the rights of citizens, it also dictates polyphonic focus. By encouraging and enabling numerous views, the process allows citizens to derail the train of thought promoted by the nation's leaders. As such, initiative creates a constant potential for a pluralistic collective agenda. In a similar vein, the multiparty systems that characterize democratic republics ultimately stimulate fragmented intranational focus. Such systems legitimate the coexistence of multiple platforms and views. Further, such systems necessarily encourage cognitive flexibility, as peaceful coexistence requires the fluidity of compromise and integration. Thus, intranational focus within democratic settings can rarely be concentrated and fixed. The philosophy upon which the arrangement is built calls for attention to difference above sameness.

Social events shape intranational focus as well. On one hand, certain events can mesmerize a collective's attention. Because of their importance to a collective's fate, some incidents can eradicate all other occurrences from the scope of immediate concern. We can refer to such events as high-focus events—instances capable of pinpointing collective attention. Conversely, certain social episodes can be so disruptive to collective existence that they atomize group concerns. By upsetting daily order and routine, breaking the bonds that unite social members, some events emphasize the individual (or smaller units such as the family) over the collective. Such instances constitute low-focus events—episodes that fragment collective attentions.

Consider events such as independence movements, victory in war, or nationalistic episodes. Within nations, these incidents constitute high-focus events. The drama of such affairs can monopolize collective concern, directing attentions away from all else but the incident in question. Further, such events place the nation in the forefront of the collective mindset; nation takes precedence over interest group or individual. High-focus events tighten intranational focus by stimulating a heightened "community of the mind."[6]

Historical accounts help to characterize the high-focus event. In his work on the American colonies, for example, Merritt (1966) links independence movements to high intranational focus. Using the self-referent language of colonial newspapers as an indicator, Merritt shows that the colonies' bid for independence generated the rapid growth of an "us against them" mentality among Americans. This mentality, in turn, served to fuse the attentions of the various groups that formed the American collective. As the independence movement gained momentum, the colonies began to redefine themselves as a single, unified body. Similarly, John Garraty and Peter Gay (1981:801–2) note that the Belgian independence movement brought a sense of unity to the populous. From its instigation in 1828 to its fruition in 1830, Belgium's struggle against the Dutch provided a single point of intranational attention for a collective that was otherwise politically and culturally fragmented.

Episodes of nationalism coalesce focus as well. Edgar Holt (1970), for example, notes that Italian nationalism surged under the Austrian domination of the 1840s, functioning to unite Italian citizens in shared purpose—namely, the opposition toward a common foe. This period promoted a singular cognitive agenda, one so intense that it is frequently identified as a stimulating factor in the victories of Mazzini, Garibaldi, and Cavour, and the ultimate success of the Italian *Risorgimento*. The British experience during World War II offers a similar illustration. Following the Battle of Britain, nationalistic pride merged British citizens and their leaders in a cognitive alliance. The combined effort integral to victory created a mental bond, one that tied the British collective to a singular point of attention.[7] As Lord Allanbrooke describes, "The nation took Churchill to their heart. He and they *were one* in their finest hour" (1959:104, emphasis added).

Incidents such as enemy invasions, large-scale disasters, revolutions, or wars in which the fate of a nation is uncertain represent low-focus events. Such incidents threaten the very organization of a

97

nation. They render a nation's standards of regulation obsolete and disrupt norms of behavior. Under such conditions, the loyalties and commitments of citizens become displaced. Indeed, low-focus events can impose such hardship on the populous that personal interest comes to replace collective loyalty; focus on the nation can become secondary to individual concerns for survival.[8]

The Mexican revolt of 1911, for example, represents a low-focus event. Recall that the resignation of Porfirio Díaz was a prime goal of that revolt, a goal that the rebels believed would fuse Mexico's Left and Right political factions. However, fusion never occurred, and civil war ensued. Mexico became a site that lacked cohesion, unity of command, and organization. Political factions disagreed on appropriate actions and suitable morals. As a result, the Mexican collective failed to develop a unified mental community. Intranational focus disintegrated to a collection of varied viewpoints promoted by competing factions (Helman 1978, Hodge and Gandy 1979). Similar characterizations apply to Iraq during the 1960s. From 1958 to 1967, the nation witnessed the assassination of King Faisal II, the overthrow of his monarchy, periods of major civil unrest under General Kassem's regime, numerous coups, and intense conflict with the Kurds. In the face of such turmoil, citizens of Iraq gravitated to multiple and often opposing cognitive poles; rather than joining the Iraqi collective in cognitive unison, the events of the 1960s splintered intranational focus (Marr 1985). And recent incidents in Bangladesh offer a similar low-focus scenario. During the short period of 1970 to 1990, the citizens of Bangladesh experienced a state of emergency, an army coup, a redefinition of the nation as an Islamic republic, a presidential assassination, the dissolution of their parliament, a tidal wade, a massive flood, and a famine. In Bangladesh, focus on individual welfare necessarily took precedence over a common collective concern. The events of this period destroyed communal ties, leaving survivors uprooted, often alone, and void of a definitive group focus (Mascarenhas 1986).

Of course, high and low intranational focus represent two extremes. Certain events can trigger more moderate levels of focus. During periods of socioeconomic development, minor political unrest, or times of social reform, for example, citizens attend to common elements: progress, development, and change. However, they also work toward a variety of secondary goals, with different sectors of the population seeing different means to an end. Thus, collective attention becomes specialized, with some population subgroups strongly focused on one set of concerns and other subgroups focused on other concerns. As such, we can identify a category called moderate intranational focus. The moderate condition renders collective attention more dispersed than it would be during high-focus events, but less fragmented than it would be during low-focus events.

The American isolationist period of the 1920s exemplifies the moderate-focus condition. Historians describe the period as one of growth—an era in which the nation enjoyed an economic boom, the expansion of its mass media, and a blossoming of art and science. These multiple avenues of development encouraged diversity of commitment. Yet diverse interests were loosely bound by a common concern with American nationalism and protectionism. Such mixed attentions rendered American focus moderate in intensity (Wiltz 1973:485–90). Moderate focus also defined Australia's post–World War II period. During that time, the Liberal government promoted economic prosperity, increased foreign investment in the nation, and the resurgence of immigration. While this strategy encouraged a variety of efforts and initiatives, it simultaneously joined Australians in a common desire to invest in their nation (Ward 1977:chap. 9). And the West Germany of the late 1960s displayed moderate focus as well. Willy Brandt's coalition government promoted an eclectic political agenda, a policy resulting in a period of economic development and sociopolitical reform. Yet although different population subgroups strove for different immediate ends, each group's ultimate goals were tied by a sense of commitment to nation at large (Laqueur 1985:chaps. 5 and 6).

In distinguishing between varying levels of intranational focus, note that each category carries with it specific social enactments. Indeed, one can associate different focus conditions with particular forms of social solidarity; each form of solidarity becomes a behavioral manifestation of a specific collective cognitive state.

Consider conditions of high intranational focus. Individuals united in cognitive space manifest this unity via specific patterns of behavior—patterns that recreate in physical space the intense and rich nature of the cognitive experience. We might characterize such behavior patterns as displays of mechanical solidarity. In high-focus settings, mechanical relations bring a collective's cognitive cohesion to the empirical realm of observable deeds. In contrast, consider conditions of low intranational focus. Low focus ensues when occurrences weaken or sever the cognitive links between collective members. In the absence of such links, behavioral expressions of bondedness fail to emerge. As such, low-focus periods are associated with anomie. The disjointed nature of the collective mindset is reflected in an atomized state of action. Finally, consider settings of moderate intranational focus. In periods of moderate focus, collective cognition allows for differentiation and specialized interests. These emphases manifest themselves in organic relations. When cognitive currents are present yet flexible, they coincide with behaviors reflecting "different, special functions which definite relations unite" (Durkheim 1915:129).

Intranational Focus and Symbolic Expression

Intranational focus is especially pertinent to the study of national symbols, for several literatures clearly link this audience condition to variations in symbolic expression. Research suggests that highly focused, highly cohesive groups generate symbols that are sparse in content and basic in design. Because they are so tightly bound, communication within such groups requires little more than symbolic shorthand. Sparse, basic symbols reference the core meanings already in the forefront of the collective's attention. Conversely, the literature suggests that fragmented groups with little or no shared focus favor symbols that are dense in content and embellished in structure. Because there is little cognitive overlap and minimal community structure among members of low-focus groups, communication requires detail and elaboration. When common ground cannot be assumed, meaning must be fully itemized.[9]

The patterns of which I speak have been empirically demonstrated in a variety of symbolic arenas, including language (see, e.g., Bernstein 1975), the graphic arts (Bergesen 1984), music (Lomax 1968, Bergesen 1979), ritual (Douglas 1970:chap. 3), and religion (Swanson 1960, 1967).[10] The argument is easily applied to national

symbols. When national leaders address an audience that is culturally homogeneous, governed by authoritative arrangements, and
unified by social events—that is, an audience characterized by high
intranational focus—they will communicate using symbols with
minimal content and basic syntactic design. Under such conditions,
the national audience enjoys a cognitive corporateness, a singular
mindset that is supported and reified by mechanical solidarity patterns. For those who are so merged, detail in communication can be
sacrificed; minimal input will suffice. Leaders targeting a highly
focused population can convey meaning simply by referencing that
which is already in the forefront of the collective's mind.

As national audience conditions shift from high to moderate, and
finally, to low intranational focus, leaders will increasingly favor
symbols with maximum information and embellished designs. The
dimensions of low intranational focus—cultural heterogeneity, political pluralism, and divisive social events—force collectives to emphasize the subgroup or the individual over the whole. Low focus
splinters the collective mindset, directing it to multiple goals, beliefs,
issues, and meanings. This cognitive fragmentation is exacerbated
by the lack of tangible social ties and bonding behavioral patterns.
Communication in such an arena requires sensitivity to audience
multiplicity. To ensure full comprehension of a message, symbols
must accommodate high detail and flexible expression. Leaders
must be able to add sufficient information to their message, combining and recombining its material, until it effectively conveys meaning to a diverse target.[11]

The content of national anthems and flags supports the patterns
just described. Periods of high intranational focus frequently are
associated with simple, often sparse symbol content. Consider the
content of "God Save the King." This anthem was adopted during a
period of high intranational focus (1745): England was culturally
homogeneous, authoritatively governed, and faced with a unity-
provoking event—the Jacobite threat to the crown. Thus, King
George II called for the adoption of a hymn that would help retain
loyalty to the crown. He selected "God Save the King," applauding
the basic nature of the anthem. Not only was it a calm, soothing piece
of music, but its lyrics conveyed a message that was singular and
simple—long live the king (Griffith 1952:24–28):

> God save our gracious King,
> Long live our noble King,
> God Save the King!
> Send him victorious,
> Happy and glorious,
> Long to reign over us,
> God save the King!

The content of Togo's anthem also displays the minimalism one would expect from a high-focus period of adoption. Although Togo was not completely homogeneous at the time of the anthem's adoption (1969), the symbol did emerge under a one-party political system. In addition, the anthem was attached to a surge of nationalism and the adoption of a new constitution, both high-focus events. Therefore, it is not surprising that the anthem's content is relentless in its single plea for unity:

> Let us put aside every bad feeling
> That hinders national unity.
> Let us fight such feelings as we fought imperialism.
> Settling accounts with people, hatred and anarchy
> Only serve to hold back the revolution.
> If we are divided, the enemy infiltrates
> our ranks to exploit us.
> Togolese! Our ancestors are calling us to unity.
> Peace, Peace, Peace, oh Togolese,
> Is what our forefathers demand of us.

In contrast, the anthem of the United States was adopted during a period of low intranational focus (1931). At this time, the American collective displayed cultural heterogeneity and democratic pluralism. In addition, the collective faced the divisiveness inherent in economic disaster. The highly detailed content of the American anthem is in keeping with the intranational focus hypothesis. The lyrics of the anthem constitute an extremely elaborate depiction of a single battle, giving a detailed account of the role of the national flag within that battle. Rather than repeating a singular sentiment, the lyrics of the American anthem provide a thick description of a historical event:

> O say, can you see, by the dawn's early light,
> What so proudly we hailed at the twilight's last gleaming,
> Whose broad stripes and bright stars,
> through the perilous fight,
> O'er the ramparts we watched, were so gallantly streaming?
> And the rockets' red glare, the bombs bursting in air,
> Gave proof through the night that our flag was still there.
> O say, does that star-spangled banner yet wave
> O'er the land of the free and the home of the brave?

Indeed, detail is so central to this anthem's lyrics that certain descriptions exceed a single stanza. Note that the painstaking account of a both battle and flag are continued in stanza 2:

> On the shore, dimly seen through the mists of the deep,
> Where the foe's haughty host in dread silence reposes,
> What is that which the breeze, oe'r the towering steep,
> As it fitfully blows, half conceals, half discloses?
> Now it catches the gleam of the morning's first beam,
> In full glory reflected now shines on the stream;
> 'Tis the star-spangled banner, O long may it wave
> O'er the land of the free and the home of the brave!

Ecuador's anthem is also a product of a low-focus era. Historians describe the period of the anthem's adoption (1948) as one of the most turbulent Ecuador has ever known (Fitch 1977:13), with severe economic depression and intense political factionalism generating widespread social disruption. Note, for example, that only one of José María Velasco's five terms as president (1934–72) was free of a military coup (Needler 1967). During this period the nation also was involved in territorial disputes with Peru. Further, some historians indicate that Ecuador was fighting attempted Nazi infiltration of the country (Burk and Maier 1973). The theoretical base upon which I am building suggests that an anthem adopted under such conditions will contain elaborate content. This proves true for Ecuador. The anthem's lyrics tell a story rather than expressing a single sentiment; further, they rely heavily on repetition, a hallmark of an information-dense anthem:

(Chorus)
We salute e're again this our homeland,
Glory be to you,
Joy and peace, your radiance bestowing,
Who, exceeding the sun, brightly shine.
We salute e're again this our homeland, (repeat)
Glory be to you, your breast o'erflowing, (repeat)
Joy and peace, your radiance bestowing, (repeat)
Who, exceeding the sun, brightly shine. (repeat)
(Verse)
Coming first were the sons of the country
Which Pichincha on high is adorning.
Who acclaimed you as their sov'reign lady
And shed blood for the sake of the land:
God looked on and accepted the sacrifice, (repeat)
And that blood was seed prolific; (repeat)
Other heroes the world observed, astounded, (repeat)
For the fight rise up on ev'ry hand. (repeat)
Rise up on ev'ry hand. (repeat)

The content of flags presents a similar story. Flags adopted during periods of high intranational focus tend toward minimalism. Japan's national flag, for example, was the product of a high-focus period (1854). At this time, Japan's emperor directed the homogeneous population to turn inward and focus solely on the internal needs of the nation. Indeed, the monarch institutionalized this policy through a number of isolationist dictums (Kennedy 1987:206–9). The singular focus of the Japanese mindset should correspond to a flag with limited ingredients. And indeed, the flag's lone red disc suspended on a white field epitomizes such conciseness (see fig. 5.1). Now consider the case of San Marino. Its flag was adopted immediately following Italy's signed acknowledgment of the nation's independence (1862). This peaceful independence movement, along with the nation's cultural homogeneity, supported a high-focus milieu. In keeping with theoretical expectations, this period produced a flag with minimal content. The flag contains only two horizontal planes, white over blue (see fig. 5.1).

Flags emerging from low-focus periods generally contain abundant content; they present information that is both substantial and highly detailed. South Africa's first national flag provides a case in

Figure 5.1. Flags from high-focus versus low-focus settings. *Above left to right:* Japan and San Marino; *below left to right:* South Africa and Zimbabwe.

point.[12] Recall that South Africa was formed from four separate units: the British colonies of Natal and the Cape, the former independent Boer states, the Orange Free State, and the South African Republic. The content of the South African flag reflects the nation's fragmented history (see fig. 5.1). In addition to its orange, white, and black stripes, the flag is ornamented by three additional flags: the Orange Free State flag, the South African Republic flag, and the United Kingdom's Union Jack. By imposing flags within a flag, the symbol maximizes informational input. Indeed, the flag s elaborate content provides distinct representation for the various components of the national whole (Crampton 1990:90).

Zimbabwe's embellished flag also is a product of a low-focus period. The symbol was adopted (1980) during a independence movement fraught with bitter and violent factionalism. Various political parties vied for control of the government, and the nation's numerous ethnic groups were continually at odds. The flag's information density aptly reflects this low-focus condition; it contains eight fields and two ornaments, and displays five different colors (see fig. 5.1). Further, the official interpretation of the flag suggests its excessive content was purposively devised in order to achieve a fair representation of the nation's diverse population. Mauro Talocci (1977:166) details the government's "two-tier" interpretation of the symbol. At the collective level, the flag's colors are said to express deference to the Zimbabwe African National Union. But individually, each color carries an additional meaning. Black represents the African majority of the population, red stands for the blood lost by those killed in the liberation struggle, green represents the nation's agricultural sector, and white stands for peace. The red star symbolizes both socialism and national aspiration, and the yellow bird signifies the nation's ancient African culture.

The link between intranational focus and symbol content is underscored when we note the ways in which drastic *changes* in focus can instigate alterations to symbol content. The flags of Kampuchea illustrate the point (see fig. 5.2). In 1970, Kampuchea was fresh from revolution and struggling to implement a republican form of government (both low-focus events). During this period, Kampuchea's leaders adopted a flag quite elaborate in content. A red canton rests on a blue field, the canton ornamented with a detailed representation of the Temple of Angkor Wat, the field decorated with three white stars. The government's official description of the flag is as explicit as the flag's content:

> The three stars of the flag are said to be symbolic of the nation, its religion and its republican government; upper, central, and lower Kampuchea; the three parts of its government (legislative, executive, and judiciary); and the triple jewel of the Buddhist religious faith (Buddha, Dhamma, Sangha). The representation of the Angkor Wat, one of the mightiest architectural ruins of the world, symbolizes the golden age of the Khmer Empire. Blue is said to characterize the justice, happiness, and honesty of the Khmer people and red, their spirit of determination and courage. Buddhism is associated in the Khmer flag with white. (Smith 1975:247)

After the revolution of 1975, the Khmer Rouge discarded this elaborate flag in favor of a more minimalist offering. Pol Pot's totalitarian "reign of terror" adopted a flag sparse in content. Its single red field

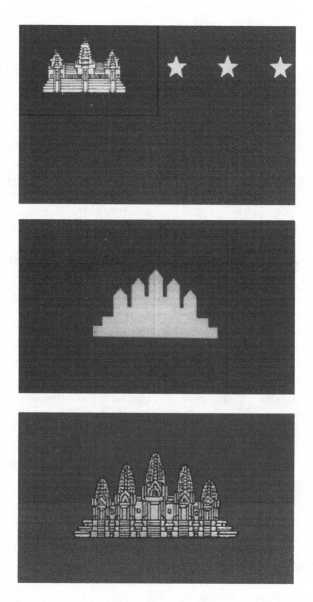

Figure 5.2. The flags of Kampuchea

(symbolic of Kampuchea's communist philosophy) was adorned only by an abstract, gold representation of the Temple of Angkor Wat. This change in content coincides with the theoretical premises presented here. As Kampuchea moved from a pluralistic republic to single-party dictatorship, the nation's focus was heightened and its symbolic voice simplified. The post–Pol Pot era brought a third national flag to Kampuchea. Adopted in 1989, William Crampton (1990:23) tells us that the new flag symbolized the increased openness of the new government and the diverse factions within the nation. The increased pluralism of the post–Pol Pot era corresponds to elaborated symbol content. The red field of the former flag was changed to a backdrop of blue and red horizontal stripes. In addition, the abstract rendering of the Temple of Angkor Wat became increasingly detailed in its rendering.

In Slovenia too, the symbols accompanying the struggle for international recognition illustrate the ways in which a change in focus can stimulate a change in symbol content. Consider that Slovenia's symbols emerged from the anomie of the Yugoslavian breakup. Nasko Kriznar (1992) documents that this low-focus period gave rise to elaborate symbol content. Using the symbols of pre-1991 Yugoslavia as a baseline, Slovenians frequently enhanced the content of Yugoslavian symbols in producing emblems of their own. For example, the slogan "Slovenia, my country" or the familiar linden leaves were added to the traditional YU symbol before the symbol was used in Slovenia. In addition, Slovene citizens experimented with new symbolic statements. Kriznar tells us: "It was not unusual for the whole back of the car to become a visual billboard. When these visual symbols started to pile up, the owner of the car ordinarily placed them upon the car symmetrically, usually in the form of a cross" (1992:3). These crosses embody symbolic forms housing maximum information input. They represent complex images containing the numerous views present within the fragmented nation.[13]

This discussion substantiates a link between intranational focus and symbol content. In the next section, I explore the impact of focus on symbol syntax. Using my sample of anthems and flags, I examine the three dimensions of intranational focus and itemize the ways in which they influence the symbolic design of a nation's identity.

Intranational Focus and Symbol Syntax

I began my analysis of the impact of focus on symbol syntax by ascertaining the level of intranational focus displayed by each nation in the sample. Classifications were made for *both* the year of anthem adoption and the year of flag adoption. This step required attention to each dimension of intranational focus: cultural configuration, political arrangement, and the unfolding of social events.

I began with cultural configuration, operationally defining the concept as the number of ethnic, linguistic, and religious groups a nation's government reports in its population statistics.[14] Data were derived from *Countries of the World and Their Leaders Yearbook*.[15] As one might expect, the data on ethnic, linguistic, and religious diversity were highly correlated.[16] Consequently, I used factors analysis to create a single summary measure representing a nation's overall cultural configuration.[17] Low values on the indicator reflect cultural homogeneity (a component of high intranational focus); increasing values reflect cultural heterogeneity (and thus, low intranational focus). Appendix B lists each nation's cultural configuration score, along with descriptive statistics for the variable.

With regard to anthems, the findings suggest only a weak positive relationship between cultural configuration and anthem syntax (r = .101; p = .47). Further, in comparing the relative effect of cultural configuration to that of previously examined variables, we find that a nation's cultural configuration affords no additional insight on the adoption of anthem designs. As table 5.1 shows, a nation's world-system position and the anthem syntax of both its neighbors and its colonial power overshadow the impact of cultural configuration. The culture variable fails to reach statistical significance, and the introduction of this new indicator to the model produces no increase in explained variance. Based on this analysis, we must conclude that *cultural configuration, as a dimension of intranational focus, is not a prime editor of anthem design.*

The findings regarding flag syntax are identical. The correlation between cultural configuration and graphic syntactic structure is positive, but weak (r = .119; p = .41). Similarly, the effect of cultural configuration is overpowered by other factors in the regression

Table 5.1. Regression Analysis of Anthem Syntactic Metastructure on Elements of Intranational Focus

Independent Variables	Model 1 (B/Beta)	Model 2 (B/Beta)	Model 3 (B/Beta)
High-focus event	—	—	−.759/−.293[a]
Low-focus event	—	—	1.015/.256[a]
(Moderate-focus event)	—	—	(.472/.148)[a]
Political arrangement	—	.732/.264[a]	.760/.274[a]
Overall cultural configuration	−.004/−.002	—	—
World-system location (periphery)	.345/.141[a]	.333/.161[a]	.478/.173[a]
Colonial power's syntax	.245/.280[a]	.284/.326[a]	.187/.215[a]
Neighboring nations' syntax	.243/.178[a]	.218/.164[a]	.210/.162[a]
R^2	.16	.21	.34
F	6.01[a]	8.89[a]	12.75[a]
N	152	149	149

model. The culture variable fails to achieve statistical significance, and its addition to the model offers no additional explanatory power. Table 5.2 highlights these results.

Taking the findings on anthems and flags together, *there is little evidence to substantiate the impact of a nation's cultural configuration on the syntactic structure of national anthems or flags.*

Political arrangement represents the second dimension of intranational focus. Authoritarian governments correspond to high intranational focus, whereas democratic governments are associated with low intranational focus. In this research, political arrangement is operationalized using a dichotomous variable; absolute monarchies, dictatorships, military regimes, and one-party states comprise the

Table 5.2. Regression Analysis of Flag Syntactic Metastructure on Elements of Intranational Focus

Independent Variables	Model 1 (B/Beta	Model 2 (B/Beta	Model 3 (B/Beta
High-focus event	—	—	−.761/−.278[a]
Low-focus event	—	—	1.168/.197[a]
(Moderate-focus event)	—	—	(.550/.199)[a]
Political arrangement	—	.369/.128[a]	.370/.129[a]
Overall cultural configuration	.020/.008	—	—
World-system location (periphery)	.658/.129[a]	.658/.128[a]	.973/.192[a]
Colonial power's syntax	.385/.364[a]	.385/.365[a]	.368/.348[a]
Space-time interaction[b]	.101/.140[a]	.093/.130[a]	.100/.140[a]
R^2	.21	.24	.30
F	13.13[a]	11.82[a]	12.84[a]
N	169	177	177

[a]Indicates that coefficients are significant at the .05 level or lower.
[b]When entered separately, the figures on neighboring nation flag syntax were B = .193; Beta = .139; p = .05. The figures for the time of adoption were B = .004; Beta = .132; p = .05.

authoritarian category of the variable (coded as 0). Parliamentary rule, presidential governments, and multiparty republics constitute the variable's democratic category (coded as 1). Data were derived from several historical sources.[18] Note that two political arrangement codes were assigned to each nation: one representing the year of anthem adoption and one representing the flag adoption year. Appendix B displays the classifications.

When analyzing anthems, the findings indicate a significant association between a nation's political arrangement and its anthem structure. Anthems adopted by democratic regimes display a mean syntax score that is significantly higher, and thus more embellished, than the mean score of anthems adopted under authoritarian governments (Democratic Mean = .215; Authoritarian Mean = −.399; t = −2.77; p = .006). This relationship holds true even when controlling for the effects of previously identified editors of symbol structure (see model 1 versus model 2 in table 5.1).[19] And adding this variable to the analysis increases the amount of explained variance in anthem syntax by 5 percent. Based on these results, *we must acknowledge a nation's political arrangement among the prime editors of anthem syntax.*

The findings for flags are identical. A nation's political arrangement is clearly linked to the syntax of its flag, with democratic regimes adopting flags that are more embellished than their authoritarian counterparts (Democratic Mean = .137; Authoritarian Mean = −.287; t = −1.98; p = .049). Further, that relationship remains significant even when considering a nation's world-system position, the flags of its neighbors, temporal cohort, or colonial power. Indeed, by adding the political arrangement variable to the regression model, we increase the explained variance in the syntactic structure of flags by 3 percent (see model 1 versus model 2 in table 5.2).

The analysis of anthems and flags suggests that *a nation's political arrangement, as a component of intranational focus, is a key editor of symbol design. The more pluralistic the view of the ruling regime, the more embellished the structure by which identity is symbolized.*

Social events represent the final dimension of intranational focus. In this analysis, I consider social events as stimulants of either high, moderate, or low focus. Recall that incidents such as independence movements, nationalistic movements, or victory in war are categorized as high-focus events. Conversely, bloody coups, economic depressions, lost wars, natural disasters, revolutions, and the like represent low-focus events. Moderate-focus events are exemplified by relatively peaceful social movements or periods of economic development. In Appendix A, I highlight specific cases from each category. Interested readers may find these descriptions a useful illustration of the coding process.

Using nine general historical sources, and a wide variety of more specific accounts, I recorded the social affairs occurring in each nation.[20] Data were collected for two historical periods: the year of each nation's anthem adoption and the year of flag adoption. Appendix B lists all social event classifications.

The analysis of anthems reveals a significant association between social events and anthem structure. A one-way analysis of variance shows that high-focus events generate the most basic anthem structures (mean = −.469), followed by moderate-focus (mean = .205)[21] and low-focus events (mean = 1.431; F = 21.09; p = .0001). This effect remains significant in the controlled analysis.[22] Further, by adding the social event variables to the regression model, we account for an additional 13 percent of the variance in anthem structure.[23] (See model 2 versus model 3 in table 5.1.)

The findings for flags are identical. A one-way analysis of variance links different categories of events to varying graphic structure (F = 4.85; p = .009). As predicted, high-focus events are associated with the most basic syntax (mean = −.320), followed by moderate-focus (mean = .231) and low-focus events (mean = .669).[24] The predictive power of social events remains significant in controlled analysis. Further, the social event variables account for an additional 6 percent of the explained variance addressed by the model (see model 2 versus model 3 in table 5.2). Thus, considering the findings on both anthems and flags, we must conclude that *intranational focus, as generated by social events, is a significant predictor of variations in anthem and flag structure. The higher the focus generated by social events, the more basic the design of a nation's symbols.*

Although certain dimensions of intranational focus can be linked to variations in symbol syntax, note that the strength of such links varies by symbol genre. In the selection of anthems, for example, the political arrangements and social events that trigger a nation's intranational focus outweigh the impact of a nation's external referents of identity. National flags, however, present a somewhat different story, as external referents of identity appear more important to the selection of visual designs.

The different usage patterns that apply to anthems and flags may help us to better understand the variable impact of intranational focus. For while both symbol genres enjoy intranational exposure, flags are considerably more central than anthems within the international arena. There are logical reasons for this pattern. Flags are tangible and portable, and thus, easily transferred from site to site and from nation to nation. As such, flags become convenient markers for explorers as they lay claim new lands; flags become the traveling vessel's primary means of identification, and so forth. In addition, flags can be expanded or reduced without damaging their integrity. Thus, they function equally well from the rooftop of an embassy, the antenna of a diplomatic limousine, or the lapel of a diplomat's jacket. Finally, as visual symbols, flags can be apprehended in a split second; they do not require performance or staging as is typical to anthems. Rapid apprehension and ease of display are key to the international arena where nations are competing for attention.

The suitability of flags to the international theater explains their clear prominence over anthems. And this international prominence, in turn, may explain why external editors of symbolic expression play a more powerful role than intranational editors in determining flag design.

Conclusion

In considering intranational focus, we highlight the ways in which a national collective is "contained" in its symbols.[25] The influence of intranational focus on symbol adoption renders anthems and flags both subjective statements and reflexive objects in the projection of the national self.

As we review the incorporation of audience into symbol, we find that where a national audience "comes from," that is, its cultural roots, may bear less effect on a nation's symbolic voice than where that audience "is," that is, its experience at the social moment during which symbols emerge. This analysis suggests that national audiences are not targeted on the basis of their ethnic, religious, and linguistic makeup. Rather, the political arrangements that guide the national body, and the social events that direct its attention, influence the communication strategies by which a population is addressed. Taken together, these factors imply that message structure is tied to a national population's community of experience rather than to its community of record.[26]

This notion of experience is key to the final chapters of this book. For thus far, our inquiry into anthem and flag design has emphasized those transmitting these symbolic messages. We have looked at international reference groups and intranational targets through the eyes of national leaders—those making the adoption choices. Now it is time to consider the impact of adopted symbols on those that experience them—their audiences.

6

"OFF KEY" STRATEGY SELECTIONS

George: You know the song they were playing on the jukebox last night
when we met?
Doris: No.
George: "If I Knew You Were Coming I'd've Baked a Cake"!
Doris: So?
George: So that's going to be "our song"! Other people would get "Be My
Love" or "Hello Young Lovers." Me—I get "If I Knew You Were
Coming I'd've Baked a Cake"![1]

Deviant Anthems and Flags

"Our song," "our place," or "our stories"—all become the symbols of
a new couple's identity. As two distinct individuals merge to form a
dyad, certain musical backdrops, physical locations, and temporal
reconstructions come to form the new couple's unique signature.

The exchange between George and Doris reminds us, however,
that identity symbolization is not an arbitrary task. Certain symbols
prove more or less appropriate to some contexts than others; certain
songs, places, and occasions, for example, seem more fitting to a new
romance than others. Indeed, in large measure, the links between
symbols and their referents are contextually driven.[2] Knowing this,
George's concern over the couple's new theme does not surprise us.

Context suggests that lovers should be denoted by songs of romance, not comedic ditties—by Sinatra, not Sousa.

George's observations on symbolization, of course, transcend the realm of the romantic dyad. Builders of national identities too can signify their nations in more or less suitable terms. National symbols can either conform to contextual norms of expression or defy them; such symbols can meet conventional expectations or disappoint them. In chapters 3, 4, and 5, we discovered the contextual norms that define appropriate national symbol designs. We learned, for example, that nations typically share the communication strategies of their neighbors and contemporaries while divesting from those of their colonial past. Economic equivalents typically choose similar strategies of expression, with the most central of economic groups exhibiting the most basic communication designs. And we noted that levels of intranational focus influence symbol syntax; similarly focused nations adopt similar designs, with highly focused nations typically choosing the most basic formats.

Taken together, these findings illustrate two important points. First, they highlight the contextual nature of collective symbolization, demonstrating that *the symbol syntax of a nation's identity is inexorably tied to the social settings from which the symbol originates.*[3] Second, the findings suggest that a nation's context delineates the boundaries of its symbolic discourse; *various settings carry strong norms of expression—expectations regarding the suitability of national symbol designs.* Some settings promote similar designs among members, others call for distinctive forms; some contexts beckon basic structures, others favor embellishment.

This chapter delves more deeply into the contextually based norms of symbol structure. I will argue that these norms classify national symbols along a continuum of normal to deviant design. Symbols whose syntactic structures meet contextual expectations— that is, their structures conform to those we would predict on the basis of the conditions from which the symbols emerge—constitute *normal symbols*. Those that defy the norms of expression—symbol structures failing to conform to expected patterns—constitute *deviant symbols*. With these distinctions in mind, we will compare symbols that fall at the extremes of the normal-deviant continuum, examining the citizen response stimulated by these contrasting types. Using historical documentation as well as data from 124 interviews, I will argue that deviant symbols prove problematic for audiences. Like the couple that draws the "wrong" love song, collectives assigned the "wrong" theme song never feel fully comfortable with their symbol. Because of their inconsistencies to the settings from which they emerge, deviant national symbols never come to be fully embraced by the national populations they represent. As such, deviant symbols lack the motivational power of their normative counterparts. Anthems and flags that initially do not "fit" their targets' circumstances never come to adequately fulfill the important functions for which the symbols were adopted. In closing, I will speculate regarding the social structural factors that might lead to the adoption of a deviant symbol.

Normal versus Deviant Symbols

Throughout this analysis, I have suggested that several social dimensions of a nation—its physical, historical, and socioeconomic location, its collective experience and the resulting focus of its population—constitute cognitive realities against which macro-level communication occurs. Further, I have argued that within each of these cognitive planes, only certain symbolic grammars appear properly located. Certain regional locations, for example, favor some structures over others; certain temporal cohorts exhibit clear syntactic preferences, and so on. In this way, social settings, and the cognitive realities they stimulate, establish the acceptable parameters of message design.

Research on human cognition provides the basis for my claims. Cognitive theorists suggest that every culture possesses a "manual" of appropriate syntactic strategies.[4] The entries of the manual itemize the formats recognized and accepted within certain social groups and settings. Just as members of a culture come to learn the entries in their culture's manuals of etiquette, romance, religion, or economic exchange, so too do members learn the contents of the manual of syntax design. Once doing so, collectives internalize their lessons in the form of cognitive schema. Such schema become frameworks that "specify types of relationships and procedures upon *the way things fit together"* (Norman and Bobrow 1975:125, emphasis added).[5] The syntax schema by which a collective operates provide guidelines with reference to the decipherable versus the indecipherable, and appropriate versus inappropriate, message designs.

Once defined, the acceptable parameters of aural and graphic syntactic design become part of the subjective stock of knowledge to which members of collectives are socially and culturally conditioned. Just as one learns the potential pool of words from which to construct sentences, the various orderings by which words can be combined, and the variety of intonations and exclamations that can tailor a message, so too does one learn rules regarding the proper use of shapes, colors, and sounds. In childhood, for example, we are taught that certain colors simply do not "match," and we are discouraged from combining such colors in drawings or in clothing outfits. Similarly, we are taught that certain notes should never be combined because they create an abrasive or "foreign" sound. Such instances constitute lessons of appropriateness, instructions on the suitability of certain graphic and aural configurations.

These lessons of appropriateness extend to the sights and sounds of national identity. Citizens are socialized to acknowledge certain aural and graphic structures as suitable to their national culture. Many Asian nations, for example, recognize music based on pentatonic scales as culturally appropriate, while labeling diatonic scale designs as foreign. Similarly, certain national collectives define particular colors or color combinations as culturally relevant. Green is tied to Islamic nations; red, white, and blue is significant to many nations with a western European tradition, etc. Once national collectives are socialized to acceptable communication patterns, they not only acknowledge the patterns but also come to expect adherence to these norms of expression.[6] As communication expectations emerge, certain settings come to exact certain communication formats; *specific symbol structures become the norm for particular contexts.*

Based on this premise, I argue that there exists both normal and deviant symbols. *Normal symbols are those whose syntactic features meet the expectations of their targets.* Normal symbols fall within the parameters of the symbolic grammar typical to the group targeted by the message; these symbols conform to the target group's rules and conventional modes of expression. In contrast, *deviant symbols display syntactic features that contradict a target group's expectations.* They fail to meet the anticipated strategies by which their audiences communicate. Thus, deviant symbols distort the symbolic grammar common to the groups represented by the symbols.

The normal-deviant distinction I am proposing for symbol structure frequently is invoked with reference to symbol content, with researchers linking content appropriateness to the social setting of a symbol's creation. On the musical front, for instance, Alan Lomax (1968:chap. 8) demonstrates that differentially structured societies learn to expect different vocal content. Raspy, guttural sounds prove the norm for cultures emphasizing male dominance and masculine assertiveness. Conversely, societies stressing sexual equality and cooperation favor the content of clear, relaxed tones. Other studies chart similar content-setting links. Both Nettl (1967) and Cerulo (1984) note, for example, that songs composed in settings fraught with aggression normally contain high proportions of loud, high tones. In contrast, low, soft tones are viewed as appropriate to songs emerging from quiet or religious settings. Each of these works implies a contextual basis for musical content, and each suggests the operation of distinct guidelines defining acceptable content.

Research on other art genres illustrates active norms of symbol content as well. Studying folk dance, Curt Sachs (1963) demonstrated that in certain cultural contexts, some dance steps are viewed as more appropriate content than others. Dances built upon long, wide steps are the norm in masculine cultures, while societies displaying a more feminine orientation favor short, narrow steps. Bergesen and Jones (1992) uncover similar content-context links in modern dance vocabularies. Their research shows that dances emerging from close-knit choreographic networks normally display minimal content—that is, few steps and few directives. In contrast, dances produced by choreographers in isolated environments typically display maximal content. Norms of content appear to govern the production of graphic symbols as well. J. L. Fisher (1961), for example, notes such patterns in contrasting the art of egalitarian versus hierarchical societies. The normative vocabulary of egalitarian societies consists of open characters, while hierarchical societies come to expect paintings built upon closed characters. More recently, Rosanne Martorella (1989) uncovered some of the art-content norms of the American corporate setting. Abstract content meets the expectations of Fortune 500 companies and large northeastern firms. In contrast, firms located in the West or Southwest regions of the nation define regional art as appropriate content for display. These studies suggest that in dance and art, too, norms of symbol content can be clearly identified and firmly tied to context.

Context-based norms of content are easily witnessed when examining national symbols. During critical transitions in a nation's history, periods involving the reevaluation of symbols, amendments to symbols are generally guided by the content norms of the era. Brazil's national anthem proves a case in point. Originally adopted in 1831, the anthem was built around highly charged lyrics reflecting the political instability of the period. Thus in 1831, the anthem's content was normal for the context from which it emerged. When Brazil became a republic in 1889, the nation's political context changed radically. At that time, the new leadership decided to reconsider the nation's symbols. Nettl (1967:183) notes that the new government came to view the standing anthem as deviant within Brazil's new political setting. Thus, amidst public support, the government abolished the original words of the anthem, soliciting new, more appropriate lyrics from the population.

The history of the German national anthem offers a similar example. The original lyrics, written prior to World War II, began with the phrase: "Germany, Germany above everything." In the prewar context, this sentiment was considered an appropriate expression of patriotism. After the war, however, the new government reexamined the anthem's lyrics, now defining them as deviant in nature. The words were viewed as explosive and unsuitable to the new image Germany was trying to project (Nettl 1967:88). As a result, the government dropped the anthem's first verse.

Currently, the French are grappling with norms of symbol content. In 1992, various citizen groups voiced serious concerns regarding the warlike lyrics of "La Marseillaise." While these sentiments are acknowledged as appropriate to their setting of creation, some citizens find them provocative and deviant in the current environment. As a result, certain activists are campaigning to replace the anthem's original content with a gentler message:

Old Version	Proposed Version
Arise you children of the Motherland	Arise you children of the Motherland
Oh now is here our glorious day	Lets sing together for liberty
Over us the bloodstained banner	Liberty, O dearest Liberty
Of tyranny holds sway. (repeat)	Your bloody ramparts have fallen. (repeat)
Oh do you here there in our fields	Oh how lucky we are to be French!
The roar of those fierce fighting men?	Lets be proud of our flag
Who come right hear into our midst	One day all rights
To slaughter sons, wives, and kin?	Will choose France as their cradle.
To arms, O citizens	Together, O citizens
Form up in closed ranks	Let us march hand in hand
March on, march on!	Sing on, sing on
And drench our fields	Until our songs
With their tainted blood.	Silence all cannons.[7]

The success of the French activists remains to be seen, but the case, like earlier examples, underscores the public's recognition of appropriate versus inappropriate content.

Norms of content surround national flag adoptions as well. Consider the Italian flag. In 1944, when Mussolini established the Italian Socialist Republic, he adopted a green-white-red tricolor flag, ornamented by an eagle crest in its center. After World War II, the government of the new Italian republic stripped the flag of its decorative ornament. Whereas the eagle crest was normative to Mussolini's government, Smith (1975:146–47) notes that Italy's new leaders viewed it as inappropriate to the nation's postwar setting and adjusted the content of the flag accordingly.

Issues of content appropriateness characterize the history of Burundi's national flag as well. When Burundi gained independence in 1962, its leaders adopted a flag containing two central ornaments: the drum, a traditional Tutsi emblem, and a sorghum plant, a well-recognized sign of prosperity. In 1967, the formation of the republic brought a greater sensitivity to the nation's intricate ethnic composition. Crampton (1990:23) tells us that the content of the national flag was reexamined at this time and defined as deviant to the spirit of the era. As a consequence, in 1967 the drum and sorghum plant were replaced by three stars. The new ornaments were said to provide a more appropriate depiction of Burundi's ethnic makeup, as each star signified the ethnic groups of the period: Tutsis, Hutus, and Twa. By changing the content of the flag in this way, Burundi's leaders and citizens bowed to normative guidelines; they purged the flag of inappropriate material, bringing the symbol's content in line with conventional expectation.

These examples suggest distinct norms governing *what* communicators say. In turning to symbol structure, I propose the existence of norms that govern *how* communicators convey their message as well. In the next section, I use my sample of anthems and flags to delineate these norms of structure, and document communicators' conscious adherence to them.

Delineating Structure Norms for National Symbols

Earlier chapters itemized five specific links between the syntactic structure of national symbols and the nature of their adoption sites:

1. Former colonies distinguish the designs of their anthems and flags from those of their colonial powers.
2. Nation cohorts adopt similarly structured flags, with more recent cohorts choosing the most embellished formats.
3. Neighboring nations adopt similar anthem and flag designs.
4. Economic equivalents in the world-system choose similar symbol structures, with movement from core to periphery associated with increased embellishment.
5. Similarly focused nations adopt similarly structured anthems and flags. In particular, political arrangements and events that increase intranational focus are associated with basic designs; decreased focus in these areas is associated with embellished designs.

In essence, these findings map clear patterns of collective symbolic expression. The systematic adoption of basic versus embellished structures in each of these contexts suggests certain social expectations with regard to message formatting—a recognition of typical versus atypical symbol design. As such, the findings illustrate definitive norms of structure; they indicate shared rules of communication that govern the definition of appropriate identity designs.

Historical accounts suggest that those selecting national symbols defer to the rules of symbol design. In selecting their anthems and flags, records indicate that national leaders acknowledge, albeit implicitly at times, that certain structures seem more appropriate than others to the adoption context. Consider the history of the Mexican anthem. In searching for the "right" piece, sources (Nettl 1967:192– 293; Mead 1980:63) note that Mexican leaders rejected several musical offerings, labeling them inappropriate to the Mexican condition. Composer Juan Bottesini made the first attempt at scoring the Bocanegra poem upon which the anthem is based. But following its first performance, national leaders dismissed the Bocanegra/ Bottesini effort, judging the music insufficiently stirring for the tumultuous times at hand. Mexican leaders next initiated a public competition in active search of appropriate music. After reviewing scores of submissions, leaders settled on a piece by Jaime D. Nunó. Nunó's music was filled with vigorous melodic lines, complex rhythms, and harmonic modulations. It was this embellished structure that Mexican leaders deemed appropriate to the nation's adoption context—structural qualities in total conformity with the communication norms of the low-focus events under which the anthem was adopted.

The history of East Germany's anthem also suggests a conscious adherence to structure norms. East German leaders called for an anthem shortly after World War II, a period of intense nationalism and rigid totalitarianism in the nation. Reportedly (see Nettl 1967:89– 90), German leaders felt that a stately tune would best bespeak the "new" nation's setting. Thus they chose Hanns Eisler's offering, an anthem built on a solemn melody and a simple, repetitive rhythm. The anthem was hailed by East Germany's Central Art Committee as a clear example of music appropriate to the social conditions at hand.[8] The government's enthusiastic approval coincides with the norms of structure for the period. The characteristics of Eisler's music fully conform to the norms governing the high-focus setting in which the anthem was adopted.

Instances of anthem replacement also illustrate structure norms at work. The Czech symbol provides a case in point. When agitating against the oppressive Austro-Hungarian regime, the Czechs discarded their standing national anthem, "Kde domov muj," in favor of a new anthem, "Hej Slované." Nettl (1967:127, 33) tells us that "Kde domov muj" was a simple, mellow, and peaceful tune perceived by the Czechs as inappropriate to their struggle. In contrast, the melody of "Hej Slované" was viewed as revolutionary, aggressive, and strongly extroverted. Consequently, its music was deemed more congruous to the rebellious setting at hand. The Czech example underscores the conscious recognition of norms connecting symbol structure and social setting. By changing anthems, the Czechs affirmed that certain modes of collective self-expression can become more or less appropriate as the setting of that expression changes.

Historical accounts of flag adoptions also suggest a conscious adherence to structure norms. Flags derived via public competition crystallize this point. For although such contests can theoretically result in acceptable flag designs, more often, national leaders amend winning submissions in an effort to render them fully appropriate. Consider Guyana's national flag competition. The actual winning design superimposed a green and yellow triangle over a red field (see fig. 6.1A). Enthralled with the entry, Guyana's leadership nevertheless made some significant changes to the flag before officially adopting it. Specifically, they reversed the ordering of the colors and added both a black and white stripe to the design. The government explained these amendments by citing the need for greater detail in correctly depicting its nation.[9] This need for increased detail should not surprise us. Embellishment represents the norm for nations located in peripheral socioeconomic contexts or those promoting democratic environments. The revisions instituted by Guyana's officials made the winning submission more congruent with the structure norms of that nation's reality.

Recent changes to Iraq's national flag present a similar scenario. On January 13, 1991, Saddam Hussein called for an embellishment of the symbol, adding to it the slogan "God Is Almighty" (see fig. 6.1B). This embellishment embodied a normative response to the decreasing intranational focus that characterized the Iraqi environment. During that period, Hussein faced external ultimatums from the United Nations Security Council, the threat of American invasion,

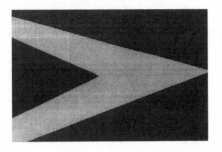

Figure 6.1a. The original (left) and final (right) designs of Guyana's national flag

and the divided sentiments of his own constituency.[10] Thus, the embellishment of the flag embodied a communication strategy change demanded by the disruptive setting. Indeed, Smith (1991:42) notes that the embellished flag became part of a conscious "psychological warfare" developed by Hussein to deal with the new Iraqi context.

The disbanded Soviet Union provides another laboratory for the present inquiry. As the reestablished republics of the region adopted (or in many cases, reclaimed) their own national symbols, we witnessed the norms of structure at work. Uzbekistan, for example, was the first Central Asian republic to declare its independence from the union; it was also the first to discard its Soviet-based symbols and adopt an independent national flag.[11] The current symbol, chosen from a pool of more than two hundred design proposals, emerged

Figure 6.1b. The original (left) and recently embellished (right) designs of Iraq's national flag

Figure 6.1c. The original (left) and recently embellished (right) designs of Uzbekistan's national flag

from a period of rapid transition: the nation was moving from submission to revolt, from totalitarianism to republicanism, from a semi-peripheral location (albeit by association) to a peripheral status. Given the norms of symbol structure identified in this book, we would expect Uzbekistan's new flag to be more embellished in design than its predecessor. Figure 6.1C shows this to be true.[12] The current design increases both the number of colors and the number of ornaments used in the flag (Smith 1992:242–44). The new flag's embellished design is in full keeping with it's adoption context.

The examples reviewed heretofore suggest that structure norms can be itemized. Further, although not continually articulated, these rules are acknowledged by those adopting national symbols. Yet the existence and acknowledgment of norms does not guarantee conformity to them. Despite established guidelines of symbol design, some nations nevertheless adopt deviant symbols. In the next section, we explore the consequences of that action.

Normal Symbols, Deviant Symbols, and Popular Reception

There is good reason to believe that variant levels of structural normalcy trigger different audience response. Communication theorists tell us that when a message runs counter to audience expectation, audience members will likely discard it. Because such deviant messages do not resonate with audiences, they often suffer the disaffection of their targets.[13] On the basis of these claims, we cannot help but conclude that normal symbols represent a superior communication tool.

The links between normal symbols and positive audience reception are not difficult to understand. By definition, normal symbols are in concert with cultural schema. Such symbols introduce no new elements to the sociocultural stock of knowledge, and require no added explication in order for their message to be received. Thus, normal symbols are highly predictable, and this predictability generates comfort, making the symbols "approachable"—easy for an audience to receive, process, and accept. As such, normal symbols increase the potential for audience attachment and enhance the likelihood of effective communication.

Deviant symbols, by contrast, fail to match our cultural schema. The syntax of such symbols strays substantially from the entries in our sociocultural manuals. Thus, deviant symbols give receivers no frame of reference within which to decipher their meaning; they provoke confusion, stimulating uncertainty and unpredictability. As a result, deviant symbols are likely to be discarded or disregarded by receivers; they are apt to dampen audience attachment and impede effective communication.[14]

Given the links between audience attachment and symbol design, national leaders should heed carefully the norms of structure existing in their nation's adoption environment. Our knowledge heretofore suggests that the more normal a symbol's structure, the greater its potential to generate strong audience connection and response. Such attachment is vital, as it is the primary source from which national symbols gain their power. Without this acceptance, national symbols cannot adequately fulfill the variety of integral functions for which they are adopted. Further, I argue that a lack of audience acceptance can lead to ineffectiveness over the life of the symbol. A deviant structure can stigmatize the symbol, thus defining it in a way that hinders a popular bond, even beyond the immediate conditions of the symbol's adoption.

My data on anthems and flags provide material with which to test this hypothesis. By reexamining each symbol in the sample, we can classify syntactic designs and assess their relative levels of deviance. Having done so, we can isolate extreme cases of syntactic structure—

the highly deviant and the highly normal—comparing public response to each design category.

Classifying Deviant Structure

Identifying normal and deviant symbol structures is an intricate task. The relative deviance of a symbol's design must be viewed with reference to the structure norms that guide five specific social contexts: the lineal, spatial, socioeconomic, political, and event.[15] In essence, a symbol's structure must be coded as normal or deviant within each of these contexts. On the basis of such information, a composite deviance score can then be calculated.

Appendix A provides a detailed explanation of the classification method. There, interested readers can follow one specific symbol through each step of the process. Those wishing to peruse the distribution of normal and deviant symbols are urged to turn to Appendix B, where each symbol's deviance score is listed.

In interpreting the findings to follow, note that the deviance scores for symbol structure can range from 0 to 5, with 0 indicating perfect conformity to structure norms and 5 signifying perfect deviance. My analysis is focused on symbols representing the extremes of this continuum; I address audience response to highly normal versus highly deviant symbols.[16]

Popular Reaction to Normal versus Deviant Symbols

When comparing normal versus deviant symbols, both historical sources[17] and interview data[18] suggest several distinct differences in citizen response. Further, my research indicates that the responses triggered by a symbol's status at adoption—normal or deviant—persist beyond the symbol's introduction. Although social contexts may change, thus bringing a symbol's structure in accord or discord with norms through time, it is a symbol's acceptance or rejection *at adoption* that appears to influence the long-term nature of the symbol's connection to the national audience it represents.

For analytical purposes, I discuss audience response to anthems and flags with reference to three key dimensions: passionate versus rational reception, sacred versus secular engagement, and voluntary versus mandated reverence.[19]

Passionate versus Rational Reception

Audience responses to normal versus deviant symbols suggests that normal symbols stir passionate, emotional reactions in their targets; they touch the "heart" of their publics. In contrast, deviant symbols trigger more temperate, rational responses; their appeal is cerebral.

Certain symbol histories document the passion inspired by normal symbols. Of Belgium's normal anthem, for example, Nettl notes that from its inception, the anthem was "a *fiery, stirring* piece of music, *noted for generating fervor* in those who hear it" (1967:96, emphasis added). Similarly, he reports the long-term appeal of Poland's normal anthem, describing it as "capable of *deeply moving* those singing it" (ibid.:119, emphasis added). Comparable observations characterize the histories of normal anthems from Bulgaria, Czechoslovakia, and Great Britain; since their adoption, these anthems have been warmly embraced by the populations they serve (see, e.g., Griffith 1952:24–39; Nettl 1967:114, 127).

Popular testimony echoes scholarly accounts. In discussing Bolivia's normal anthem, for example, a cultural attaché described it as "one of the most *beloved* hymns in the nation. Truly! Since it came into being, there is no one who doesn't know it or who is not moved by it!" In a similar vein, an Egyptian representative said of his nation's normal anthem: "Our symbols, especially the anthem, are especially important to us. They *touch our hearts* . . . literally . . . because they are related to our long heritage. Since their adoption, they are known by everyone—even small children." Such reports alert us to the emotional appeal normal anthems garner upon their adoption as well as the long-term power of that connection.

Deviant anthems are met with much less vigor. Although citizens are generally attached to these symbols, the nature of such bonds is far less electrifying than that which ties citizens to normal symbols. In reviewing the deviant anthems in my sample, for instance, I noted that the publics they serve historically have directed their emotion toward other songs. For example, Norwegians prefer the folk song "Sonner of Norge det aeldgamie rige" to the nation's deviant anthem. Similarly, Sweden's deviant anthem competes with several songs, "Ur Svenska hjertans djup en gang" and "Sverige, Sverige, fosterland" among them.[20] Venezuelans report greater affection for the song "Alma Aanera" than they do for their deviant anthem. And citizens of Paraguay prefer a folk song entitled "Lovely Country" to the nation's deviant anthem (see Griffith 1952, Mead 1980, Nettl 1967, and Reed and Bristow 1985 for details). In this regard, U.S. readers will no doubt note the frequency with which "America the Beautiful" or "God Bless America" are performed in place of the "Star-Spangled Banner." Indeed, several grass-roots movements have attempted to replace the United States' deviant national anthem with one of these alternatives. Mead (1980) reminds us that the "Star-Spangled Banner" won congressional confirmation in 1931 only after the statute proposing the anthem was amended so as to cite "America" ("My country, 'tis of thee") as the "unofficial" anthem.

Personal testimony underscores the restrained reactions to deviant anthems. An embassy official from Sierra Leone, for example, described citizen reactions toward his nation's deviant anthem in this way: "We respect our anthem. We would, at the very least, stand when it is played. And certainly, those that don't can be . . . yes, they are called to task, for we never want to desecrate the anthem. But we feel more reverent than emotional about it. There are no sentimental bonds with the symbol . . . there never have been." Similarly, a Norwegian official described reactions to his nation's deviant anthem: "Emotional, yes, I guess, sometimes . . . maybe. I would say about 50 percent of citizens feel that attached. But the other 50 percent are more respectful than emotional . . . do you know what I mean?"

Note that some deviant anthems fail to achieve even a rational attachment with their audiences; rather, citizens appear nearly detached from them. One researcher told me, for example, that during lengthy visits to Indonesia, he was continually amazed by the low regard those citizens had for their nation's deviant anthem: "I remember attending a public parade. When the anthem was played, citizens couldn't care less; they paid little attention, expressed no reverence. I asked a few people why they felt so little attachment to the song. They told me that they viewed it as a Western accoutrement imposed on them rather than rising from them." Similarly, a Zambian attaché had this to say of his nation's deviant anthem: "With the exception of the political elites who are active in the government, most people sing the anthem just for the sake of singing it. They don't understand what it is. They don't necessarily see it as a symbol that captures Zambia." In each of these cases, we witness anthems that seemingly never connect with their targets. The symbols are generally revered, but citizen fervor toward them never reaches the heights enjoyed by normal symbols.

In comparing normal and deviant flags, we find a similar phenomenon. Whereas normal flags generally evoke passion, deviant flags elicit a more reserved response. "The Great Australian Flag Debate," for example, highlights the intense passion a normal flag can generate. Since its adoption in 1909, the Australian flag has enjoyed the enthusiasm of the nation's citizens. But over the past ten years, a lobbying group known as AUSFLAG has campaigned vigorously to change the flag.[21] The group has sponsored several flag design competitions and unfurled several prototypes for public viewing. AUSFLAG proponents have been quite vocal in their cause. Note, for instance, the directness of Leo Schofield's words, published in an Australian newspaper during one of AUSFLAG's campaigns: "There are powerful reasons why we should modify the current flag. It is not uniquely Australian. It is virtually indistinguishable from that of New Zealand. It is an Imperial flag that signifies our subservience to Britain. . . . However, I doubt if our present Prime Minister has the stomach, the taste, or the good sense to make the change."[22]

AUSFLAG's efforts inevitably trigger heated public debate. Note the following emotional responses to Schofield's pleas for change: "In case you do not know, the Union Jack in the corner of our flag represents our heritage. . . . Our flag is the best looking of all of them when flying. I am proud of it!" (signed "an Oz fanatic") and "The Union Jack in the top corner [of the flag] reminds us that under it, many of the first inhabitants were treated as animals, and many of our forebears were forced to leave their homelands to come here." These emotional debates often transcend the pages of the newspaper. For example, when Harold Scruby, Mosman's deputy mayor and chairman of AUSFLAG, used government property to display alternatives to the nation's current flag, the mayor of Mosman, Peter Clive, used the law to block Scruby's initiative. According to newspaper accounts, "The Mayor of Mosman, Alderman Peter Clive, has instructed that a flag being promoted by the deputy mayor, Alderman Harold Scruby, is not to be flown from any council property. He told Tuesday night's council meeting he would take steps to ensure Mosman Council was disassociated from moves by Alderman Scruby to have a new Australian flag." The passion that binds most Australians to their normal flag may well win out in the end, for at the present time, some officials (and some AUSFLAG members) seem doubtful that the current symbol will ever be changed.[23] This suggests that once adopted, the passionate reaction generated by a normal symbol is difficult to dismantle.

The Australian case is hardly unique. My interviews with foreign diplomats and citizens regarding other normal flags revealed emotional bonds of equal strength. For example, in speaking of his nation's normal flag, a Brazilian attaché told me: "For us, our national symbols, both flag and anthem, well, they are Brazil. We are very attached to them, very attached indeed. You see, for us, they mean anything that is Brazil." A Mexican official expressed similar sentiments in discussing her nation's normal flag: "Mexico is a very religious country, yes. You will see shrines and statues all over the place, especially to Our Lady of Guadalupe. She is a figure of the people. I would put the flag in the same category as her. Mexicans have for all time been very devoted to the flag. They love it, they truly love it."

Deviant flags generate a very different reaction. Although respected, public response toward them is more rational than passionate. For example, in speaking of his nation's deviant flag, a Kuwaiti official told me:

> Kuwaitis are just not attached to the flag as you would see in the United States, for example. I could not believe what I saw with your flag when I first arrived here! Our people do not fly the flag at home. Its uses are restricted to the public sphere, you know, government buildings. . . . Display increases a bit on National Day. And of course, you saw a lot of the flag when we were liberated from Iraq. But I would characterize our feeling toward the flag as one of healthy respect. We never disgrace it, but we are not fanatical about it. It has never been so.

An Argentine representative made similar assessments in commenting on his nation's deviant flag: "We are not fanatical about the flag.

We respect it, but we don't do it so emotionally!" And an exchange student from South Korea said of public reactions to her nation's deviant flag: "It has always been as if we respect the flag out of habit rather than true feeling."

Historical studies suggest that some deviant flags fail to stimulate any noteworthy attachments, documenting cases in which citizens seemingly disengage from their symbols. In writing of public response toward the Union Jack, for example, Firth (1973:366) notes that the symbol occupies "the sphere of the mundane . . . Britain treats the flag neither with reverence or despite." Similarly, Crampton (1990:138) suggests that Burma's deviant flag has suffered public indifference from its inception. Both the Shans and the Karens, groups that comprise the majority of the populus, dismissed the flag upon its adoption. Each group then set about designing its own symbols as part of a rhetoric for independence and statehood. Such cases further underscore the lackluster response that frequently plagues the deviant symbol.

Sacred versus Secular Engagement

Throughout this book, I have repeatedly noted the sacred status of national symbols. And both historical writings and personal testimony on anthems and flags remind us of the unique position these symbols occupy in the communities they serve. Note that both normal and deviant symbols are referenced with a near-religious reverence. For example, a British exchange student said of her nation's normal anthem: "People just automatically stand up, out of respect, when the anthem is played. Sometimes, I'll be at home, alone mind you, and I will hear the anthem on the telly and find myself standing up—it's mind boggling, but there I am, standing up in my own living room! . . . Other national songs exist—'Rule Britannia,' 'I Vow to Thee My Country'—but they simply don't hold the respect, they're just not taken as seriously as 'God Save the Queen.'"

Similarly, a Mexican cultural attaché had this to say of Mexico's normal flag: "Sometimes, in very special marketplaces, you will see a shrine to Our Lady of Guadalupe, the patron Saint of Mexico, and right next to that statue, there is always the flag. These displays make the flag holy, if you know what I mean. They show that Our Lady and the flag are at the same level." But by the same token, a representative of the Ivory Coast expressed similar sentiments about his nation's deviant anthem: "The national anthem is a very special symbol. It must always be treated with respect. Not to do so is to commit . . . well, blasphemy. There's no other word for it." Venezuela's deviant flag too was described with such respect. An exchange student told me: "I cannot say enough about the importance of the flag. It is a holy and special symbol of our people."

Because of their sacred nature, national symbols are said to be misplaced in the profane sphere. Whether we define the profane as that which is antagonistic to the sacred (e.g., Durkheim 1915:53) or as that which is secular or ordinary (see, e.g., Stanner 1967:217–40), national symbols are thought to be incongruous with the profane. However, my comparisons of normal and deviant symbols suggest a necessary amendment to that position. My data indicate that some symbols do exhibit a secular component. Although all anthems and flags enjoy a sacred status, normal symbols often reside in both the sacred and secular arenas. Citizens frequently report a "hands-on" experience with normal symbols—one not enjoyed by their deviant counterparts.

The secular side of normal symbols is best revealed in usage. In listing appropriate uses for national anthems and flags, citizens represented by normal symbols described both official and informal settings. Respondents from Bolivia, Brazil, Colombia, Costa Rica, Ecuador, Egypt, Finland, Great Britain, Guatemala, Hungary, Kuwait, Mexico, and Peru told me that their nations' normal symbols are likely to be found both in formal government sites and in everyday arenas such as marketplaces, sporting events, and theaters. The normal anthems of these nations are often sung daily in the schools, or performed prior to popular entertainment functions. These nations' normal flags are frequently displayed in homes or incorporated into items of clothing.

Conversely, respondents represented by deviant symbols described restricted usage. In nations such as Guatemala, Ivory Coast, Kuwait, Norway, Paraguay, Sierra Leone, South Korea, Sweden, and Zambia, anthems and flags rarely leave the official public domain. Rather, the deviant symbols of these nations are unveiled *for* citizens rather than being used *by* them. The remarks of some South

Korean exchange students illustrate the point: "We were amazed, truly amazed, to see the variety of places Americans display their flag, the frequency with which it is displayed. In Korea, the flag is displayed in the home only on national holidays. Public buildings are the only locations in which one would expect to see the flag flown daily." Similarly, these students told me that they were appalled by Americans who wore the flag on their clothing or displayed it in a tattoo: "In Korea, the flag is a sacred thing. To make it a part of popular culture artifacts constitutes a sign of disrespect."

In some ways, the absence of deviant symbols from the secular domain tells us something about the nature of their sacredness. The inaccessibility of deviant symbols suggests that their sacredness may be viewed as an endangered commodity, that their power and aura may be threatened by unlimited contact. If such is the case, restrictions on free symbol usage may represent a form of protectionism. By confining anthems and flags to the sacred arena, nations act to insulate their symbols, and thus themselves, from potential defilement or desecration.

In contrast, the secular dimension of normal symbols implies a confidence in their sacred status. The diffusion of normal symbols into the secular domain suggests a nation's security in its symbols; it indicates a belief that a symbol's power cannot be drained by public contact. Consequently, normal symbols project a "user-friendly" quality. They provide citizens with a tangible opportunity to experience their nation—an open invitation to don their collective self.[24]

Voluntary versus Mandated Reverence

If a nation's confidence in the sacredness of its symbols varies by the symbols' status—normal versus deviant—then normal and deviant symbols will be maintained by different mechanisms. Indeed, my research indicates that devotion to normal symbols occurs on a largely voluntary basis. In contrast, respect toward deviant symbols is generally mandated by law.

During interviews, citizens represented by normal symbols frequently noted the voluntary nature of their veneration. For example, a Costa Rican official told me, "Our anthem is automatically treated with due solemnity and respect." Similarly, a cultural attaché from

Chile said, "Disrespect for the national anthem is not punishable by law, so to speak, but it is passively prohibited." And a Hungarian citizen reported, "If there are laws regulating the anthem, I don't know of them . . . no, they are not highly publicized. We don't need laws to get respect for the anthem. It's too important to us. We would never defile it." Comments on normal flags were quite similar. For example, a Greek information officer told me, "All official references discuss the flag as an expression of the nation, discussing the need to honor it, but they are not harsh statements, not like a law. People are very attached to the flag. It is not necessary to threaten them for respect." These reports suggest that when a nation feels secure in the sacredness of its symbols, it can allow respect for a symbol to emerge *from* the people. Thus in the normal symbol's environment, public attachment develops naturally; it need not be officially imposed.

When the sacredness of symbols appears tenuous, symbols must be constantly buttressed. As such, the sacred status of deviant symbols must be continually reestablished and reinforced. I discovered a variety of mechanisms operating in this regard. For example, deviant symbols' contents and designs were often carefully outlined in national constitutions. Note the following description of Ethiopia's deviant flag: "The flag of the People's Democratic Republic of Ethiopia is of rectangular shape with the colors green above, yellow in the middle, and red below. Particulars shall be determined by law" (quoted in Smith 1988:9). And this description of Niger's deviant flag: "The national emblem shall be the tricolour flag with three horizontal stripes. The upper stripe being orange, the middle stripe white with an orange disc in the centre, and the lower stripe green" (*Constitutions of African States* 1972:vol. 2, p. 1130). Often, constitutions strictly outlined acceptable uses for a symbol. Consider the constitution of Cyprus:

> The Republic shall have its own flag of neutral design chosen jointly by the President and Vice President of the Republic.
>
> The authority of the Republic and any public corporation or public utility body created by or under the laws of the Republic shall fly the flag of the Republic and they shall have the right to fly on holidays together with the flag of the Republic either the Greek or the Turkish flag at the same time.

The Communal authority and institution shall have the right to fly on holidays together with the flag of the Republic either the Greek or the Turkish flag at the same time.

Any citizen of the Republic or any body corporate or uncorporate, other than public whose members are citizens of the Republic, shall have the right to fly on their premises, the flag of the Republic or the Greek or the Turkish flag without restriction. (Peaslee 1965:140)

By specifying anthems or flags within the national constitution—itself a sacred symbol—national leaders ensure that deviant anthems and flags enjoy sanctity by association. A symbiotic relationship develops as the sacred references the sacred.

Formal laws and regulations also are used to buttress the sacredness of deviant symbols.[25] Frequently, appropriate protocol toward deviant symbols is codified, thus mandating respect toward them. As one Zambian official told me: "There are laws that mandate the singing of our anthem in official gatherings of thirty or more. If thirty or more people are present, their meeting *must* begin with the anthem. These laws are strictly enforced." Similarly, an official of the Ivory Coast told me, "Of course there must be laws governing the use of our anthem and our flag. We cannot allow any blasphemy of these symbols." An Argentine citizen informed me of the strict regulations governing public behavior toward the nation's deviant flag: "You cannot fly the flag just anywhere. That is not likely. It is to be flown only on public buildings. And of course, there is strict reaction to burning the flag . . . But no country would allow such a thing, no?" And consider just part of the elaborate three-page "Flag and Coat-of-Arms Regulation" in force within the Bahamas:

Where any person—
   (a) mutilates, cuts, tears, burns or in any way defaces whether by writing, printing or stamping thereon or otherwise; or
   (b) by any spoken words insults or brings contempt or ridicule,
the National Flag . . . such person, unless he can prove that the act was done with lawful justification or excuse or the words were spoken without intent to insult or bring into contempt or ridicule the said flags or the Coat of Arms, or any representation thereof, shall be guilty of an offense and liable on summary conviction to a fine not exceeding five hundred dollars or to imprisonment for a term not exceeding six months or to both such fine and imprisonment.

Such mandated reverence toward deviant symbols is taken quite seriously. When infractions of symbol regulations occur—no matter how unusual the offense—public officials take immediate note and sanctions are pursued. Consider the following problem described by a Kuwaiti attaché:

> Citizens are forbidden by law to fly the flag on their homes. There are some rare occasions when this law is less than strictly enforced. On National Day, officials would probably ignore illegal flying of the flag. . . . After the war with Iraq, however, some unusual displays of the flag emerged in Kuwait. The people were excited. They displayed the flag at our liberation. This was tolerated for awhile, but eventually, it was discouraged. Some people, though not many, actually tried to circumvent the law by painting the flag on their homes! I wonder how our government will deal with issues of protocol. If the flag is painted on homes, it cannot be removed from rain or darkness. It's a tough one, but something will be done soon, I'm sure.

By comparing the regulation of normal and deviant symbols, we learn that the sacred aura of deviant symbols is never left to chance. Rather, nations choose to formalize and legalize a symbol's special position, suggesting that only then is a symbol's sacredness ensured.

Why Do Communicators Deviate?

The existence of deviant national symbols is surprising. For throughout this book, I have argued that symbol structure is purposively selected. Given this intention, one must wonder why a structure that contradicts audience expectation—a communication error—would knowingly be chosen by symbol adopters.

The vast literature on symbolic expression offers some insight on the issue. Research suggests that certain settings may beckon deviant messages. First, some studies show that *communicators deviate from normative guidelines when they feel a loss of control over their social environment.* In earlier work (Cerulo 1984), I demonstrated this pattern as it occurs among musicians. Specifically, I examined the structure of classical compositions written during World War II, comparing pieces written by composers shielded from battle versus composers directly exposed to combat conditions. Although all the musicians were faithful to the norms of composition in their prewar works, only those shielded from combat continued to be bound by these rules during the war. Composers directly exposed to battle broke with compositional norms, introducing new techniques and styles into their music.

In the war-music study, I note that composers in combat zones experienced a sudden lack of control over their environment. These individuals were regularly exposed to direct, often surprise, attack. Physical danger and visible devastation became prominent features of their surroundings. The composers' communication networks were totally destroyed and their everyday rituals disrupted. In essence, combat zone composers experienced a near-constant sense of uncertainty and a loss of mastery over their personal destiny. Faced with this reality, the composers sought control in other areas of their lives, as Ernest Becker (1973:89–90) notes, a common response to such conditions.[26] When an individual is entrenched in a collective problem that no longer holds the potential for collective control, he or she creates an alternate environment in which personal control can be exercised. For combat-zone composers, that alternate environment was a musical one. Their craft provided a means by which to regain power. These composers recaptured control by restructuring their music in a manner that was not expected by their audience. In this way, control over information substituted for the control of events.

It may be that a similar process is at work in the selection of national symbols. When nations occupy powerless positions, their leaders may choose deviant modes of expression in an effort to capture some dimension of control. For such leaders, the symbolic realm may constitute the alternate environment to which Becker refers, a locale apart from the sociopolitical and socioeconomic realms that dominate the powerless. National leaders can achieve exclusivity in this alternate environment by projecting a nonconventional voice, a nonnormative design that only the senders can fully predict. In this way, the transmitting nation creates a moment of power in the symbolic arena, a point at which the transmitter is in complete control.

We can offer a second explanation for the adoption of deviant symbols. Research *links an individual's lack of connectedness to a propen-*

sity for deviance. Consider the variety of arenas in which this relationship proves true. Studies of juvenile delinquency, for example, demonstrate that isolated individuals frequently engage in deviance. Those lacking social bonds are released from the power of norms, freeing them to engage in rule-violating behaviors (see, e.g., Becker 1963, Hirschi 1969, Lemert 1953, Lott and Lott 1961). In the realm of science too, research links isolation to deviance—but here, deviance in the form of innovation.[27] Connectedness stresses the routine, whereas isolation releases individuals from the status quo, enabling them to pursue the different, to take the risk associated with the introduction of innovation (see, e.g., Burt 1987, Coleman et al. 1966, Kuhn 1970, Rogers 1983). Isolation and deviance have also been paired in the study of social perceptions. Isolates are more likely than the well-connected to mischaracterize qualities and behaviors of themselves and others (see, e.g., Cerulo 1990, Ross 1977).

These findings are relevant to the study of deviant anthems and flags. For just as isolation helps to stimulate deviant behaviors such as crime, innovation, and mischaracterization, so too may isolation motivate deviant symbolization. Isolated nations may experience release from the communication norms that govern the world community, leaving leaders of these nations free to experiment with highly variant strategies. For such leaders, the absence of strict "shoulds," may allow a variety of expressive possibilities to enter the foreground.

A third explanation for the adoption of deviant symbols comes from research suggesting that *deviant communication strategies best capture audience attention,*[28] thus heightening the potential for message effectiveness.[29] Normative strategies are less effective in this regard because of their clarity. Processing a clear message often requires little active effort from receivers, risking a passive receiver response known as "mindlessness" (Langer 1978; also see Guiraud 1975:13; Marcus and Zajonc 1985:9; McGuire 1985), or "habituation"—situations in which information is so routine that receivers process it without conscious reflection on the material (see, e.g., Bogart 1973; Leukel 1972:385–86). Deviant strategies overcome problems of habituation. By presenting the unexpected to receivers, communicators force audience members to readjust their interpretive frameworks. When bombarded with deviant images and designs, receivers members must work to apprehend the message. This active response is likely to increase cognitive activity, message recall, and subsequent action.

The link between deviant communication strategies and audience attention may help us to better understand the adoption of deviant symbols. If national leaders perceive their audiences to be distracted, despondent, or weary, if they view their targets as dispersed, they may choose to project identity symbolizations in ways that reactivate receivers. Note that many of the adoption contexts examined thus far bespeak such dispersion. Settings of cultural diversity, democratic multiplicity, revolution, or direct attack—all of these milieus can constitute difficult communication environments. Those faced with such conditions may employ the novelty of deviance as a tool for the successful captivation of an audience.

These three schools of thought suggest hypotheses for future research. Clearly, the adoption of deviant structures demands further investigation.[30] By pursuing the premises presented here, as well as further conceptualizing the problem, our understanding of deviant communication choices can only be enhanced.

Conclusion

Many of the national anthems and flags highlighted in this chapter tell the tale of identity in "a different voice." These symbols defy the communication strategies prescribed by their social circumstances, representing their nations via deviant modes of expression. I have speculated on the source of this deviance. But more importantly, I have attempted to demonstrate that the practice of deviant symbolization is not without consequences. Deviant symbols do not enjoy the fervent reception or the intense attachment of their more normal counterparts. Deviant symbols simply do not "work" as well as normal ones. Given this knowledge, one cannot help but ponder the fate of symbols that "don't work." Such questions lead us to broader inquiries on symbol change. It is to this issue of symbol replacement that the next chapter directs us.

7

CHANGING VOICE

DESPITE THE DYNAMIC nature of our personal identities, symbols of the self often are quite stable. We retain our childhood nicknames long beyond their functional applicability. We cling to college rings, favorite sweaters, or the first dollar ever earned even though these items represent events long behind us. Once we embrace such symbols, we rarely part with them. For although these articles may not typify our current selves, they nevertheless represent important pieces of our history, making them hard to discard.

When Associative Relationships Lose Their Charge

Like the signifiers of personal identities, national identity symbols, once adopted, are rarely cast aside. Despite the fact that certain symbols refer to specific events—mere moments in the lengthy history of a nation—these symbols are generally retained for the life of the nation. Indeed, in the history of nations, remarkably few (approximately 15 percent) have changed their anthems and flags.[1] The same is true for other national symbols. With regard to the nation, the bond between symbols and that which they represent—what Saussure referred to as an associative relationship—proves hard to destroy.

The rarity of national symbol change renders it a remarkable phenomenon. For knowing the intensity with which national symbols are embraced, we cannot help but wonder what situations and events are capable of disturbing that appeal. This chapter is devoted to a better understanding of the issue. Using the historical accounts and interview data described in chapter 6, I explore the elements that appear to motivate national symbol change.

Associative Relationships and Change

To understand symbol change, we must reexamine the notion of *associative relationships*. This concept, introduced by Saussure, refers to the link between a symbol and that which it signifies.[2] Associative relationships denote a bond that virtually enables communication, for it is this link between symbol and referent that deems the two elements, in essence, interchangeable ([1915] 1959:66–75).[3]

Saussure did little to further detail associative relationships. His only elaboration concerned the *nature* of the symbols within these relationships; he was adamant in his belief that symbols are, at inception, abstract and arbitrary signs. Here, I offer additional considerations. Certain characteristics of both the symbols and referents that constitute associative relationships must be reviewed in order to adequately characterize the permanence of their bond. Specifically, we first must determine if the symbol is a static or a dynamic entity. Second, we must locate the symbol, placing it in both the spatial and temporal sphere, or solely in the temporal. Third, we must note the symbol's social relevance—high or low—within both present experience and the memory of the collective from which it emerges. Finally, we must assess a symbol's level of abstractness; counter to Saussure, I argue that the abstractness of symbols can vary, and thus, must be considered.

These four specifications bring multidimensionality to the associative relationship. This point is key, for I argue that variations along these dimensions can lead to different types of links between symbols and their referents, with some links more recalcitrant to symbol change than others. To fully understand these distinctions, we must discuss each of the aforementioned dimensions of the associative relationship in greater detail.

Static versus Dynamic Referents

The people, objects, moods, or values to which we attend can be classified on the basis of activity: static or dynamic. In the *static condition,* referents are constant. They do not change or grow, but remain stable, projecting a quality of permanence. Concrete, inanimate objects provide good examples of static referents. Consider that a chair, a table, or a desk will serve its life undergoing little or no change. To be sure, these objects may suffer scratches and nicks; they may be refinished, repainted, or relocated from one room to another or from house to house. Yet the entity's form, the essence of the chair, table, or desk, will remain largely the same as it was at its inception. To destroy that essence, we would have to destroy the object itself.

In the *dynamic condition,* the referent is in constant flux. The entity is not a stable element, but one always "under construction." Whether developing or decomposing, the key to the referent's dynamism lies in its continual modification. Personal identity exemplifies a dynamic signified, for an individual's identity is an emergent quality that is always "becoming." Each day's experience, each year's triumphs and failures, bring new dimensions and new emphases to the core of the individual, her/his beliefs, values, and goals. Although the presence of identity remains constant, that which constitutes it is always changing.

Spatial and Temporal Locations of the Referent

The entities we signify can also be located with reference to spatial and temporal planes. The *spatial plane* is restricted to entities that we perceive via the senses, what Kant called "empirical intuition" (1929:43–56). Empirical intuition demands current tangibility. Hence, referents emerging from the spatial plane always have a "here and now" quality. In contrast, the *temporal plane* encompasses entities that no longer exist or those that have not yet become.[4] Thus, referents in the temporal plane cannot be externally perceived. We experience them via "pure intuition"; their reality is internally based (Kant 1929:43–56). We may discuss or envision such entities within the confines of the present, but our thoughts and words refer to something beyond our current spatial plane. Thus in the temporal realm, the link between symbol and referent crosses the line between present and past or present and future.[5]

Some referents enjoy both a spatial and temporal reality. They exist in the here and now, they enjoy a past, and they may be projected into the future as well. Other referents have only a temporal reality; they used to be or they may yet be, but they are not now (Kant 1929:53). So, for example, as a living being, I exist in both the spatial and temporal plane. While alive, I can be apprehended via the senses; being seen, touched, and heard by others and by myself constitutes my empirical reality. While alive, I have a temporal existence as well. I can be referenced as memory, or become the subject of future fantasy. When I die, I will lose my spatial relevance. Yet I can continue to live in the temporal plane via memory or fantasy. Thus as a nonliving being, my reality shifts from space and time to a solely temporal existence.

Social Relevance of the Referent

Individuals apprehend stimuli, experience thoughts and feelings every moment of every day. Some of these perceptions are "asterisked" as important, while others are dismissed. We can speak of entities that capture our special attentions as relevant. Such entities hold meaning for our personal or social circumstance; they speak to our needs and understandings or offer insight into our condition. Irrelevant entities, in contrast, are easily overlooked. Their connection to our interests never becomes clear; their link to our lives is never recognized.[6]

Both relevant and irrelevant entities can be symbolized, yet only the relevant retain the central attention of their audience. Irrelevant entities become the ground against which relevant figures are perceived. An example from the world of music clarifies the point. In the 1700s, several musicians held stature in Vienna; at this time and place, Adlasser, Bonno, Gassmann, Mozart, Muller, Salieri, Weigl, and Wranitzky all were relevant entities. When they ceased to be living beings, however, Mozart alone retained relevance. Within the temporal plane, Mozart is recalled as unique against the backdrop of his contemporaries. To be sure, the aforementioned composers are no less real than Mozart. Yet in the passage of time, they have become subordinate to Mozart's image. Thus, they have been dismissed from our collective attention as irrelevant referents.

Abstractness of the Symbol

In writing of associative relationships, Saussure saw neither a necessary connection nor a natural reflection between a symbol and its referent. Rather, he considered all symbols as abstract entities (1959:67–69). Many have taken exception to Saussure's position on this point. Some have offered evidence in contradiction of the claim (see, e.g., Lévi-Strauss 1963, Jakobson and Waugh 1979, Hodge and Kress 1988). Others have offered theoretical alternatives to Saussure's premise. The Peircian system of classification, for instance, enumerates different levels of signification in which the signifier can be more or less abstract, a more or less accurate reflection of the object it represents.[7] Hodge and Kress promote a similar notion, proposing a continuum of signs that proceeds from more to less abstract (1988:22).

Saussure's critics alert us to the fact that the relative abstractness of symbols must be taken into account. Symbols that concretely reflect their referents are perceived differently than abstract symbols that merely reference the entities they represent. In this way, varying levels of abstraction can result in diverse links between a symbol and its referent.

Reconsidering Associative Bonds

The nature of the ties between symbol and referent cannot be assumed. Rather, the dimensions along which these entities vary give rise to four different types of associative bonds: charged, blocked, dormant, and suspended (see table 7.1). These distinctions are important because each type of bond differentially influences a symbol's susceptibility to change.

A *charged associative bond* is one in which the ties between symbol and referent are energized. The relationship is alive with meaning, as referent and symbol form a fully integrated unit. Charged bonds are the product of very specific conditions. First, they are confined to

Table 7.1. Classification of Associative Relationships

Referents	Symbols Abstract ↔ Concrete	
Static		
Spatial and temporal		
Relevant	Charged	Charged
Irrelevant	Dormant	Dormant
Temporal only		
Relevant	Charged	Charged
Irrelevant	Dormant	Dormant
Dynamic		
Spatial and temporal		
Relevant	Charged	Blocked
Irrelevant	Dormant	Suspended
Temporal only		
Relevant	Charged	Blocked
Irrelevant	Dormant	Suspended

relevant signifieds. Without relevance, the referent would fail to capture audience attention and its symbol would be discarded or ignored.

When signifieds are dynamic in nature, charged bonds are contingent on the presence of highly abstract symbols. In the dynamic condition, symbols must be sufficiently malleable so as to accommodate change to the entities they represent. If concrete symbols are paired with dynamic referents, they can become too closely linked to earlier forms of a changing entity. When such mismatching occurs, the bond between symbol and referent can be lost; the symbol can become obsolete, and thus, vulnerable to rejection.

Finally, charged associative bonds can occur when referents exist in both space and time, or when referents enjoy only a temporal existence. However, symbols associated with the latter condition are known as *dangling signifiers*.[8] Dangling signifiers can be empirically experienced, laying claim to an independent life of their own. Yet although the dangling signifier exists in the present, its referent is confined to either the past or the future. Consequently, the dangling signifier has the power to remove its target audience from the here and now and transport it to a reality that has been or will be.

The relationship between an existing marriage (the referent) and a wedding ring (the symbol) exemplifies a charged associative bond. An existing marriage represents a dynamic referent; it is emergent, developing, and ever-changing. Further, an existing marriage is highly relevant; it holds important consequences for the participants, and it frames the interaction for those to whom the couple relates. Finally, an existing marriage has both a spatial and temporal presence. It takes on a specific form in the here and now, yet it can be referenced with regard to what it was in the past and what it will be in the future. Under these conditions, any symbol of an existing marriage must favor abstraction if it is to remain charged. The wedding ring meets this requirement. Circular bands of gold or silver have no inherent meaning; they offer no concrete reflection or detail. Rather, they are highly abstract and neutral in character. As such, the meaning of the wedding ring can be defined and redefined as that which it signifies changes. The abstractness of the ring makes it possible for the bond between referent and symbol to retain its power in the face of shifts and alterations.

Note that when a marriage is dissolved by death or divorce, the wedding band becomes a dangling signifier. Although its spatial referent—the existing marriage—is lost, the wedding band does not lose its meaning or power. It simply refers its audience to a new, solely temporal location. The abstract nature of the wedding ring explains this symbol's extended life. Because the symbol can accommodate reinterpretation, the ring that once signified joy can be reconstructed to signify happy memories, pain, a bad decision, or anger.

Of course, symbols of charged relationships need not always be abstract. If a referent is concrete, then a concrete symbol can be as highly charged as an abstract one. Because concrete referents maintain stability, symbolizing them in a flexible way becomes unnecessary. But under such conditions, the relevance of the referent is key. If a concrete symbol is to maintain its charge, the object to which it refers must sustain the attention of its audience.

The charged associative relationship presents little likelihood for symbol replacement. Such relationships represent a perfect match between referent and symbol, keeping the ties that bind the two components alive and vibrant.

Dormant associative bonds occur when referents lose their relevance. Dormant symbols are appropriately matched to their referents, but that which the symbols signify has become temporarily uninteresting to the audience. Consequently, dormant associative bonds characterize the unremarkable, in both the spatial and temporal arenas.

Popular culture fads aptly illustrate the dormant condition. Recall the Pet Rock phenomenon of the 1970s. During that product's (the referent) tenure, its logo, Pet Rock (the symbol), retained meaning. However, when the product lost its appeal, the Pet Rock logo disappeared from our daily consciousness. Although the product may regain popularity in the future, both the symbol and referent currently remain beyond the bounds of our immediate attention. The associative bond that links symbol to referent is dormant; it is not actively apprehended or processed by an audience.

Certain Crayola crayons offer a similar example. Recall that in 1990, Crayola retired eight of the colors in their collection: maize, raw umber, lemon yellow, blue gray, violet blue, green blue, orange red, and orange yellow. The company held a special ceremony at its corporate headquarters, bidding adieu to the once popular eight and welcoming several new colors to the crayon collection. Each retired color name and the color it represents now comprise a dormant associative relationship. As each color was laid to rest, so too was its symbol, and the relationships receded to the back of our minds. The referents become irrelevant, thus releasing their symbols from our attentions.

Note that what is irrelevant today may regain relevance tomorrow. And because *dormant relationships* can be resurrected, *their signifiers are not susceptible to change*. If a referent recaptures its original relevance, its symbol will likely return to the consciousness of the audience in its original form.

Blocked associative bonds are confined to relevant, dynamic referents. They occur when concrete, literal symbols come to represent important entities that change by nature. This match creates a disequilibrium that the associative relationship cannot withstand. For as the referent undergoes amendment, its symbol remains petrified, increasingly removed from that which it signifies. Under such conditions, the connection between symbol and referent is blocked, losing the power it once possessed.

Certain corporate logos illustrate the blocked condition. Consider the original logo (the symbol) of RCA (the referent). The symbol revolved around Little Nipper, the quizzical puppy pictured in Barraud's painting, *His Master's Voice*. In the logo, the dog sits, stumped by the sound of a gramophone. When this symbol was introduced in 1929, it clearly captured the nature of RCA, a company devoted to the production of sound. However, over the next sixty years, RCA grew and diversified, becoming involved in areas such as photovoltaics, navigation, and data communications. Consequently, when GE acquired RCA in the 1980s, it deemed Little Nipper too confining an image for the company. The concreteness of Nipper and the gramophone blocked adequate representation of RCA's new, broad scope. As a result, corporate officials dropped the symbol, replacing it with a more abstract, alphabetic "RCA" design.[9] The history of the Johnson Wax logo presents a similar story. Note that the company describes the logo (consisting of two vertical diamonds inside a J) as "an integral and distinctive part" of the company (Goldwasser 1986:190–91). Yet as the company moved beyond the production of wax products, officials worried that a logo so concretely reflective of the Johnson name could damage sales. Specifically, executives were concerned that consumers might be hesitant to buy and use personal products on themselves if these products were associated with wax. Consequently, the company began deleting the logo from its personal care line, substituting the words "Rydelle Laboratories, Inc." (Rydelle Laboratories, Inc. is a subsidiary of Johnson Wax, one with low public visibility.) In so doing, this changing entity rejected a highly concrete self-representation, opting for a more abstract design.

Blocked connections between referents and symbols render the symbols vulnerable to change. In this condition, changes to the referent render its concrete representation obsolete; such symbols are drained of their energy, losing the potential to effect their target audience. As such, new symbols are likely to emerge as a method of recharging the associative relationship.

Suspended associative bonds are born of unstable conditions as they match concrete symbols with dynamic entities. But the weakness of suspended bonds is exacerbated because they encompass irrelevant referents. Concurrent instability and irrelevance threaten the viability of the associative bond. So devastating is the destruction that if the referent regains relevance, it does so with new and different representation.

Certain "on the job" signifiers illustrate the suspended condition. Consider the connection between a worker (the referent) and the nameplate on her/his office door (the symbol). Such a nameplate indicates, in concrete terms, that the referent is part of a firm or institution. When an individual leaves a job, the nameplate is quickly removed from the office door. The symbol's personalized, concrete nature makes it impossible to retain once its referent departs. Thus, the relationship between symbol and referent is permanently suspended.

Suspended associative relationships are necessarily connected to symbol change. As old referents pass away, and new referents emerge, symbols too must die and new symbols must be born.

National Symbols, Associative Relationships, and Change

The distinctions I have drawn among various associative bonds provide immediate insight on the low rate of national symbol change. Most of the bonds linking symbols to nation are charged in nature. Thus, the protective field provided by charged associative bonds renders most national symbols recalcitrant to change.

In analyzing symbol-nation links, note that the burden of a charged relationship rests largely on the nature of the symbol. This is because the condition of the referent is confined by the characteristics of nationhood. Nations are emergent entities, and thus dynamic by definition. This quality necessarily denotes the ingredients of charged representation. Provided a nation retains its relevance, it will require a sufficiently abstract symbol. Most national symbols conform to this requirement. From genre to genre, the large majority of national symbols are broad, general, and abstract in nature.[10] In examining national anthems, for example, we find that the lyrics of most anthems reference the general rather than the particular, the amorphous rather than the crystallized. Consider the lyrics of Argentina's national anthem:

Hear, oh mortals! the sacred cry:
Freedom, freedom, freedom!
Hear the noise of broken chains;
See the throne of Equality the noble.

The qualities cited here—freedom and equality—are broad, intangible, and flexible. Thus these words can come to mean anything that suits the nation's current purposes. Other anthems offer similar references. Consider the lyrics to Fiji's anthem:

Blessings grant, Oh God of nations, on the isles of Fiji,
As we stand united under noble banner blue.
As we honor and defend the cause of freedom ever,
Onward march together, God Bless Fiji.

Or consider the lyrics to Zambia's anthem:

Stand and sing of Zambia, proud and free,
Land of work and joy in unity,
Victors in the struggle for the right,
We have won freedom's fight, All one, strong and free.

All of these symbols are flexible because they describe the nation in amorphous terms. Despite change and development, a nation's struggles always can be perceived as "for the right," its people always described as "noble," and its cries of war always heard as "sacred." The abstract, adaptable nature of these lyrics ensures the continued charge of the relationship between the words and the nations they represent.

Like anthems, the content of most flags is sufficiently abstract to meet the criteria of charged associative relationships. The flag of Bangladesh, for example, features a single red disc symbolizing the struggle for independence. The Jamaican flag's green, black, and yellow fields represent agriculture, mineral wealth, and triumph over hardship (Crampton 1990:16, 58). The red canton of Togo's flag is officially described as "the colors of charity, of fidelity, of love, of those cardinal virtues which inspire love of fellow humans and the sacrifice of one's life" (quoted in Smith 1975:287). And the black stripe of Trinidad and Tobago's flag signifies strength, unity, and purpose, as well as the wealth of the land (Smith 1975:288). These examples indicate that there is no literal connection between the content of flags and that which they represent. Unlike concrete pictures or words with highly specific referents, each flag's abstract elements allow the symbol to remain highly charged. The components are sufficiently general such that their meaning can be made over to capture a variety of circumstances that might befall their referents.[11]

Although the large majority of anthems and flags, and the nations they represent, are bound by charged associative relationships, variant associative ties sometimes emerge. The demise of the Soviet Union, and the reemergence of Armenia, Estonia, and the other republics, for example, brought many dormant relationships to the foreground. The original symbols of these nations became temporarily irrelevant within the world community when the entities they signified were subsumed by the Soviet Union. When these nations were reinstated as independent republics, however, both symbols and referents returned to the forefront of active world attention. As such, dormant ties became recharged. The original anthems and flags of these republics were again acknowledged as meaningful entries on the social scene.

In some cases, nations and symbols are bound by blocked or suspended relationships. And here lies the key to understanding instances of national symbol change, for *the replacement of a national symbol appears confined to the blocked and suspended conditions.* When a nation changes but its signifier remains rigid, national symbols are amended or replaced in order to recharge the ties that bond symbol to referent.

Throughout this book, I have discussed instances of anthem change. Recall, for example, the replacement of lyrics in the Brazilian or West German anthems. In reviewing these two cases, we must note that change resulted from blocked associative bonds. The original lyrics of each anthem specified concrete events; the words detailed situations that could not be reconciled with the changing realities of their referents. Thus the symbols came to provide inaccurate representation. The bonds between symbols and referents became blocked, leaving these symbols vulnerable to change.

Similarly, Nettl writes of the change to Austria's anthem, noting that the highly specific nature of the music spurred a blocked relationship: "When the Austrian Republic was established after the close of World War I, the new rulers took it to be incumbent upon them to put an end to the old Haydn melody. *It had too much of an Hapsburg flair about it.* So in 1920 the Austrian composer Wilhelm Kienzl was approached, and he provided the music for Karl Renner's text, "Deutsch-Oesterreich, du herrliches Land, wir lieben Dich" (1967:65, emphasis added). The "Hapsburg flair" of the original Austrian anthem rendered the symbol inappropriate to the non-Hapsburg milieu of the nation's post–World War I setting. Thus, the mismatch of concrete symbol with dynamic referent blocked the charge that joined the two. As such, a new anthem became the only path toward regaining a charged associative relationship.

In Burkina Faso, anthem replacement emerged from suspended associative bonds. The nation's former anthem was a product of its old identity, the Upper Volta. Further, that anthem was concrete in nature, making specific references to a defunct entity. Note the lyrics to the first line of the anthem: "Proud Volta of my forefathers" (Cartledge et al. 1978:470). Because of its concrete nature, this symbol could not be transferred to the new nation, Burkina Faso. Once losing its referent, the anthem had no other fate but change.

Flag changes present similar examples. Changes to the Norwegian flag, for instance, resulted from a blocked associative relationship. Hallvard Traetteberg (1978:79–81) tells us that Norway's original flag contained concrete references to Sweden. The symbol was built upon traditional Swedish colors and longstanding Swedish ornaments. While Norway remained tied to Sweden, the nation's concrete flag remained appropriate. But as Norway moved toward independence, its concrete symbol proved incongruous with the nation's new and changing condition. The blocked charge that resulted from the mismatch of nation and symbol triggered symbol change.

Blocked bonds spurred flag change in Congo as well. Upon independence in 1959–60, Congo adopted a green, yellow, and red striped flag, signifying the nation's pan-African ideology. In the late 1960s, when socialism overtook Congo, the nation divorced itself from its past politics. With the new socialist emphasis, the concrete pan-African references of the original flag proved misplaced, and the symbol became a candidate for change. Thus, Congo replaced its original flag with a variation of the Soviet flag (Crampton 1990:31).

In some instances, flag change is situated within suspended associative relationships. Consider the case of Zanzibar. Zanzibar's original flag, adopted in 1963, consisted of a plain red field bearing a green disc and two yellow cloves. The clove ornaments were intended to concretely signify the source of the islands' prosperity. But in October of 1964, Zanzibar united with Tanganyika to form Tanzania, and the entity of Zanzibar ceased to exist. Thus, the concrete nature of Zanzibar's flag made it an inappropriate symbol of the new nation, Tanzania. Detached from its referent, the content of the old symbol was left vulnerable to change.

Although blocked or suspended associative relationships leave symbols vulnerable to change, their presence alone does not necessarily mandate such change. Frequently, nations adopt concrete symbols and retain them for a substantial part or the whole of their existence. Thus, *we must view blocked and suspended associative bonds as necessary but insufficient conditions for symbol change.* Additional factors must be considered in order to determine the absolute conditions of change. Toward that end, I argue that blocked and suspended associative relationships must be spurred by specific social circumstances if they are to result in symbol replacement.[12]

Social Stimulants of Symbol Change

In searching for the stimulants of symbol change, I examined several historical cases of anthem and flag replacement. Further, I analyzed *all* anthems and flags replaced during the past twenty years (see table 7.2). During this investigation, I found that certain factors and events routinely accompanied symbol change: the physical redefinition of a nation, the political redefinition of a nation, the redefinition of a nation's leadership, and the association of a national symbol with multiple referents. These four phenomena appear capable of instigating the types of blocked or suspended bonds that result in symbol replacement.

When blocked or suspended associative relationships result from the *physical redefinition of a nation,* the likelihood of symbol change is high. Physical redefinitions occur when nations make acquisitions, merge with other nations, suffer enemy infiltration, and so forth.

Table 7.2. Changing Anthems and Flags

Nation	Nation			
	Old Anthem Syntax	Deviance Score	New Anthem Syntax	Deviance Score
Afghanistan	.14	2	−1.60[a]	1
Bulgaria	−1.57	4	−.47	1[a]
Burkina Faso	−.81	4	.72	4
Congo	−.02	4	−.97[a]	2[a]
Egypt	−.20	4	−.76[a]	1[a]
Ethiopia	1.01	5	−.08[a]	3[a]
Iraq	−.11	2	−1.93[a]	3
Kuwait	−1.90	3	−.80	0
Nigeria	−.15	4	−.35[a]	3[a]
Romania	−1.75	2	−.66	2
Somalia	.01	3	−.38[a]	2
Togo	1.37	2	−2.37[a]	2
Yemen, Arab Republic	−.05	2	−1.30[a]	2
Yemen, People's Democratic Republic	−1.81	2	−.79	1
Yugoslavia	.26	3	−.07[a]	1
Zimbabwe	−1.78	4	.74	3[a]

Nation	Flags			
	Old Flag Syntax	Deviance Score	New Flag Syntax	Deviance Score
Afghanistan	1.26	4	1.58	3[a]
Benin	−.12	3	−1.56[a]	3
Burkina Faso	−.37	3	−.49[a]	3
Congo	−.60	4	−.30	2[a]
Haiti	−.47	4	−1.40[a]	4
Iran	−.47	3	.31	3
Kampuchea (time 1)	.81	3	−.96[a]	2
Kampuchea (time 2)	−.96	2	.09	2
Laos	−.85	3	.02	2
Lesotho	−.33	5	.68	2[a]
Libya	−.02	4	−4.27[a]	2[a]
Mozambique	2.83	4	2.83	2[a]
Namibia	1.40	2	.88[a]	3
Romania	1.09	3	−1.16[a]	2
Syria	−.02	2	.87	2
Zimbabwe	.98	1	1.41	1

[a]Indicates a change in the predicted direction.

Such events alter a nation's tangible, visible identity and ultimately mandate a change in the nation's representation.

The history of Great Britain's Union Jack or the emergence of Tanzania's flag offer clear examples of this condition. In Britain's case, the acquisition of new territories introduced new groups and cultures into a preexisting entity. In the Tanzanian case, the merging of preexisting nations gave birth to a new, hybrid culture. But in both instances, the reconstruction of a national self disturbed the relationship between referent and symbol. In the face of such disequilibrium, symbol change became necessary to revitalize associative relationships.

When a nation reassesses that for which it stands, *political redefinition* ensues. A drastic shift in political arrangement (i.e., the transition from a democracy to a dictatorship) or a shift in political philosophy (i.e., imperialism to socialism) exemplify the circumstance. Such redefinitions of the national self can put nation and symbol at odds; if blocked or suspended associative relationships result from the nation's new stance, symbol change will occur.

In Romania, political redefinition instigated a change of the nation's anthem. Nettl (1967:115–17) tells us that Romania's first anthem resulted from a public competition waged in 1861. At that time, national leaders solicited a "theme song" for Alexandru Ioan Cuza, the ruling monarch. Eduard A. Huebsch's composition "Traiasca Regele" (Long Live the King), won the competition. His anthem remained in use through Alexandru's reign, as well as the tenure of King Carol I. In 1947, Romania witnessed a major change in political policy—the conversion to socialism. As a result, the concrete anthem referencing imperial days became an inappropriate signifier of Romania. In order to recharge the relationship between nation and symbol, the Huebsch anthem was discarded and a new one adopted in 1953.

The history of South Vietnam's flag presents a similar scenario. The nation's first flag was adopted by a puppet regime ruling during the Japanese occupation of the country. It consisted of a yellow field (historically, an imperial color for the nation) and three thin red horizontal stripes, the traditional hieroglyph for "Land of the South" (Smith 1975:297). Thus, the nation's first flag was steeped in a strong imperial tradition. In 1969, the National Liberation Front changed the flag. No longer controlled by colonial powers, and fighting for autonomy, NLF leaders found the old flag's concrete references to imperialism unsuitable to the nation's current condition. Therefore, the symbols of the "old" South Vietnam were released, and new ones—symbols better signifying the changing entity—were adopted in their place.[13]

In Dahomey, the transition from a democratic presidency to a communist dictatorship instigated a suspended associative relationship that demanded rectification. Originally, Dahomey flew a flag consisting of two horizontal stripes, yellow over red, and one green vertical stripe at the flag's hoist. The flag was highly concrete in that it referenced the nation's pan-African ideology. But Dahomey's conversion to Marxism in 1975 resulted in a new political structure. This redefinition of the national referent suspended the ties that had previously bound Dahomey to its symbols. The relationship between referent and symbol was recharged only with the leadership's adoption of a new national name—Benin, and a new national flag based on the ruling party's colors.

Blocked or suspended associative bonds are sometimes spurred by the *redefinition of a nation's leadership*. When a leader comes to define a nation, shifts in "personnel" can greatly alter that for which the nation stands. Under such conditions, the symbols that signified a fallen leader, and thus the nation, can be rendered obsolete.

Haiti provides a case in point. When Dr. François Duvalier seized control of the country in 1964, he adopted a new national flag (a black and crimson vertical bicolor flag). The dictator cast the flag in concrete terms, proclaiming: "I am the Haitian Flag One and Indivisible" (Smith 1990:129). Duvalier's departure rendered Haiti's flag an inadequate signifier of the nation. With Duvalier's demise, the nation to which the flag referred, in essence, ceased to exist. Thus as new leadership defined a new nation, a different symbol was required.[14] In a similar vein, the change of Iran's national anthem was instigated by a leadership change. Because the former anthem was simply a hymn to the shah, the shah's demise in 1980 suspended the significance of the symbol.

Some associative relationships become blocked or suspended when *a nation's symbol develops links to a second referent*—an individual, institution, or event with an overwhelmingly negative connotation. Under such conditions, the symbol ceases to function. Rejected as painful or undesirable, the symbol is replaced by a newer, fresher, less burdened image.

Several of the symbol changes examined here resulted from this "dual referent" phenomenon. Consider the case of the Austrian anthem. Austrian leaders felt compelled to replace their anthem shortly after World War II. Though longstanding and beloved by the population, the anthem took on a different meaning after the war. According to Nettl, it was as if the anthem grew "contaminated because it had been in Hitler's mouth" (1967:66). In the minds of the people, the symbol became more strongly associated with Hitler than with Austria. This negative association blocked the power derived from the symbol's original referent. As a result, Austrian leaders were forced to resignify their nation.

The replacement of Bulgaria's national anthem poses a similar example. A cultural attaché of the nation explained the change in this way: "The old anthem was a beautiful and moving song. We just hated to give it up. However, in the recent past, the song was often used by the fascist regime. That government made use of the anthem, in particular, during public executions. So you see, we just couldn't use it now. The associations are much too, well, unpleasant." When Bulgaria's anthem became attached to a violent fascist regime, the original bond between nation and referent was disrupted. Consequently, the anthem was necessarily discarded and a new, less burdened image was developed.

Lesotho's current national flag, too, resulted from a dual referent condition. Lesotho's original flag, adopted upon independence (1966), used colors of the then-dominant National Party—blue, white, red, and green. After a time, the flag became more closely linked to the party than to the nation it was adopted to signify. Consequently, the bond between symbol and nation was blocked. Crampton (1990:63) tells us that after the coup of 1986, national leaders introduced a new flag designed to recharge the connection between nation and symbol. In the new flag, the three colors are derived from the nation's motto, and the flag was ornamented with more traditional emblems of the nation.

In outlining these four social conditions, we identify the initiators of a two-stage process of symbol change: as these factors upset the symbol-referent balance, they create a disequilibrium that demands symbol change for its resolution. To complete our understanding of symbol change, we must turn our attentions to one final aspect— the nature of that change. Using my data on anthem and flag structure, the next section searches for patterns in symbol change, consistent methods of altering expression once the need for change is acknowledged.

The Nature of Symbol Change

In comparing the structures of old anthems and flags with those of their replacements, three particular patterns of change consistently emerge. First, "original" symbols generally are highly detailed and highly concrete. Second, replacement symbols are frequently less concrete than their predecessors, moving from the detail of embellished syntax to the abstractness of basic design. Finally, when change occurs, symbols tend to become more normative in design.

Consider first the concreteness of original symbols. Throughout this chapter, I have argued that concrete national symbols are most susceptible to change. Because of their detail, concrete symbols are simply too rigid to adapt to shifting national conditions. Case histories presented earlier in the chapter support the viability of that premise. But my data on symbol structure provides an opportunity for a more systematic inquiry.

Table 7.2 lists data on anthems and flags that have changed during the past twenty years. Note the syntactic structure scores for both old symbols and their replacements. In essence, these scores operationalize concreteness, for the more embellished a symbol's syntax, the more concrete and detailed the symbol's design (chapter 2 outlined these connections). The table shows that 69 percent of discarded anthems and a striking 100 percent of discarded flags possessed moderate or embellished—that is, concrete—syntax. Few of the symbols replaced were basic or abstract in design. Now note the data on replacement symbols. Sixty-three percent of the replacement anthems, and 44 percent of replacement flags are more basic, more abstract than their predecessors. *Thus overall, new symbols tend to be more basic, more abstract in design than those they replace.*

If we concede that abstractness represents the ideal condition for national symbols, then the syntax scores of replacement symbols raise an interesting point. The findings show that replacement anthems are more likely to achieve abstractness than replacement flags. As such, anthem changes seem more functional than flag changes. Whereas new anthems move toward flexibility, new flags seem just as likely to mirror previous design "mistakes."

Comparing usage patterns for anthems and flags may help us explain this phenomenon. Recall that flags, more than anthems, are the currency of the international arena. Given the breadth of the international audience, national leaders may be more conservative in changing flags than they are in manipulating anthems. Once a flag has been diffused and internalized by the world community, leaders may choose to minimize alterations to the symbol so as not to disrupt their nation's international image. In essence, the broad scope of flag exposure may discourage drastic measures in the exercise of change.

I turn now to the normalization trend. Consider the sixteen nations that changed their anthem during the past twenty years (table 7.2). Nearly half (44 percent) replaced anthems with deviant designs (i.e., their deviance score was >4). Similarly, when we examine the sixteen nations in which flag change occurred, we find that more than a third (38 percent) replaced symbols with deviant structures.

These data show that when deviant symbols undergo change, they are likely to become more normative in design. In examining deviant original symbols, note that 86 percent of their anthem replacements and 83 percent of their flag replacements move toward increased normalcy.[15] These findings suggest that the normalization of structure may serve as a strategy for recharging symbols. When blocked or suspended associative relationships contain deviant anthems or flags, leaders may "inject" the symbols with conventionality in an attempt to render them more suitable, and thus more strongly bound, to their referents.

Conclusion

This chapter searched for the factors that instigate the rare condition of symbol change. I have argued that such change rests in the associative relationship binding symbol to nation. If the charge of that relationship is disturbed, symbols can become vulnerable to replacement. Yet such disruption is not easily achieved. Only certain social circumstances appear capable of instigating the conditions of change.

When viewed in this way, the low rate of national symbol change becomes easier to understand. The conditions of change are narrow and highly restrictive. In lieu of the right provisions, national symbols, like the nicknames and mementos of our personal histories, cling to that which they signify—their bonds not easily severed, their meaning not easily forgotten.

8

FINAL NOTES ON IDENTITY DESIGNS

THIS BOOK BEGAN with a story of adoption, notes on the designing and redesigning of Guyana's national flag. In describing the shuffling of colors and shapes, the addition and deletion of elements, I posed the question: "What was it about these colors, and the order in which they were presented, that rendered the final version of the Guyanese flag the one and only suitable representation of the nation?" We are in a better position to answer that question now.

We have discovered a clear logic guiding the selection of national symbols. Senders knowingly choose some designs over others, their choices systematically linked to the social conditions from which the symbols emerge. Specifically, we have learned that space and time have an impact on symbol design. Regional and temporal clusters become reference groups for the symbolic expression of identity. We have discovered that lineage influences symbol design. Symbol structure serves as a tool of demarcation, distinguishing or splitting colonies from their colonizers. Socioeconomic location, too, affects the sight and sound of a nation. Position breeds clear patterns of expression, with those on the periphery exhibiting the most embellished message designs. And the condition of a symbol's target influences symbol design. The more homogeneous or intense the cognitive focus of the target, the less elaborate symbol structure need be. This is true for focus generated by both political systems of authority and specific social events.

This study also addressed issues of symbol reception. We discovered that receivers respond to symbol designs in patterned and predictable ways—patterns that are linked to the norms that guide symbolic expression. This research delineated the boundaries of "normal" symbolic discourse and explored the consequences of deviating from such norms. Indeed, when the norms of national identity expression are violated, we found that national audiences became somewhat disengaged from their symbols.

Finally, we noted that symbols of national identity are rarely discarded. Yet this study documented the highly specific conditions under which change sometimes does occur. I demonstrated that the immediate cause of change is located in the disruption of the associative relationships that link symbol to nation. Further, I identified the social factors capable of triggering such disruption: the physical or political redefinition of a nation, a change in national leadership, or the intrusion of a second referent for the symbol.

At this writing, nationhood is still alive and well. Existing nations continue to highlight their unique identities; they continue to fervently fight to reaffirm their borders and protect their possessions. Further, new nations are continually emerging. Indeed, while writing this book, I updated my sample several times to accommodate the symbols of new nations. Amidst both the prevalence of nationhood and ever-increasing international exchange, national symbols remain central to sociopolitical and socioeconomic dialogue. They remain key to defining a nation, sustaining its presence, and motivating it to action. Knowing this serves to emphasize the importance of effective symbol selection. To choose a deviant symbol, or one with a blocked or suspended charge, is to risk the loss of a symbol's immense power in both the domestic and the international arenas.

The nation, like all other entities, exists in an environment that is increasingly reliant on audio-visual communication. In such a world, nonverbal symbols—anthems, flags, monuments, and the like— may replace verbal rhetoric as the currency of control. The notion is not so far-fetched, for no words could match the impact of some of the recent national images the world has seen: the falling of the Berlin Wall, the dropping of the Soviet flag, the handshake that brought peace to the Israelis and Palestinians. In such an environment, those who master the art of symbol design may become the masters of international dialogue. Indeed, the fight for control may be waged with sight and sound. As such, a full understanding of our "weapons" is vital. Communication effects will be enhanced or tempered only when we fully comprehend the nature of the message.

At a more general level, this study suggests several future research sites, with issues of communication effectiveness central to them all. First, we would do well to learn more about the norms of message structure. Identifying the "appropriateness" of various shapes and sounds to specific social settings represents a new research path. The results provided by this study are fruitful, but they are limited in scope. Context and rules beyond those that guide national identity await our discovery. We must explore additional settings and more varied messages, noting the patterns of expression that each can spur. In addition, we must explore more fully the ways in which symbol structure can vary within a single context. Within a locale such as war, for example, how do the sights and sounds of defeat differ from those of victory? Or survival from those of death? By increasing the scope of our inquiry, our understanding of message structure will be greatly enhanced.

Second, the meaning of symbol structures requires more serious attention. Is it possible to match specific meanings with particular aural and graphic designs? Can we chart the sounds of happiness, sensuality, or valor? Can we map the look of love, violence, or unity? The measures of structure offered in this book provide the tools needed for such an inquiry. For if we can precisely categorize differences in sound, shape, and color, we can systematically match symbolic designs with the perceptions of those who see and hear them. In this way, we will begin to link symbol structures to particular cognitive and emotional responses. We will discover what particular images and sounds mean to those who apprehend them.[1]

Third, recall that several differences between aural and graphic design emerged from this study. For example, a nation's anthem and flag were rarely similarly designed. Further, anthem and flag structures were sometimes susceptible to different influences: temporal cohorts influenced only flag structures; anthem structures were most susceptible to intranational "editors," whereas flags seemed more responsive to international factors, and so forth. These distinctions remind us that much about nonverbal communication remains to be discovered. Although some general patterns exist between genres, each medium also displays significant peculiarities. As verbal communication loses its edge over nonverbal strategies, we must enhance our knowledge of the nonverbal arena. The similarities and differences between audio and visual messages require additional specification. Moreover, new communication arenas demand our attention. Can we find codes of expression within the tactile system or the olfactory system?[2] Can we determine the relative effectiveness of various genres? These questions remain to be answered.

Finally, I have suggested throughout this book that the process of identity construction proceeds similarly at the level of both the collective and the individual. This implies that it may be time to rethink some of the analytical divisions we have heretofore taken for granted. Elsewhere, I have illustrated the flaws inherent in categorizing social interaction according to purely *objective criteria*—that is, the size of a group or the status of its participants (Cerulo and Ruane 1996; Cerulo et al. 1992:113, 126–27; see also Beniger 1987). I have suggested instead that social interaction be classified according to the *processes* by which it occurs and the *effects* it generates. If I am right, there is much to be gained by merging our study of collective and individual identity construction. Dismantling the boundary between the macro and micro spheres may sharpen our understanding of the complex patterns that organize social life.

Durkheim (1915:274) wrote that "a society's symbols are determinants of its conduct." Evidence of that insight surrounds us daily. Nations, as well as churches, political parties, corporations, and, indeed, all collectives continue to employ symbols to identify, inspire, and motivate. In exploring national symbols, I have attempted to shed some light on the ways in which social structure guides the selection of these symbolic voices, and the way these voices, in turn, direct social conduct. But although my work has brought new information to the foreground, the research agenda before us remains full. Only through continued, systematic investigation will we come to fully understand the complex interaction between the social and symbolic spheres.

APPENDIX A

Measurement Information

Measuring Symbol Syntax

Given the importance of syntactic structure to symbolic communication, devising a way to measure structure represents a central research task. This section offers my own technique. With the aid of selected anthems and flags, I offer a step-by-step illustration of a measurement method for music and graphic syntax.

Music

Melody provides the clearest site in which to illustrate my measurement strategy. We can think of any melody as a succession of single musical notes—a series of pitches arranged horizontally on the musical staff. These notes are arranged in arithmetic relation to one another[1] and display a logical and discernible sequence of musical sound. It is this sequence that determines the melody's syntactic structure.

To properly locate a melody's syntactic structure along the basic-embellished continuum, we must measure four primary characteristics: the frequency of motion in the melody; the magnitude of that motion; the method by which motion is constructed—that is, smooth (conjunct) or jagged (disjunct); and the presence of melodic ornamentation—that is, the decoration of central melody notes. (For more detail, see, e.g., Apel 1974, Ringer 1980, Siegmeister 1965, and Westergaard 1975.) These characteristics operationalize the basic-embellished continuum of structure.

Pitch-time plots provide the means for measuring frequency, magnitude, method of motion, and ornamentation. Readers can refer to figure 2.1B for pitch-time plots of "God Save the Queen" and "La Marseillaise," the anthems I will use to illustrate my points. Recall that both of these anthems are written in the key of G—they use the notes of the G scale. Therefore, to graph these melodies, each of their pitches must be ranked according to the following values:

G = 0	G# = 1	A = 2	A# = 3	B = 4	C = 5	C# = 6
D = 7	D# = 8	E = 9	F = 10	F# = 11	G = 12	

Once ranked, each pitch can be matched with the appropriate beat of the anthem at which it appears. This process produces the following data matrix for "God Save the Queen":

Note	X Axis: Beat of Anthem	Y Axis: Pitch Ranking
G	1	0
G	2	0
A	3	2
F#	4	−1
G	5.5	0
A	6	2
B	7	4
B	8	4
C	9	5
B	10	4
A	11.5	2
G	12	0
A	13	2
G	14	0
F#	15	−1
G	16	0, etc.

The ranking system results in the following data matrix for "La Marseillaise":

Note	X Axis: Beat of Anthem	Y Axis: Pitch Ranking
D	intro	−5
D	intro	−5
D	intro	−5
G	1	0
G	2	0
A	3	2
A	4	2
D	5	7
B	6.5	4
G	7	0
G	7.75	0
B	8	4
G	8.75	0
E	9	−3
C	10	5
A	12	2
F#	12.75	−1
G	13	0, etc.

The pitch/time graphs provide a visual image of the two anthem melodies. But more important, the graphs illustrate the melodic lines as a function of pitch with respect to time. Thus mathematically, we can analytically determine properties of the line segments connecting each two consecutive points of the line. I have devised a number of formulae for this purpose. Such calculations provide the desired information on the frequency, magnitude, and method of each anthem's melodic motion, as well as information on melodic ornamentation.

To calculate the *frequency of melodic motion* we use the formula:

$$\text{FREQ} = \frac{1}{m}(p + t)$$

where
p = the total number of peaks in the graph of the melody
t = the total number of troughs in the graph of the melody
m = the total number of measures in the melody

The frequency score calculates the number of peaks and troughs in a melody, and thus indicates the number of directional changes in a melody. This information shows how dynamic the melody is. The higher the frequency statistic, the greater the amount of movement in the melody. Note that the formula divides the total number of peaks and troughs by the total number of measures in the melody, thus standardizing the score. (Measures are groups of beats marked off from one another by bar lines.)

The frequency value for "God Save the Queen" is .93; this melody changes direction slightly less than one time per measure. In comparison, "La Marseillaise" has a frequency score of 1.46; its melody changes direction approximately three times every two measures.

The formula for the *magnitude of melodic motion* is:

$$\text{MAG} = \frac{1}{m} \sum_{i=1}^{n} H_i$$

where
m = the total number of measures in the melody
n = the total number of peaks or troughs in the melody
H = the height of the ith peak or the depth of the ith trough.

By calculating the average size of each directional change in the melody, this formula determines how drastic movement is. Using the pitch-time plot, the formula simply sums the absolute values of the height of each melody peak and the depth of each melody trough. Dividing that value by the number of measures in the melody yields a mean score that tells us the average "musical area" covered in each melody.[2]

"God Save the Queen" displays a magnitude score of 4.43, whereas "La Marseillaise" has a score of 7.75. Consequently, movement in the French anthem is nearly twice as drastic as that in the British anthem.

There are two different methods by which to construct melodic *motion*: conjunct and disjunct motion. Conjunct motion is smooth, with notes proceeding in successive or nearly successive degrees up and down the musical scale. Conversely, disjunct motion is jagged and leapy; in disjunct melodies, notes are separated by large intervals.

To determine the relative conjunctness or disjunctness of a melody, we use the formula:

If $|\Delta P_n| < Q$, melodic line motion is conjunct.
If $|\Delta P_n| > Q$, melodic line motion is disjunct.

Q = 4.0 if the movement between $\triangle P_n$ is in the same direction as $\triangle P_{n-1}$.

Q = 3.0 if the movement between $\triangle P_n$ is in a different direction as $\triangle P_{n-1}$.

$\triangle P_n$ is defined as $(P_n - P_{n-1})$; P_n = the pitch of the nth note.

These figures allow us to classify each interval in a melody as conjunct or disjunct by comparing $|\triangle P_n|$, the distance spanned by each interval, to the value of Q. (I selected values for Q based on music theory regarding conjunct and disjunct intervals.)[3] When all classifications are made, we simply tally the total number of intervals falling into both the conjunct and disjunct categories.

According to this formula, 92 percent of the consecutive melodic intervals in "God Save the Queen" are conjunct; 8 percent are disjunct. In comparison, only 76 percent of the consecutive melodic intervals in "La Marseillaise" are conjunct; 24 percent are disjunct—three times the number found in "God Save the Queen." Humming the first line of each anthem illustrates the relative jaggedness and leapiness of "La Marseillaise" as compared to "God Save the Queen."

Finally, the formula for *melodic ornamentation* is:

$$\text{ORN} = \frac{N\,(\sqrt{r})}{v}$$

where
N = the total number of notes in a melody
r = the total instances of ornamentation in a melody
v = the total number of verbal syllables in a melody

Ornamentation represents a decoration of central melody notes. Each time a single syllable is represented by multiple notes of different pitch ranks, we have an instance of ornamentation. This formula captures the degree ornamentation found in a melody. Specifically, it taps two aspects of the phenomenon. First, the formula captures the mere presence of ornamentation, noting the ratio of notes to verbal syllables in a melody.[4] Second, the formula captures the frequency with which the technique of ornamentation occurs; it gives extra emphasis to melodies with many instances of ornamentation versus melodies with few, or just a single, instance. We provide this emphasis by weighting the formula with the square root of the total instances of ornamentation in the melody.[5] Both presence and frequency are integral to a proper analysis of ornamentation. Without simultaneously considering both aspects of ornamentation, a melody that is ornamented in only one location could conceivably be perceived as more embellished than one displaying several distinct instances of ornamentation.[6] This formula ensures that the latter of these two phenomena receives a higher score.

Certain criteria help us interpret the ornamentation statistic. If ornamentation = 1, the number of notes and syllables are equal, meaning there is no ornamentation. If ornamentation >1, musical notes outnumber verbal syllables, meaning the anthem is ornamented. Ornamentation = 1.82 in "God Save the Queen." "La Marseillaise" has a slightly higher ornamentation score—1.88.

Frequency, magnitude, method of motion, and ornamentation each address a different component of a melody's syntactic structure. But to effectively grasp the essence of a melody, we must also explore the relationship between these four elements. The sample of national anthems collected for this study (see chapter 2) helps us do so.

Earlier, I described basic syntactic structure as stable, fixed, and low in information density. When dealing with musical melodies, these qualities translate to low frequencies of directional change, low magnitudes of change, conjunct methods of musical motion, and low rates of melodic ornamentation. Embellished melodies exhibit opposite qualities along these dimensions. Table A.1 supports this conceptualization. The correlation matrix shows that the four dimensions of melodic syntax are positively correlated, thus indicating a direct relationship among all of the measures.[7] Knowing this, we can construct a single summary measure that will enable us to analyze melodic syntactic structure along the basic-embellished continuum.

In constructing this summary measure, however, we must remain mindful that certain correlations between the four individual measures of melody are low to moderate. This indicates some independence between the measures, making a simple additive method of combining them inappropriate. To overcome this problem, I standardized the four individual melody measures and factor analyzed them. Based on the loadings for the first factor,[8] I assigned a weight to each of the four measures. I then added the weighted measures to form a summary scale representing melody's syntactic structure: *Melody's Syntactic Structure = .62 Frequency + .65 Magnitude + .35 Disjunctness + .27 Ornamentation*. Of course, these factors may vary somewhat if a different sample of music

Table A.1. Correlation Matrix for the Individual Measures of Melodic Syntax

	Melodic Frequency	*Melodic Signature*	*Melodic Disjunct*	*Melodic Ornament*
Melodic frequency	1.000			
Melodic magnitude	.788	1.000		
Melodic disjunct	.189	.420	1.000	
Melodic ornament	.277	.155	.011	1.000

is used. However, when comparing the melodic syntactic structure of "God Save the Queen" and "La Marseillaise," we find that the former is comparatively more basic in design (−2.478) than the latter (−.203). Indeed, were we to hum the melodies to these anthems, we could hear this difference.

To capture the syntactic structure of phrasing, harmony, form, dynamics, and rhythm, I developed measures similar to the melody indicators discussed here. Readers interested in learning more about the construction and validity of the measures will find detailed descriptions in Cerulo (1988b, 1989b).

We have seen the usefulness of combining the four melody indicators to form a single summary measure of melodic structure. Similarly, it will be useful to combine the summary indicators for each of music's dimensions (e.g., melodic syntactic structure, phrase syntactic structure, harmonic syntactic structure, etc.) to form a single summary measure of a musical symbol's syntactic metastructure.

For the data on national anthems, the summary measures of melody, phrasing, harmony, form, dynamics, and rhythm were positively correlated.[9] Because the correlations were of varying strengths, again indicating some independence between the measures, I used the factor analysis technique described above, generating the following formula: *Music's Syntactic Metastructure = .60 Melodic Syntax + .14 Phrase Syntax + .35 Harmonic Syntax + .07 Form Syntax + .36 Dynamic Syntax + .60 Rhythmic Syntax.*[10] Again, these factors may vary somewhat if a different sample of music is used. Yet when comparing the musical syntactic metastructure of "God Save the Queen" and "La Marseillaise," we find that the former is comparatively more basic in design (−2.267) than the latter (+.625).[11]

Graphics

To properly locate a graphic image along the basic-embellished continuum, we must attend to its structural density, structural stability, and levels of structural distortion. Each of these components is multidimensional, containing aspects easily quantified and measured. As I describe this measurement process, readers may find it useful to visualize the Libyan and American national flags. These flags represent prototypes of the basic-embellished continuum's extremes. Thus, comparing the flags will help readers crystallize the qualities captured by my measures.

Three measures tap the relative density of graphic syntax: a symbol's total number of colors, its total number of fields, and the proportion of secondary colors used in the image. We determine a symbol's *total number of colors* (represented by test statistic N) by counting the number of distinct hues contained in the image. Albert Munsell's (1946) color theory provides the range of hues: red, yellow-red, yellow, green-yellow, green, blue-green, blue, purple-blue, purple, and red-purple. In this study, white and black represent separate hues as well. As such, each symbol can contain as many as twelve different colors.[12]

The Libyan flag contains only one color: green (N = 1). In contrast, the American flag contains three colors: red, white, and purple/blue (N = 3). Thus, the American flag projects more color information than its Libyan counterpart.

To calculate a symbol's *total number of fields* (represented by test statistic F), we attend to the way in which the symbol is divided, counting the number of planes contained in the symbol. These sections represent distinct segments of information.

The Libyan flag has only one field (F = 1). Its single, unadorned plane presents only one center of information. In contrast, the American flag contains fourteen fields (F = 14)—thirteen horizontal stripes and a single canton (the rectangular segment containing the fifty stars).

To determine the *proportion of secondary colors* in a symbol, we use the formula:

$$P_s = \frac{S}{N}$$

where
S = the total number of secondary colors in a symbol
N = the total number of colors in the symbol

The proportion is derived by dividing the number of secondary colors found in a symbol by the symbol's total number of colors. (Note that the measure refers to the *number* of colors used in the symbol rather than the area encompassed by each color.)

Because the Libyan flag contains only green, 100 percent of its colors are secondary (P_s = 1.00). In contrast, the American flag contains three colors: red, white, and purple/blue. Red and white are primary colors,[13] but purple/blue is a secondary color. Thus, 33 percent of the colors used in the American flag are secondary (P_s = .33).

Recall that my definition of basic graphic syntax suggests that it is lower in density than embellished structure. Therefore, we expect that basic symbols will display few colors, few fields, and a low proportion of secondary colors. When analyzing my sample of flags, the correlation coefficients for the three dimensions of density—all positive—confirm this contention (see table A.2A).[14]

Given this information, we can analyze graphic density using a single summary measure reflecting the basic-embellished continuum. I used the factor analysis method described earlier to create such a measure:[15] *Graphic Density = .63 Total Color + .55 Total Fields + .55 Proportion Secondary Colors.*[16] The lower the value of this measure, the lower the density of the symbol's structure. When we use this indicator to compare the graphic density of the Libyan and American flags, we find that former is comparatively more basic in design (−1.829) than the latter (1.688).

The relative stability of a symbol's graphic syntax rests on several components of color contrast: the degree of contrast, the complexity of contrast, hue contrast intensity, value contrast intensity, and chroma contrast intensity. To calculate the first of these qualities, *degree of contrast* (represented by test statistic C), we count the total number of points in an image where colors meet.

Table A.2a. Correlation Coefficients for Graphic Density

	Total Colors	Total Fields	Proportion of Secondary Colors
Total colors	1.000		
Total fields	.345	1.000	
Proportion of secondary colors	.356	.212	1.000

Since the Libyan flag contains only one hue, there are no junctures of color, and thus, no contrast (C = 0). Conversely, colors meet several times in the American flag. Red and white meet twelve times, red and blue meet four times, and white and blue meet fifty-four times. Therefore, the American flag has a high degree of contrast (C = 70), presenting more visual stimuli to process than the Libyan flag.

When contrast is present in an image, it is important to determine its nature. Toward that end, we can distinguish *simple* from *complex* contrasts. A simple contrast juxtaposes colors of the same hue. Because the meeting of like hues is easily processed by the human eye, simple contrasts create a sense of stability in the symbol. Complex contrasts, on the other hand, occur between colors of different hues. These matches are visually jarring and require more effort from viewers when processing. (For more information, see Munsell 1946:37–40; Stockton 1983:6–8.)

Once distinguishing simple from complex contrasts, we can calculate the *proportion of complex color contrasts* in a symbol using the formula:

$$P_X = \frac{x}{C}$$

where
x = the total number of complex color contrasts in a symbol
C = the total number of points in a symbol at which color contrast occurs

This formula simply divides the total instances of complex contrasts by all contrast occurrences.

Because Libya's flag contains only one color, there are no complex color contrasts (P_X = 0). However, all of the colors in the American flag stem from different hues, making all points of contrast complex (P_X =

1.00). Thus, the American flag presents more elaborate material for viewers to process than its Libyan counterpart.

A graphic symbol's stability also rests on the intensity of contrasting colors. Contrast intensity varies across three dimensions: hue, value, and chroma. Hue indicates a color's position on the color wheel; it characterizes a color's attributes—that is, red, blue, or green-yellow. Value refers to a color's relative lightness or darkness—the shade of the color. Chroma refers to a color's relative brightness or dullness—the color's radiance.

Albert Munsell (1946) devised a method of classifying a color's hue, value, and chroma. The system specifies these qualities via three symbols. For example, the green of the Libyan flag is specified as G5/8 The G refers to the hue of the color—in this case, green. The 5 notes the color's value on a 10-point scale, where 1 = dark and 10 = light. Here, 5 denotes a color of moderate shade. Finally, the 8 specifies the color's chroma, again on a 10-point scale, where 1 = dull and 10 = bright. Here, 8 indicates a highly radiant color.

Munsell's classifications provide the necessary information with which to construct measures of a symbol's hue, value, and chroma contrast intensity. The first of these measures, *hue contrast intensity,* captures the magnitude of the differences presented by the hues located at each point of color contrast in a symbol. The greater the contrasts in hues, the higher the hue contrast intensity. To calculate these differences, we first assign numerical ranks to white, black,[17] and the ten colors on the color wheel. These number assignments begin with 1 and ascend by units of one as we move clockwise around the color wheel:

Red	= 1	Blue/Green	= 6
Yellow/Red	= 2	Blue	= 7
Yellow	= 3	Purple/Blue	= 8
White	= 3	Black	= 8
Green/Yellow	= 4	Purple	= 9
Green	= 5	Red/Purple	= 10

With this information in hand, we can calculate hue contrast intensity using the formula:

$$I_H = \frac{\sum_{i=1}^{n} |h_n - h_{n-1}| \sqrt{C}}{C}$$

where
h = the hue intensity of a color
C = the total number of points in a symbol at which color contrast occurs

The formula first calculates the differences in the hue intensity ranks found at every point of color contrast. These differences are then summed and multiplied by the square root of the symbol's degree of contrast. (This step gives added weight to those symbols displaying high incidence of differentiation versus those that display only a single point of contrast.) Lastly, the formula divides the numerator by the total number of contrast points in the symbol, thus standardizing the data. Ultimately, we achieve a mean score indicating the average intensity of a symbol's hue contrast.

Since there are no points of color contrast in the Libyan flag, hue contrast intensity is non-existent ($I_H = 0$). However, the presence of three distinct hues and multiple points of contrast make hue contrast intensity in the American flag considerably higher than that of the Libyan flag ($I_H = 38.49$).

Value contrast intensity captures the magnitude of the shade differences found at each point of color contrast. We calculate it using the formula:

$$I_V = \frac{\sum_{i=1}^{n} |v_n - v_{n-1}| \sqrt{C}}{C}$$

where
v = the value intensity of a color
C = the total number of points in a symbol at which color contrast occurs

The mechanics of this formula are identical to those executed in the hue contrast measure. But here, the formula produces a mean score indicating the average intensity of shade differentiation found in a symbol. The greater the contrast of these shades, the higher the value contrast intensity.

Because of its single color design, value contrast intensity is non-existent in the Libyan flag ($I_V = 0$). However, the same statistic is quite high for the American flag (I_V = 31.55), tapping that symbol's relative embellishment.

Chroma contrast intensity captures the relative brightness of adjacent colors. The following formula calculates this quality:

$$I_R = \frac{\sum_{i=1}^{n} |r_n - r_{n-1}| \sqrt{C}}{C}$$

where
r = the chroma intensity of a color
C = the total number of points in a symbol at which color contrast occurs

Like the formulae for hue and value contrast intensity, this formula provides us with the average magnitude of chroma contrast in a symbol. The greater the average distinction between color brilliances, the higher the chroma contrast intensity. As one might imagine, chroma contrast intensity for the Libyan flag is absent (I_R = 0), but quite high for the American flag (I_R = 31.55).

Table A.2B contains the correlation coefficients for the five dimensions of graphic stability. Because these variables are positively correlated, we can combine them to form a summary measure; factor analysis yields the following formula: *Graphic Stability = .51 Degree of Contrast + .12 Proportion of Complex Contrast + .50 Hue Contrast Intensity + .49 Value Contrast Intensity + .48 Chroma Contrast Intensity.*[18] The lower the value of this measure, the more stable the structure of the symbol. When we use this measure to compare the graphic stability of the Libyan versus the American flag, we find that the former is comparatively more basic in design (−7.539) than the latter (5.206). This clearly meets with expectation, given the placid design of the Libyan flag relative to its American counterpart.

Graphic distortion, the last dimension of graphic syntactic structure, consists of two key dimensions: geometric inconsistency and ornamentation. *Geometric inconsistency* addresses the relative discrepancy among a symbol's building blocks. Inconsistency occurs when contradictory shapes are introduced into established field patterns. Thus, a geometrically inconsistent symbol might display a single vertical field over several horizontal fields; it might exhibit a triangular field over a collection of horizontal fields. These inconsistencies disrupt the symbol's

Table A.2b. Correlation Coefficients for Graphic Stability

	Degree of Contrast	Complexity of Contrast	Hue Contrast Intensity	Value Contrast Intensity	Chroma Contrast Intensity
Degree of contrast	1.000				
Complexity of contrast	.078	1.000			
Hue contrast intensity	.831	.215	1.000		
Value contrast intensity	.850	.208	.727	1.000	
Chroma contrast intensity	.751	.070	.770	.691	1.000

dominant geometric design; they create visual disparities requiring the increased attention of those processing the symbol. As such, geometric inconsistency renders symbol structure more elaborate in design.

To capture a symbol's level of geometric inconsistency (represented by test statistic G), we count the number of contradictory geometric fields in a symbol. Neither the Libyan nor the American flag contain such contradictory sections. The Libyan flag is a single, unadorned plane; the American flag is comprised solely of horizontal, rectangular fields. Therefore, in both instances, geometric inconsistency is absent (G = 0).

Ornamentation can also increase graphic distortion. Adding decorations to a symbol disrupts the flow of its foundational shapes and lines; such decorations demand more careful processing on the part of a symbol's receivers. As such, ornamentation adds to the embellishment of graphic syntax.

To calculate a symbol's level of ornamentation (represented by test statistic O), we count the number of emblems or decorations imposed on the symbol's field. For example, both the hammer and sickle of the Soviet Union's flag would be defined as emblems. Similarly, the seven stars of Venezuela's flag constitute distinct emblems. Libya's flag contains no decoration; it is free of ornamentation (O = 1). On the other

Table A.2c. Correlation Coefficients for Graphic Distortion

	Geometric Inconsistency	Total Ornaments
Geometric Inconsistency	1.000	.044

hand, the American flag contains fifty stars, making ornamentation quite extensive (O = 50).

Table A.2C contains the correlation coefficients for the two dimensions of graphic distortion.[19] Using factor analysis, we derive the following summary measure: *Graphic Distortion = .71 Geometric Inconsistency + .71 Level of Ornamentation.*[20] The lower the value of this measure, the less distorted the structure of the symbol. When we use this measure to compare the graphic distortion of the Libyan versus the American flag, we find that the former is comparatively more basic in design (−1.153) than the latter (1.971).

Recall that in developing a measure for music's syntactic metastructure, I combined the summary indicators for the individual elements of music: melodic syntactic structure, phrase syntactic structure, and so on. In the same way, we can combine the three summary measures described above—graphic density, graphic stability, and graphic distortion—to form a single indicator designed to measure a graphic symbol's syntactic metastructure. As in all previous calculations, factor analysis provides the tool for this task. (See table A.2D for correlations between the measures.) Based on my sample of 180 national flags, I generated the following formula for the measurement of graphic syntactic metastructure: *Graphic Symbol's Syntactic Structure = .55 Graphic Constancy + .67 Graphic Stability + .51 Graphic Fixedness.*[21] The lower the value of this measure, the more basic the structure of the symbol; the higher the value, the more embellished the structure.

Table A.2d. Correlation Coefficients for Graphic Metastructure

	Graphic Density	Graphic Stability	Graphic Distortion
Graphic density	1.000		
Graphic stability	.592	1.000	
Graphic distortion	.172	.528	1.000

Using this measure, we can pursue one final comparison of the Libyan and American national flags. The metascore of the former indicates a highly basic design (-4.271); the score for the latter suggests great embellishment ($+3.449$). This finding clearly confirms any visual perusal of the two flags (for more detail, see Cerulo 1992).

Classifying Social Events

Social events were classified as high, moderate, or low in focus. Classifications were made with reference to the year in which a nation adopted its anthem, and again, for the year of flag adoption.

High-focus events included incidents capable of concentrating the thoughts and actions of the national body, or those mobilizing the population toward a similar goal. These included occurrences such as independence movements, periods of nationalism, victory in war, and so forth.

Consider some examples from this group. The Netherlands, for instance, adopted its anthem in 1624. One historical source describes events of the period as follows:

> Frederick Henry, prince of Orange, stadholder, and commander in chief, resumed the course of victory (for the Netherlands). He completed the recapture of the towns recently regained by the Spaniards and extended the territory under the States-General to the key fortress of Maastricht on the Maas (Meuse) well to the south. At the same time, the Dutch navy won a series of victories over the Spaniards. . . . He ended the suppression of the Remonstrants, with whose religious views he sympathized, without exasperating the Contra-Remonstrants beyond repair. On the other hand, he established a firm grip over the policies of the republic. (*Encyclopedia Britannica Macropedia* 1985:vol. 23, 334; for additional information, see Templer 1972)

Victory over one's enemies, the tempering of domestic squabbling, and the centralization of national political policy bespeak unity and consolidation. As such, these events characterize the period as one of high focus.

Similarly, when Poland adopted its flag (1919), social affairs concentrated intranational focus. During this period, the constitutional Sejm (parliament) was formed, the "Little Constitution" was passed, and the nation witnessed a new cooperation between the New Democrats and the Peasants, a milestone achieved under Paderewski's newly formed government. The nation also acquired the Prussian sector. All of these incidents redirected the national population, bringing a new sense of cohesion to the Polish people (*Cambridge History of Poland* 1971).

New beginnings for a nation generally trigger high intranational focus. Consider, for example, the climate in East Germany during the year in which the nation adopted its anthem (1949): "The transformation of the East German people's council into the provisional people's Chamber on October 7, 1949, marked the establishment of the German Democratic Republic. It was a period of *strong national faith* in the future of the new Fatherland" (Nettl 1967:88, emphasis added). Similarly, the Bahamas, Chad, Jamaica, the Philippines, and Western Samoa represent just a few of the many nations achieving independence at the time in which they adopted their national symbols. When the transition is peaceful, independence remakes a collective and defines a new, cohesive entity. As such, the declaration of independence functions to bind citizens in the moment; it directs the national attention to one target.

Low-focus events threaten, demoralize, or disrupt the public. Such events generate fragmentation rather than unity; they diffuse citizen populations, rendering them a collection of individuals with isolated concerns rather than a joint body with a single cognitive mindset. Low-focus events include bloody coups, economic depression, lost wars, natural disasters, and revolutions.

Consider some examples from this category. The year of anthem adoption in Mexico (1854) began with a bloody coup mounted by Santa Anna. Before the year was over, the Mexican people also witnessed Santa Anna's dramatic demise at the hands of Juan Álvarez (Meyer and Sherman 1987). Such rapid shifts in control, and the violence and turmoil surrounding them, kept the Mexican collective in a state of disequilibrium. As such, the events of the period generated cognitive fission rather than fusion among the Mexican population.

Similarly, the adoption of both the Portuguese anthem and flag (1910–11) occurred amidst low-focus events. The symbols emerged immediately following the overthrow of the Portuguese monarch. This era of the Portuguese Republic is generally noted by historians for its great instability (Wheeler 1978). Only eighteen years in length, the period saw forty-eight different governments, seven different presidents (only one of whom completed his term), twenty-five coup d'états or revolutions, and several political assassinations (Malefakis 1985:444). Within such a milieu, collective bonds were necessarily disrupted and citizen attentions turned inward.

Bloody conflict between the Tutsi and Hutu permeated the adoption period of both Rwanda's (1961) and Burundi's (1967) national flags. In both nations, the rivalry between the two groups created an environment of turmoil, frequent power shifts, and violent struggle (*Chronicle of the World* 1989:1213, 1158). The populations of both nations were faced with events that served to sever citizen ties and redirect attentions toward individual survival. Events rendered the collective focus in both Rwanda and Burundi dispersed and anomic.

Moderate-focus events include incidents such as relatively peaceful social movements and periods of economic development. Although some conflict may be generated by events in this category, the incidents do not disrupt the daily routine of the collective. Rather, the collective interacts in an atmosphere of organic solidarity—one that demands split attention to both individual interests and the ties that bind those interests to the larger body.

Historical sources characterize the period in which Spain adopted its national anthem (1770) as one of moderate focus:

> Acts such as the limitation of future entail, which preserved the great estate over generations, the limitation of the privileges of the Mesta, and the right to enclose olive groves and irrigated land showed that the reformers believed primarily in the right of private individuals to do what they liked with their own. . . . Patriotic societies, organized with government encouragement, were meant to provide the provincial basis for a progressive society and to familiarize Spaniards with European advances in technology and agriculture. (*Encyclopedia Britannica Macropedia* 1985:vol. 28, 51; for more information, see, e.g., Petrie 1971)

This description depicts a pluralistic environment, one in which groups are loosely bound, while simultaneously pursuing variant interests.

Costa Rica, too, experienced a period of varied development during the year in which its anthem was adopted (1853): "A constant stream of oxcarts carried coffee from the Meseta Central to Pacific ports and ships bound for Europe. This trade brought British investment. Farmers with even small acreage could derive an adequate if simple existence, and the ground was laid for a society that demanded schools and roads from its government and found political participation necessary to achieve these goals" (*Encyclopedia Britannica Macropedia* 1985:, vol. 15 700; for more information, see Biesanz 1982). In this case, national attentions were divided and multiple goals were presented at the macro level. Yet these goals were ultimately directed toward the same end. So although collective attention in Costa Rica lacked the pointedness triggered by high-focus events, the collective eye was still beckoned to a common target, albeit in a more casual and relaxed fashion.

The year in which Ireland adopted its national anthem (1926) was also a period of moderate focus. The national body attended to the enactment of judicial reform, the establishment of a police force, and the peaceful reconciliation of Northern Ireland and the Irish Free State (Mc-Cracken 1958). These events, although multiple and not without conflict, allowed for routinized activity and areas of overlapping collective attention. Hence, they characterize a collective focus that is moderate in strength.

The moderate-focus condition contains a subcategory: mixed focus. Mixed focus captures periods in which high-focus and low-focus events exist simultaneously. During such periods, collective attention may be riveted to a single issue of primary national concern while the collective may be struggling with the fragmentation and destruction caused by the event in question. In this way, mixed focus depicts an environment in which concern for collective and individual interests are concurrently optimal.

The French anthem and flag were adopted during a period of mixed focus (1794–95). On the one hand, the Revolution and its authoritarian aftermath heightened collective attention. Yet the national population was factionalized regarding the postrevolutionary agenda, and atomized by the new government's terror tactics (Garraty and Gay 1981:763–73). In essence, this period in French history put collective and individual interests in direct competition.

Mixed focus also characterized the nine-year period surrounding the adoption of the original South African anthem and flag (1927–36). Premiere Herzog was working to emancipate South Africa from imperial control; he fostered rapid growth in an economic nationalism and worked to eradicate conflict between the nation's political parties. All of these events bespeak high focus. Yet concurrent to such incidents, the population experienced an economic depression and the intense factionalism caused by segregation policies (*Cambridge History of the British Empire* 1963; Gwendolen 1977). These alternating circumstances promoted a "tug of war" for the population's attention, a condition characteristic of this mixed category.

The case of Zambia, too, exemplifies mixed intranational focus. Zambia's anthem and flag were adopted upon the nation's declaration of independence, typically a high-focus event. However, several low-focus events accompanied Zambian independence: "When Zambia achieved its independence, it was, despite the Copperbelt, a poverty-stricken and backward country with severe class, regional, ethnic, and rural-urban divisions. During the period of the transference of power, Lozi separatism was a serious problem, and in 1964 open warfare broke out between the millenarian Lumpa (Leshina) Church and the state" (*Encyclopedia Britannica Macropedia* vol 27:976; for more information see, e.g., Roberts 1976). This juxtapositioning of independence with factionalism and poverty created a mixture of cognitive states.

Measuring Deviant Symbol Structure

In this section, I use the national anthem of the Ivory Coast to describe the measurement of structural deviance. This symbol is particular useful for this purpose, as it is a prototype of deviant syntactic structure.

Recall that the relative deviance of anthem structure is determined with reference to the structure norms guiding five specific social contexts: lineal, spatial, socioeconomic, political, and event. The position of the Ivory Coast's anthem in each of these domains is reviewed below.

Lineal Context

In chapter 3, we discovered that nations tend to adopt anthems whose structures diverge from those of their colonial powers. Thus in the lineal context, differentiation represents the norm and similarity expresses deviance. To classify an anthem as normal or deviant with reference to lineal norms of structure, I compare the anthem's syntax score with that of its colonial power. If the anthem's standardized syntax score falls at or within .25 standard deviations above or below the standardized syntax score of its colonial power's anthem, I consider the two scores similar, and classify the anthem under scrutiny as deviant.[22] If the anthem falls beyond this preset limit, I code its structure as normal.

Now consider the case of the Ivory Coast. This anthem displayed a standardized syntax score of +.53. Its colonial power, France, possesses a score of +.78. The difference between these two scores equals .25. According to the present coding scheme, the structure of the Ivory Coast's anthem must be classified as deviant within the lineal context.

Spatial Context

In the spatial context, a normal symbol is one whose syntactic structure resembles others of the "neighborhood." Knowing this, I classified an anthem's structure as normal when the standardized form of its syntax score fell within 1.25 standard deviations above or below the standardized average score for all bordering nations.[23] Scores exceeding this "cutoff" point were categorized as deviant.[24]

Note that the national anthem of the Ivory Coast displays a standardized syntax score of +.53. The standardized mean for the Ivory Coast's neighborhood, however, is −.85. The distance between these two score equals 1.38 standard deviations. Because that difference exceeds the 1.25 preset limit, I classify the Ivory Coast's anthem as a deviant to its region.

Socioeconomic Context

Recall that embellished syntax represents the normal structure for nations located in the periphery of the world-system, whereas basic syntax is typical of core nations; more moderate symbol designs proved the norm for semiperiphery nations. Identifying deviant symbols within this socioeconomic context entailed a two-step process. First, I recoded the measures of syntactic metastructure. Symbols whose scores fell within the first third of the basic-embellished continuum were coded as basic; scores within the second third of the continuum were designated as moderate; all other scores were classified as embellished. In step two, I compared each symbol's syntax classification—basic, moderate, or embellished—with the category considered the norm for that nation's world-system location. If the symbol's observed and expected structure were in accord, the symbol was classified as normal. If the symbol's observed and expected structure were discordant, the symbol was labeled deviant.

The Ivory Coast's anthem (+.53) represents a moderate syntactic design. Given the nation's peripheral socioeconomic status, this design contradicts our expectation of embellishment. Based on the discordance between the Ivory Coast's observed and expected syntax status, the anthem must be classified as deviant to its socioeconomic setting.

Political Context

The coding process outlined for socioeconomic context can be applied to the political arena as well. To determine the deviance of a national symbol's structure, we compare a symbol's actual syntax status—basic, moderate, or embellished—to the status expected under a specific political arrangement. Recall that basic syntactic structure represents the norm for authoritarian governments, whereas embellished designs are typical to democratic regimes. When we apply this standard to the anthem of the Ivory Coast, we must classify the symbol as deviant. Its structure is moderate in design, yet expectation demands embellishment.

Event Context

The analysis of social events suggested that basic syntax is the norm for high-focus events, moderate syntax is typical to moderate-focus events, and embellished syntax is appropriate to low-focus events. Knowing this, we must classify the Ivory Coast's anthem as deviant within this context. The anthem's moderate syntax contradicts the norms of basic structure typical to the setting of the anthem's adoption—namely, the high-focus event of peaceful independence.

After considering the Ivory Coast's anthem within the five pertinent contexts, I tallied the anthem's occurrences of deviance, thus calculating a composite deviance score for the symbol. Because the anthem proved deviant to each of the five contexts of its adoption, its deviance score equals five.

APPENDIX B

Nation Data

Table B.1. Nation Data

Nation	Music Score	Graphic Score	Colonial Power	Anthem Adoption Year	Flag Adoption Year	Ideology at Anthem Adoption	Ideology at Flag Adoption	Regional Lumping of Symbols N†
Afghanistan	-2.102	1.580	England	1978	1980	I†	C†	N†
Albania	.526	-.297	Turkey	1912	1946	*	C	F
Algeria	-1.698	.074	France	1963	1962	I	I	F
Andorra	.311	-1.167	France	1914	1866	*	*	B
Angola	-.715	.405	Portugal	1975	1975	S	S	A
Anguilla	*	-.536	England	*	1967	*	*	*
Antigua and Barbuda	-.786	1.238	England	1981	1967	*	*	*
Argentina	.592	-1.806	Spain	1813	1816	*	C	N
Armenia	*	-.613	U.S.S.R.	*	*	C	C	*
Australia	-.229	1.619	England	1984	1909	D	D	B
Austria	-1.188	-2.015	*	1947	1945	D	D	N
Azerebijan	*	1.235	U.S.S.R.	*	1918	I	C	*
Bahamas	.713	.950	England	1973	1973	D	D	B
Bahrain	-1.037	-2.594	England	1971	1933	I	I	B
Bangladesh	*	-2.285	France	1971	1972	*	I	*
Barbados	-1.755	.716	England	1966	1966	*	*	B
Belgium	1.859	-.823	Germany	1938	1830	D	D	B
Belize	-.243	1.806	England	1981	1981	*	*	B
Benin	-.109	-1.558	France	1960	1975	C	C	F
Bhutan	.329	.690	Italy	*	1965	*	*	B
Bolivia	1.580	-1.509	Spain	1842	1888	*	*	B
Botswana	-.038	-.562	England	1966	1966	D	D	F
Brazil	2.388	.544	Portugal	1922	1971	D	D	A

Brunei	-1.266	.947	England	1951	1959	*	*	B
Bulgaria	-.631	1.184	Turkey	1964	1971	C	C	B
Burkina Faso, Republic of	.926	-.491	France	*	1984	P	C	N
Burma	-.018	1.897	India	1948	1974	D	S	F
Burundi	.048	1.609	Belgium	1962	1967	*	*	A
Cameroon	1.731	-.274	France	1957	1975	P	P	A
Canada	-.978	-1.008	England	1980	1965	D	D	F
Cape Verde	*	1.842	Portugal	*	1974	P	P	N
Central African Republic	*	1.724	France	*	1958	P	P	*
Chad	-1.134	-1.208	France	1960	1959	D	P	B
Chile	1.478	.131	Spain	1941	1817	*	*	F
China, People's Republic of	-1.323	-1.084	*	1949	1949	C	C	A
China, Republic of	.150	-.392	Japan	1929	1928	*	*	B
Colombia	1.161	-1.141	Spain	1905	1861	*	*	B
Comoros	1.083	-.005	France	1978	1978	I	I	B
Congo	-1.278	-.296	France	1969	1969	P	C	B
Costa Rica	2.600	2.131	Spain	1853	1964	*	*	B
Cuba	-.245	1.794	Spain	1868	1902	D	D	B
Cyprus	1.471	-1.181	Turkey	1960	1960	*	*	B
Czechoslovakia	.585	.451	*	1919	1920	S	S	B
Denmark	-.527	-1.500	*	*	1854	*	*	B
Djibouti	-.482	1.403	France	1977	1977	I	I	B
Dominica	.058	3.119	England	1978	1978	D	D	F
Dominican Republic	1.803	.227	Spain	1900	1844	*	*	N
Ecuador	2.947	-1.020	Spain	1948	1900	*	*	B

Table B.1. Nation Data *continued*

Nation	Music Score	Graphic Score	Colonial Power	Anthem Adoption Year	Flag Adoption Year	Ideology at Anthem Adoption	Ideology at Flag Adoption	Regional Lumping of Symbols
Egypt	-1.001	.449	England	1979	1972	D	I	B
El Salvador	2.478	-.770	Spain	1953	1972	D	D	A
Equatorial Guinea	.032	.813	Spain	1968	1968	*	*	F
Estonia	.495	-.719	U.S.S.R.	1917	1920	C	C	F
Ethiopia	-.125	-1.509	Italy	1975	1941	P	*	F
Fiji	-1.443	2.217	England	1970	1970	*	*	A
Finland	.902	-1.273	Sweden	1848	1920	*	*	B
France	.624	-1.098	*	1795	1794	D	D	B
Gabon	-2.224	-.986	France	1960	1960	*	*	B
Gambia	-.296	-.261	England	1965	1965	D	D	B
Georgia	*	-.520	U.S.S.R.	*	1917	C	C	*
German Democratic Republic	-2.065	-.971	*	1950	1959	S	S	B
German Federal Republic	1.237	1.507	*	1922	1949	*	D	N
Ghana	.566	.370	England	1957	1957	P	P	B
Greece	1.471	1.610	*	1864	1978	*	D	B
Grenada	*	2.358	England	1974	1974	P	P	F
Guatemala	2.061	-1.140	Spain	1887	1968	*	*	B
Guinea	-1.220	-1.509	France	*	1958	P	P	F
Guinea-Bissau	2.660	.469	Portugal	1974	1973	P	P	A
Guyana	.078	.012	England	1966	1966	P	P	B
Haiti	.374	-1.404	France	1904	1986	*	*	F

Honduras	1.092	1915	Spain	1949	*	*	N
Hungary	-.581	1844	*	1957	*	*	B
Iceland	1.892	1874	Denmark	1915	*	*	A
India	*	*	England	1947	*	*	*
Indonesia	.545	1949	Netherlands	1945	I	I	N
Iran	-.724	1980	*	1979	I	I	B
Iraq	-2.530	1981	Turkey	1963	*	*	N
Ireland	.317	1926	England	1937	D	D	Z
Israel	.678	1948	England	1948	*	*	B
Italy	1.960	1946	*	1946	*	*	A
Ivory Coast	.687	1960	France	1959	*	*	A
Jamaica	.347	1962	England	1962	*	*	B
Japan	*	*	*	1854	*	*	*
Jordan	-1.425	1946	England	1928	I	I	F
Kampuchea (Cambodia)	-.818	1976	France	1989	S	S	B
Kenya	-.433	1963	England	1963	P	P	F
Kiribati	-.951	1979	England	1979	*	*	A
Korea, Democratic People's Republic	.759	1947	Japan	1948	C	C	B
Korea, Republic of	.564	1948	Japan	1950	*	*	B
Kuwait	-1.083	1978	England	1961	I	I	B
Laos	-1.245	1947	France	1975	C	C	B
Latvia	-.697	1874	U.S.S.R.	1922	S	S	B
Lebanon	.758	1927	Turkey	1943	I	I	B
Lesotho	-2.911	1967	England	1987	*	*	B
Liberia	-2.288	*	U.S.	1847	D	D	N
Libya	-3.046	1969	Turkey	1977	I	I	N

Table B.1. Nation Data *continued*

Nation	Music Score	Graphic Score	Colonial Power	Anthem Adoption Year	Flag Adoption Year	Ideology at Anthem Adoption	Ideology at Flag Adoption	Regional Lumping of Symbols
Liechtenstein	-2.267	-.284	Switzerland	*	1937	*	*	A
Lithuania	-.883	-1.444	U.S.S.R.	1918	1922	C	C	B
Luxembourg	.135	-1.098	Germany	1895	1972	*	*	A
Madagascar	1.358	-1.016	France	1958	1959	*	*	B
Malawi	-.452	.631	England	1964	1964	P	P	B
Malaysia	-.851	2.286	England	1957	1963	*	*	B
Maldives	-1.178	-.584	England	1972	1965	I	I	F
Mali	-1.820	-1.509	France	1962	1961	P	P	A
Malta	-.410	-.673	England	1923	1964	*	*	N
Mauritania	*	-1.405	France	*	1959	I	I	A
Mauritius	.888	-.402	England	1968	1968	*	*	*
Mexico	2.384	1.395	Spain	1854	1968	*	S	B
Monaco	-.260	-2.594	France	1867	1881	*	*	B
Mongolia	1.038	-.153	*	1950	1949	C	C	F
Moracco	*	-1.558	Spain	*	1915	*	*	N
Mozambique	.881	2.838	Portugal	1975	1983	*	*	F
Namibia	*	.874	Germany	*	1990	*	*	*
Nauru	-.547	-.178	England	1968	1968	*	*	F
Nepal	-.505	-.114	England	1899	1962	*	*	B
Netherlands	-1.129	-1.098	*	1626	1937	*	*	A
New Zealand	.090	1.991	England	1940	1902	*	*	B
Nicaragua	2.040	-.682	Spain	1821	1971	*	*	B
Niger	-.145	-.226	France	1961	1959	*	*	N

Nigeria	-.470	-.984	England	1978	1960	*	*	B
Norway	-1.471	.118	*	1864	1821	*	*	N
Oman	-1.303	-.292	England	1970	1970	I	I	B
Pakistan	.529	-.262	England	1954	1947	*	I	B
Panama	1.335	.962	U.S.	1903	1903	*	*	B
Papua New Guinea	-.609	1.435	England	1976	1971	*	*	*
Paraguay	.328	1.568	Spain	1846	1842	*	*	F
Peru	2.050	-2.015	Spain	1821	1825	*	*	F
Phillipines	-.850	1.168	Spain	1899	1898	*	*	B
Poland	-.233	-2.594	Germany	1927	1919	D	D	F
Portugal	1.155	.766	*	1910	1911	*	*	N
Qatar	-2.873	-2.323	England	1954	1949	I	I	A
Romania	-.877	-1.160	*	1977	1965	S	S	F
Russia	*	-.875	*	*	1883	*	*	B
Rwanda	1.088	.424	Belgium	1962	1961	P	P	F
San Marino	-1.692	-2.368	Italy	1894	1797	*	*	N
Sao Tome	1.452	1.632	Portugal	*	1975	P	P	N
Saudi Arabia	-.391	-.678	*	1950	1938	I	I	N
Senegal	*	-.524	France	*	1960	P	P	*
Seychelles	2.305	-1.147	England	1978	1977	S	S	B
Sierra Leone	.833	-.724	England	1961	1961	*	*	B
Singapore	-.062	-.232	England	1959	1959	*	*	B
Solomon Islands	-2.300	1.425	England	1978	1977	*	*	A
Somalia	-.505	-1.849	England	1960	1954	*	*	B
South Africa	1.145	1.860	England	1936	1927	*	*	B
Spain	-.222	-2.093	*	1770	1785	*	*	B
Sri Lanka	.989	1.228	England	1952	1972	*	*	*
St. Christopher	*	1.460	England	*	1967	P	P	*

Table B.1. Nation Data *continued*

Nation	Music Score	Graphic Score	Colonial Power	Anthem Adoption Year	Flag Adoption Year	Ideology at Anthem Adoption	Ideology at Flag Adoption	Regional Lumping of Symbols
St. Lucia	.211	.029	England	1967	1967	*	*	B
St. Vincent	-1.032	.617	England	1979	1985	D	D	A
Sudan	1.410	1.425	England	1956	1970	I	I	N
Surinam	-.349	.128	Netherlands	1876	1959	*	*	B
Swaziland	*	1.638	England	*	1967	*	*	*
Sweden	1.520	-1.273	*	1885	1906	D	D	B
Switzerland	-.835	-2.148	*	1961	1889	D	D	B
Syria	1.190	.871	France	1936	1980	I	I	B
Tanzania	.915	.280	England	1961	1964	*	*	N
Thailand	*	-.354	*	*	1917	*	*	*
Togo	-3.104	.787	France	1979	1960	P	P	A
Tonga	-1.125	-1.434	England	1874	1875	*	*	A
Trinidad and Tobago	-.398	-.334	England	1962	1962	*	*	F
Tunisia	1.402	-1.317	France	1958	1835	I	I	A
Turkey	2.189	-1.555	*	1921	1936	I	I	N
U.S.S.R.	.930	-1.632	*	1943	1923	C	C	N
Uganda	.508	1.524	England	1962	1962	*	*	B
Ukraine	.068	-1.861	U.S.S.R.	1917	1918	C	C	A
United Arab Emirates	.255	1.522	England	1971	1971	I	I	F
United Kingdom	-2.267	.925	*	1745	1801	*	*	A
United States	-.985	3.448	England	1931	1960	D	D	B
Uruguay	1.709	1.674	Spain	1845	1830	*	*	B
Vanuata	-1.177	2.198	France	1980	1980	*	*	B

Venezuela	−1.192	1.559	Spain	1881	1954	*	*	N
Vietnam, Democratic Republic of	.855	−2.148	France	1946	1955	S	S	N
Vietnam, Republic of South	*	−.333	France	*	1969	*	*	*
Vietnam, Socialist Republic of	.855	−2.148	France	1976	1976	S	S	N
Western Samoa	−1.180	.561	New Zealand	1962	1949	*	*	B
Yemen, Arab Republic of	−1.704	.566	England	*	1962	I	I	A
Yemen, People's Democratic Republic of	−1.050	1.689	England	*	1967	I	I	F
Yugoslavia	−.104	.363	Turkey	1945	1946	S	S	B
Zaire	.948	−.240	Belgium	1972	1971	P	P	N
Zambia	−1.558	1.243	England	1964	1964	*	*	A
Zimbabwe	.948	1.412	England	*	1980	P	P	F
Mean	−.015	−.016	—	1935	1942	—	—	—
Median	−.038	.002	—	1954	1960	—	—	—
Mode	—	—	England	1962, 1978	1959	I	I	B
Standard deviation	1.303	1.377	—	52.948	45.037	—	—	—
Minimum	−3.105	−4.271	—	1626	1785	—	—	—
Maximum	2.948	3.449	—	1984	1990	—	—	—

Nation	World-System Position at Anthem Adoption	World-System Position at Flag Adoption	Cultural Configuration	Political Arrangement at Anthem Adoption	Political Arrangement at Flag Adoption	Event Focus at Anthem Adoption	Event Focus at Flag Adoption	Anthem Deviance Score	Flag Deviance Score
Afghanistan	P‡	P‡	1.245	A§	A§	H"	L"	1	3
Albania	P	SP	1.157	A	A	H	m	3	2
Algeria	P	P	.969	A	A	H	H	1	4
Andorra	P	P	.916	D	D	m	m	2	3
Angola	P	P	2.081	D	D	M	M	2	2
Anguilla	*	P	*	*	D	*	H	*	4
Antigua and Barbuda	P	P	1.626	D	D	H	m	*	2
Argentina	P	P	1.720	D	D	M	H	3	5
Armenia	*	*	*	*	*	*	*	*	*
Australia	C	P	.961	D	D	m	m	2	1
Austria	C	C	.415	D	D	M	H	2	3
Azerebijan	*	*	*	*	A	*	M	*	*
Bahamas	P	P	1.448	D	D	M	M	3	4
Bahrain	P	P	1.302	A	A	H	m	3	2
Bangladesh	P	P	1.442	*	D	*	H	*	3
Barbados	P	P	.981	D	D	H	H	3	3
Belgium	C	SP	1.305	D	D	L	H	1	3
Belize	P	P	1.653	D	D	H	M	4	2
Benin	P	P	1.122	D	A	H	H	3	3

Bhutan	P	P	1.449	*	*	*	m	*	3
Bolivia	P	P	1.098	A	D	L	m	1	2
Botswana	P	P	1.359	D	D	H	H	3	4
Brazil	P	SP	1.129	D	D	L	M	0	1
Brunei	P	P	1.360	A	A	M	H	3	3
Bulgaria	SP	SP	1.170	D	A	m	H	1	3
Burkina Faso, Republic of	P	P	1.774	*	A	*	H	*	3
Burma	SP	SP	1.948	D	A	M	M	1	4
Burundi	P	P	1.358	D	D	M	L	2	0
Cameroon	P	P	2.702	D	D	M	m	2	2
Canada	C	C	1.441	D	D	H	m	3	3
Cape Verde	P	P	1.266	*	D	*	H	*	2
Central African Republic	P	P	1.768	*	D	*	M	*	4
Chad	P	P	1.897	D	D	H	H	3	2
Chile	P	P	1.088	D	A	m	M	1	3
China, People's Republic of	P	P	1.726	A	A	H	H	2	4
China, Republic of	P	P	1.794	A	A	M	M	3	2
Colombia	P	P	.574	D	D	m	m	1	2
Comoros	P	P	1.277	D	D	M	M	2	2
Congo	P	P	2.070	A	A	M	M	2	2
Costa Rica	P	P	.792	D	D	m	m	1	2
Cuba	SP	SP	.429	A	M	M	H	1	2
Cyprus	P	P	1.358	D	D	H	H	1	4

Nation	World-System Position at Anthem Adoption	World-System Position at Flag Adoption	Cultural Configuration	Political Arrangement at Anthem Adoption	Political Arrangement at Flag Adoption	Event Focus at Anthem Adoption	Event Focus at Flag Adoption	Anthem Deviance Score	Flag Deviance Score
Czechoslovakia	SP	SP	1.518	D	D	M	M	1	3
Denmark	C	C	1.043	*	D	*	H	*	3
Djibouti	P	P	1.390	D	D	H	H	3	1
Dominica	P	P	1.286	D	D	H	H	3	2
Dominican Republic	P	P	.415	A	A	m	H	2	4
Ecuador	P	P	1.996	D	A	L	m	0	2
Egypt	SP	SP	1.155	D	D	M	m	1	1
El Salvador	P	P	1.384	D	D	L	M	1	2
Equatorial Guinea	P	P	1.825	A	A	M	M	3	2
Estonia	P	P	*	D	D	H	H	3	5
Ethiopia	P	P	1.729	A	A	L	H	3	4
Fiji	P	P	1.552	D	D	H	H	3	1
Finland	SP	SP	1.153	A	D	m	M	1	2
France	C	C	.605	A	A	M	M	2	3
Gabon	P	P	1.607	D	D	H	H	3	4
Gambia	P	P	1.858	D	D	H	H	3	3

Georgia	P	P	*	*	A	*	L	*	4
German Democratic Republic	SP	SP	.725	A	A	H	L	2	2
German Federal Republic	C	C	.725	D	D	L	L	1	3
Ghana	P	P	1.676	D	D	H	H	3	3
Greece	SP	P	.732	D	D	m	m	3	1
Grenada	P	P	1.528	D	D	H	H	*	2
Guatemala	P	P	1.577	D	A	L	L	O	4
Guinea	P	P	1.850	*	D	*	H	*	3
Guinea-Bissau	P	P	1.989	D	D	M	M	2	2
Guyana	P	P	2.063	D	D	H	H	3	3
Haiti	P	P	1.157	A	D	m	H	2	4
Honduras	P	P	.885	A	A	L	m	2	3
Hungary	SP	SP	1.355	A	A	m	H	1	3
Iceland	SP	SP	.000	D	D	H	m	3	1
India	P	P	2.076	*	D	*	M	*	2
Indonesia	P	P	2.073	D	D	H	H	4	3
Iran	SP	SP	1.928	A	A	H	H	2	3
Iraq	SP	SP	1.236	A	A	L	L	3	2
Ireland	SP	SP	.910	D	D	m	H	2	3
Israel	P	P	1.593	D	D	H	H	3	3
Italy	C	C	.537	D	D	L	m	3	2
Ivory Coast	P	P	2.260	D	D	H	H	5	4
Jamaica	P	P	1.709	D	D	H	H	3	3
Japan	SP	SP	.732	*	A	*	H	*	3
Jordan	SP	P	1.103	D	D	H	H	3	1

Nation	World-System Position at Anthem Adoption	World-System Position at Flag Adoption	Cultural Configuration	Political Arrangement at Anthem Adoption	Political Arrangement at Flag Adoption	Event Focus at Anthem Adoption	Event Focus at Flag Adoption	Anthem Deviance Score	Flag Deviance Score
Kampuchea (Cambodia)	P	P	1.517	A	A	H	m	3	2
Kenya	P	P	2.122	D	D	H	H	3	3
Kiribati	P	P	1.890	D	D	H	H	4	1
Korea, Democratic People's Republic	P	P	.928	A	A	H	H	3	4
Korea, Republic of	SP	SP	.808	D	D	H	H	2	4
Kuwait	SP	SP	.792	A	A	m	M	0	4
Laos	P	P	1.301	A	A	H	M	1	2
Latvia	P	P	*	A	D	m	H	2	3
Lebanon	P	P	1.852	D	D	m	H	2	3
Lesotho	P	P	1.661	D	A	H	m	3	2
Liberia	P	P	2.065	*	D	*	M	*	2
Libya	SP	SP	.979	A	A	H	H	2	2
Liechtenstein	SP	SP	.910	*	D	*	m	*	1
Lithuania	P	P	*	D	D	H	H	3	4
Luxembourg	C	C	1.098	D	D	m	m	2	2
Madagascar	P	P	1.441	D	D	H	H	1	5

Malawi	P	1.679	D	D	H	H	3	3
Malaysia	SP	1.966	D	D	H	m	2	3
Maldives	P	.720	D	D	H	H	4	3
Mali	P	1.347	D	D	H	H	2	3
Malta	P	.720	D	D	M	H	3	3
Mauritania	P	.971	*	*	*	H	*	3
Mauritius	P	1.551	D	D	H	H	2	3
Mexico	SP	.979	D	D	L	m	0	1
Monaco	P	.845	A	A	m	m	3	2
Mongolia	P	1.640	A	A	m	m	4	3
Moracco	P	.993	*	*	*	m	*	2
Mozambique	P	1.801	A	A	H	m	3	2
Namibia	P	1.771	*	*	*	H	*	3
Nauru	P	1.536	D	D	H	H	3	4
Nepal	P	2.169	A	A	m	H	2	3
Netherlands	C	1.241	A	A	H	M	1	3
New Zealand	C	1.355	D	D	H	m	3	2
Nicaragua	P	1.429	D	D	M	m	1	3
Niger	P	1.497	D	D	H	H	3	4
Nigeria	P	2.445	D	D	H	H	3	3
Norway	SP	.974	D	D	M	M	4	3
Oman	SP	1.709	A	A	H	H	2	2
Pakistan	SP	1.645	D	D	H	H	3	2
Panama	P	1.471	D	D	M	M	1	1
Papua New Guinea	P	2.153	D	D	H	m	3	3
Paraguay	P	.991	A	A	m	m	4	3

Nation	World-System Position at Anthem Adoption	World-System Position at Flag Adoption	Cultural Configuration	Political Arrangement at Anthem Adoption	Political Arrangement at Flag Adoption	Event Focus at Anthem Adoption	Event Focus at Flag Adoption	Anthem Deviance Score	Flag Deviance Score
Peru	P	P	1.004	A	A	L	H	1	2
Phillipines	P	P	1.305	D	D	H	H	3	2
Poland	SP	SP	1.000	A	D	m	H	1	3
Portugal	SP	SP	.294	D	D	L	M	2	2
Qatar	SP	SP	.792	A	A	m	m	3	3
Romania	SP	SP	1.718	A	A	H	H	2	2
Russia	*	C	*	*	A	*	m	*	3
Rwanda	P	P	1.157	D	D	M	L	1	3
San Marino	P	P	.294	D	D	H	H	3	2
Sao Tome	P	P	.294	*	D	*	H	*	1
Saudi Arabia	SP	SP	.294	A	A	m	m	1	2
Senegal	P	P	1.678	*	D	*	H	*	3
Seychelles	P	P	1.115	D	D	L	M	0	2
Sierra Leone	P	P	1.561	D	D	H	H	4	3
Singapore	SP	SP	1.944	D	D	H	H	2	2
Solomon Islands	P	P	2.224	D	D	H	H	2	4
Somalia	P	P	.415	D	A	M	m	2	2
South Africa	SP	SP	1.988	D	D	M	M	2	2
Spain	C	C	.504	A	A	m	m	2	3
Sri Lanka	P	P	1.612	D	D	m	H	*	2

St. Christopher	P	P	.924	*	D	*	H	*	2
St. Lucia	P	P	1.229	D	D	H	H	3	4
St. Vincent	P	P	1.865	D	D	H	m	3	2
Sudan	P	P	1.654	D	A	H	L	2	3
Surinam	P	P	1.797	D	D	m	m	3	2
Swaziland	P	P	1.619	*	D	*	H	*	1
Sweden	C	C	1.686	D	D	m	m	4	3
Switzerland	C	C	1.146	D	D	m	m	3	4
Syria	P	SP	1.815	D	D	H	m	2	1
Tanzania	P	P	1.986	D	A	m	M	2	2
Thailand	P	P	2.010	*	A	*	m	*	3
Togo	P	P	1.478	A	D	H	M	2	2
Tonga	P	P	1.166	D	D	H	H	2	4
Trinidad and Tobago	P	P	1.435	D	D	H	H	3	4
Tunisia	P	P	1.157	D	A	H	H	2	3
Turkey	SP	SP	1.518	D	A	L	H	3	4
U.S.S.R.	SP	SP	2.157	A	A	M	H	1	3
Uganda	P	P	1.815	D	D	H	H	3	2
Ukraine	SP	SP	*	D	D	H	H	2	3
United Arab Emirates	SP	SP	1.480	A	A	M	M	2	5
United Kingdom	C	C	1.282	A	D	H	M	1	4

Nation	World-System Position at Anthem Adoption	World-System Position at Flag Adoption	Cultural Configuration	Political Arrangement at Anthem Adoption	Political Arrangement at Flag Adoption	Event Focus at Anthem Adoption	Event Focus at Flag Adoption	Anthem Deviance Score	Flag Deviance Score
United States	C	C	1.739	D	D	L	m	4	2
Uruguay	P	P	1.119	D	D	L	M	0	2
Vanuata	P	P	1.114	D	D	H	M	2	2
Venezuela	P	SP	.910	D	A	m	m	4	4
Vietnam, Democratic Republic of	P	P	1.951	A	A	H	H	5	1
Vietnam, Republic of South	P	P	1.951	*	D	*	M	*	2
Vietnam, Socialist Republic of	P	P	1.951	A	A	M	M	4	2
Western Samoa	P	P	1.080	D	D	H	H	2	3
Yemen, Arab Republic of	*	SP	.000	*	A	*	H	*	2
Yemen, People's Democratic Republic of	*	SP	.000	*	A	*	L	*	3
Yugoslavia	SP	SP	1.744	A	A	m	m	1	1
Zaire	P	P	2.367	A	A	H	H	2	3

Zambia	P	2.572	D	D	M	M	5	2
Zimbabwe	P	1.680	*	D	*	M	*	2
Mean	—	1.379	—	—	—	—	—	—
Median	—	1.430	—	—	—	—	—	—
Mode	P	.295	D	D	H	H	3	2,3
Standard deviation	—	.527	—	—	—	—	—	—
Minimum	—	0	—	—	—	—	0	0
Maximum	—	2.703	—	—	—	—	5	5

*Indicates missing data

C = Communism; D = Democracy; I = Islam; S = Socialism; P = Pan-Africanism

A = Anthem; F = Flag; B = Both; N = Neither

C = Core; SP = Semi-Periphery; P = Periphery

A = Authoritarian; D = Democratic

H = High; M = Moderate; m = Mixed; L = Low

NOTES

Introduction. National Symbols

1. This narrative is based on correspondence between Whitney Smith, the flag's designer, and Lynette Dolphin, chair of Guyana's National History and Arts Council. Guyana's flag was adopted on January 26, 1966.

2. I refer to a tradition beginning with Saussure ([1915] 1959), moving through theorists such as Barthes (1967), Eco (1976), Jakobson (1968), Leach (1976), Ledrut (1973), Lévi-Straus (1963), Prieto (1975), Sebeok (1974), and Vygotsky (1962), a tradition further specified in areas such as architecture (e.g., Broadbent 1973, Jencks 1973), art (e.g., Gombrich 1981, Lotman 1977), cinema (e.g., Metz 1971), fashion (e.g., Delaporte 1979), music (e.g., Molino 1975, Nattiez 1990), poetry (e.g., Riffaterre 1978), and text (e.g., Derrida [1967] 1980, [1972] 1981), and invigorated by social scientists such as Gottdeiner (1985), and Hodge and Kress (1988).

3. Weitman, for instance, notes the striking predominance of the aggression theme in flags. Consider that 80 percent of all national flags contain the color red, a traditional indicator of aggression; lethal animals appear in flags nearly four times as frequently as nonthreatening animals; weapons of warfare ornament flags with greater frequency than other objects (1979:359). Similarly, Zikmund (1969) and Mead (1980) show that the lyrics of more than 180 anthems can be reduced to six major subjects: pastoral beauty, call to arms, edification of leader, patriotism, peace, or the struggle for independence. These examples represent a small part of an extensive literature devoted to the content of various national symbols. See, for example, Barraclough (1969), Boli-Bennett (1979), Cartledge et al. (1978), Elting and Folsom (1968), Firth (1973), Gregory (1975), Griffith (1959), Lichtenwanger (1970), Nettl (1967), Pedersen (1971), Piggott (1937), Sousa (1890), Smith (1975), Talocci (1977), and Yeoman (1974).

4. Also see Agulhon (1981:30–31), Garbus (1989:370), and Giddens (1985:214).

5. A process often referred to as *reciprocal reflection;* see Cassirer (1955:77, 99) or Modell (1969:11–31).

6. Both Gottdeiner (1985) and Schudson (1989) promote a similar approach in studying the efficacy of symbols.

7. For support of this argument with regard to political symbols, see, for example, Cherry (1961:116), Deutsch (1953:93), Deutsch et al. (1957:7, 55), Merritt (1966:60–190), Moore (1975:223), and Shannon (1951). For more general support, see, for example, Bergesen (1979:334–37; 1984:194–97), Bernstein (1975:chap. 8), Douglas (1970), and Swanson (1967:chaps. 3–4). Also, see a larger review of this literature in Corner (1986).

1. We Pledge Allegiance

1. Lamartine, of course, repudiated the plain red flag of the 1848 revolutionaries, calling it a "flag of blood . . . dragged through the blood of the people in '91 and '93" (quoted in Smith 1975:137).

2. Hodge and Kress (1988:4) call these *logonomic rules*. They guide the production, display, and use of symbols.

3. Brooks (1926:chap. 1), Gordon (1915:chap. 1), and Smith (1975:32–59) provide further detail.

4. National anthems first appeared in central Europe and South America during the late eighteenth century.

5. Further, the symbols enable the ontological security so necessary to modern existence.

6. Schlesinger (1993, 1994) notes this phenomenon at the metanational level, discussing the use of symbols and media in attempts to create a European identity.

7. In this way, national symbols accomplish what Schutz (1951) refers to as synchronicity. The symbols focus independent actors' streams of consciousness on a single element, thus unifying their thoughts and emotions.

8. Of course, rulers have used symbols to motivate action well before the establishment of nations. Julius Caesar (100–44 B.C.), for example, used stories, myths, lavish symbolic spectacles, and coins to stimulate loyalty and stir the people toward continued support of his military actions. Interestingly, Caesar contended that coins could best motivate citizen action as they were seen by the widest possible range of subjects under the ruler's control (Jowett and O'Donnell 1986:41).

9. Griffith (1952:50) notes: "For several years after the revolution, 'La Marseillaise' was forbidden by the French government because of fear of its effect on the passions of the excitable French people."

10. Note that this monument was originally intended to symbolize the glory of conquest. However, it has subsequently been reinterpreted to honor citizen sacrifice.

11. Barr's performance included a crude bodily gesture, reportedly mimicking informal baseball rituals.

12. The Russian flag replaced the Soviet flag at the United Nations on December 27, 1991.

13. Symbols served this function for prenational entities as well. Explorers claimed new territories by planting royal flags and banners on foreign soils. Similarly, early map makers indicated control of a region by dotting lands with the flags of their claimers.

14. Manipulation is similar to semantic distortion, and juxtapositioning to syntactic or sequential distortion. See Cerulo (1988a:95–96; 1995).

15. During the 1980s, the Supreme Court found flag burning an acceptable form of political expression, fully permissible and noncriminal. Such a ruling legitimates the protest function of national symbols.

2. Syntactic Structure

1. Note that I use *symbol* where Saussure would use *sign*.
2. Saussure referred to these connections and distinctions as *syntagmatic* relationships—bonds that link the elements of any single message to one another ([1915] 1959:123).
3. Schoenberg's twelve-tone technique of composition replaced traditional principles of melody, harmony, and tonality. Every twelve-tone work is based on a series of notes containing all twelve chromatic tones. These tones resound in a special succession chosen by the composer.
4. For reviews of this massive literature, see, for example, Barey (1965:93), Barthes (1967, 1977), Blau (1993), Cassirer (1955:94, 96), Cherry (1961:66), Eco (1976, 1985), Gombrich (1960, 1981), Henrotte (1985:660–61), Hervey (1982:219), Koffka (1935:184), Kurzweil (1980), Leach (1976:10, 45–49, 58–59), Merritt (1966:xiii), Meyer (1967:chap. 1), Sless (1986:chaps. 1–3), and Zerubavel (1985:47; 1987:347–48). Also review note 2 in the introduction.
5. Leach (1976:33) writes that in interpreting a nation's anthem or flag, "meaning will depend on contrast."
6. Clashing primary colors generate motion; see Munsell (1946) and Stockton (1983).
7. Notes are similar to what Leach calls *signum* (1976:12–13) or what Saussure defines as a *sign* ([1915] 1959:66).
8. One can think of limited instances in which pitches are sounded as independent units—that is, train whistles or dinner bells. If we concede that such occurrences are music and not simply "noise," we must still acknowledge the role of dimensions such as duration of the sound or repetition of the sound in bringing meaning to the pitch. See Cerulo (1988b, 1989b).
9. For more on composition rules, see, for example, Dahlhaus (1980a, 1980b) and Lindley (1980). Dalhaus (1980a:179) states that these general rules were established as early as 1600 and have been sustained through the 1900s.
10. For additional support of the basic-embellished contrast in music, see, for example, Bergesen (1979), Lomax (1968), Meyer (1956:chap 6; 1967:chap. 1), Moles (1966), Nattiez (1990), and Youngblood (1958). Readers may notice similarities between my approach and that of researchers using the concept of symbolic "codes." Although the characteristics of my continuum differ from those constructed by other scholars, my approach is based on works such as Bergesen (1979, 1984), Bernstein (1975), Douglas (1970), Eco (1976), and Saussure ([1915] 1959). For a good review of such literature, see Corner (1986) or Giles and Wiemann (1987).
11. Cerulo (1988b, 1989b) contains other validity demonstrations.
12. To be included in the sample, an anthem must follow a Western tonal music tradition—that is, be built using the diatonic scales. Anthems based on other musical

systems would destroy the stylistic uniformity of the sample, making comparative analysis unreliable.

13. Literature on stylistic trends in art supports this line of thought. For example, revolutionary changes initiating the Renaissance period in music were mirrored in the visual arts and literature, suggesting an imitative or relativistic quality to symbolic expression.

14. For reviews of this massive literature, see, for example, Cerulo (1995); Hall (1966); Knapp et al. (1987); Leukel (1972); Littlejohn (1983); McLuhan (1965); and Rimmer (1986). Differences between communication genres also have been demonstrated in specific substantive areas, such as media agenda-setting (see, e.g., DeFleur and Ball-Rokeach 1982; McLeod et al. 1974; and Shaw and McCombs 1977), and various forms of advertising (see, e.g., Biocca 1991, Lang 1990, Mansfield and Hale 1986, and Rothschild et al. 1986).

15. From the song "Putting It Together," a part of the Broadway score for *Sunday in the Park with George.*

3. "Editors" of National Symbol Structures

1. The terms figure and ground derive from Gestalt psychology. The figure is the focal point of a message or setting. The background or ground is defined as the framework or context in which the figure is projected. See, for example, Ellis (1950:88), Koffka (1935:184), Kohler (1947:202), and Latner (1973:26–32).

2. One can, of course, point to more iconic border symbols. The Great Wall of China, for example, constructed under the orders of Emperor Zheng in 221 B.C., was designed to insulate the newly unified China. Similarly, the Berlin Wall was constructed in 1961, to contain East Germany and insulate it from outside capitalist influence.

3. Although my focus is on symbol selection, my argument is compatible with recent studies of reception and interpretation. See, for example, Ang (1985), Beisel (1993), DeVault (1990), Fiske (1984), Griswold (1987), Iser (1978), Lamont (1987), Liebes (1988), Long (1986), Radway (1984), Schudson (1989), Sewell (1992), and Stryker (1980).

4. I defined a colonial power as the nation responsible for granting a country its independence. I sometimes included nations that forcibly occupied previously free countries, thus significantly influencing their destiny. *Chronicle of the World* (1989) provided the data.

5. The colonies that comprised the U.S.S.R. dropped out of this analysis because my sample included these nations' pre-Soviet symbols. Also, Japan's colonies were not considered here because Japan's anthem is not included in the data.

6. I analyzed only those anthems adopted *after* that of the colonizer.

7. Because I am dealing with symbol populations rather than samples, tests of significance are technically inappropriate. Yet I offer them as interpretive tools with which to review the findings.

8. T-test results for these six groups are as follows: Belgium and colonies, t = −3.57, p = .07; France and colonies, t = −3.33, p = .003; Great Britain and colonies, t =

13.52, p = .000; Italy and colonies, t = −3.43, p = .04; Spain and colonies, t = 5.45, p = .000; Turkey and colonies, t = −3.92, p = .01.

9. T-test results for these seven groups are as follows: Belgium and colonies, t = 2.63, p = .10; France and colonies, t = 2.23, p = .03; Germany and colonies, t = −2.32; p = .04; Great Britain and colonies, t = −2.14, p = .04; Japan and colonies, t = 5.43, p = .03; Spain and colonies, t = 6.99, p = .000; United States and colonies, t = −6.77, p = .09.

10. The variables representing anthem adoption year and flag adoption year were not normally distributed. Therefore, I am reporting Spearman correlation coefficients. With regard to anthems, note that correlations increase slightly when outliers are dropped from the data. If one drops the anthem of the Netherlands, for example, adopted in 1626 (119 years prior to any other anthem in the sample), r = −.361; p = .02. Similarly, if one excludes the four anthems adopted prior to 1800 from the analysis (France, Netherlands, Spain, and the United Kingdom), r = −.391; p = .01.

Note at this time that the effects of outliers was fully examined throughout all analyses. The removal of outliers never resulted in a significant change in findings.

11. Data were derived from the *Chronicle of the World* (1989).

12. This approach is one of many suggested by Agresti and Finlay (1986:381–82). Note that all other variable pairs showed correlations of +/−.288 or below, with no indications of multicollinearity.

13. Although anthems of colonizers and former colonies are significantly different from one another, they also share certain broad stylistic similarities. So, for example, if a mother country's anthem is embellished, former colonies' anthems are also embellished, albeit significantly more or less embellished. Therefore, although syntax may be a vehicle by which new nations split themselves from the symbolic image of their colonial power, there appears to be some limitations regarding the degree of difference a new nation is willing to project.

14. All other variable pairs showed correlations of +/−.263 or below. Note that since ideology demonstrated no connection to flag syntax, the variables are not included in models 3 or 4.

15. Recall that neighborhood syntax score and adoption year are correlated. Therefore, to capture the effect of both space and time on flag syntax, I will utilize an interaction term in future analysis. This term is constructed according to the following formula:

$$\frac{\text{neighboring nations flag syntax} \times \text{flag adoption date}}{1000}$$

For this variable, the mean = −.056, with a standard deviation of 1.913 and a range of −3.85 to 6.78.

4. Socioeconomic Pockets and the Structure of National Symbols

1. This position is most evident in works written prior to 1848.

2. Technically, the *relations of production*—ties that emerge as individuals develop and utilize raw materials and technologies to achieve their productive goals.

3. Modernization theory best characterizes this position.

4. Most notably, Braudel.

5. Most notably, Andre Gunder Frank.

6. This summary is based on Frank (1969), Mann (1980:299), Ruggie (1983), Thomas and Meyer (1984:465), Wallerstein (1979:53; 1983; 1984:59), and Wellman (1983:162–63).

7. Braudel introduced this terminology.

8. Labor intensiveness refers to nonmechanized labor.

9. For critiques of this stance, see, for example, Kumon (1987), Modelski (1978), Ray (1983), Skocpol (1977), Thompson (1983), and Zolberg (1983).

10. White and White (1965) and Williams (1990) make similar arguments.

11. Balibar (1988::89) makes a similar observation.

12. Interestingly, Tambiah also suggests that when nations sway from this relation perspective, it often spells economic, political, and social disaster. In the case of Sri Lanka, he writes: "In the post-Independence decades, Sri Lankans have tended to rest on their colonial laurels, and to lose their sense of proportion as to their own real situation in South and Southeast Asian politics. Sri Lanka has increasingly become a backwater island which, in turning inward, has become a self-destructive pressure chamber" (1986:2). Kennedy (1987:7–10) made similar observations regarding conditions in China during the 1400s.

13. For some notable examples from this massive literature, see Berger (1972); Berger (1979); Bernstein (1975); Bradac and Mulac (1984); Burt (1987); Cicourel (1976); Duncan (1972); Eder and Enke (1991); Eidinger and Patterson (1983); Givens (1983); Goffman (1981); Kollack et al. (1985); Labov (1966); Leffler et al. (1982); Meltzer et al. (1971); Rogers (1972); Rogers and Schumacher (1983); Rosa and Mazur (1979); Schegloff (1968); Stryker (1980); Tannen (1990); Trimboli and Walker (1982); Tromel-plotz (1981); White (1992); and Wiemann (1985). For good review articles on this topic, see Capella (1987); Giles and Wiemann (1987); and Knapp et al. (1987).

14. Superstructure, in Marxian terms.

15. In many ways, the delicate balance of which I speak is institutionalized, as many national symbols require approval from a world community agency before they can be legitimately adopted. Coats of arms and national flags, for example, must be approved by the College of Arms in England.

16. Put in another way, embellished syntactic structure provides the best opportunity for peripheral nations to explain what others are presumed not to know—to provide a step by step blueprint of the dismantling of colonial-imposed reality and the implementation of indigenous policy.

17. I use "tools" in the spirit of Swidler (1986).

18. Ramirez (1987) and Wuthnow (1987) make similar points in discussing national myth construction.

19. Reed and Bristow (1985) provide all lyric translations in this book.

20. Taken from earlier cited correspondence; see intro, note 1.

21. The findings also indicate no significant distinctions in the anthem structures of core and semiperipheral nations. In the realm of anthems, the semiperiphery appears to mirror core tactics (t = .74; d.f. = 48; p = .46).

22. In this equation, world-system location is a dummy variable in which 1 = periphery nations (n = 110) and 0 represents all others (n = 50). I coded the variable in this way because of the resemblance between core and semiperiphery anthems.

23. Measures of association for world-system position and other variables in the equation range from .02 to .25; further, there was no suggestion of multicollinearity.

24. The mean graphic score for the semiperiphery sector lies midway between the mean core score and the mean periphery score. This suggests that those adopting flags in semiperiphery nations are equally influenced by the designs of those both above and below them in the world economic hierarchy. Unlike the findings on anthems, these results offer some support for the notion that the semiperiphery acts as a "bridge" between the core and the periphery.

25. In this variable, 1 = periphery nations (n = 123), while 0 = all others (n = 55).

26. Because the variables representing region and adoption period were correlated, I constructed an interaction term (multiplicative in design), allowing for their simultaneous entry into the model. See chapter 3, note 15.

27. Measures of association for world-system position and other variables in the equation range from .01 to .24; further, there was no suggestion of multicollinearity.

5. Of the People, For the People

1. Here, "effective" refers to messages that accomplish the sender's goals.

2. In areas as varied as the arts, attitude change, behavior manipulation, entertainment, propaganda, and public policy, communication and culture scholars urge thoughtful attendance to the link between audience structure and message design. See, for example, Abelson and Karlins (1970); Barthes (1967); Beisel (1993); Cassirer (1968); DeVault (1990); Fiske (1984); Gaertner (1955); Gans (1974); Goffman (1959:3–4, 35); Griswold (1987); Hovland (1959); Hovland et al. (1953); Iser (1978); Jowett and O'Donnell (1986); Lamont (1987); Liebes (1988); Long (1986); Marcus and Zajonc (1985:154–55); Martorella (1982, 1989); McGuire (1969); Mead (1934:253); Peterson (1979); Radway (1984); Schudson (1989); Sewell (1992); Toffler (1964); Weaver (1928); Zimbardo and Leippe (1991); and Zimbardo et al. (1977).

3. Similar claims include Comte's idea of consensus, Cooley's notion of collective view, and Wundt's concept of *Volksseele* (the group soul).

4. Watkins (1991) makes a similar point with reference to national communities and changing demographic patterns.

5. Swanson (1960, 1967) and Hammond and Williams (1979) offer additional support.

6. See Cerulo and Ruane (1996) and Cerulo et al. (1992) for more on the phenomena that stimulate cognitive community.

7. Simmel (1955), Coser (1956), and Lauderdale (1976) note that external oppression can lead to ingroup solidarity.

8. The term *individual* is intended to encompass other micro-level social units as well—the family being the most obvious.

9. For a good review of this literature, see, for example, Corner (1986), Giles and Wiemann (1987), and Steinfatt (1989). For more general discussions linking audience context to message format and style, see Beisel (1993), DeVault (1990), Fiske (1984), Griswold (1987), Iser (1978), Lamont (1987), Liebes (1988), Long (1986), Radway (1984), or Schudson (1989).

10. Also see Collins (1988) and Coser (1991).

11. Wagner-Pacifici and Schwartz (1991) support this premise.

12. My data were analyzed before the adoption of South Africa's new national flag in 1994.

13. Kriznar (1992:5) also notes that those promoting different political arrangements propose symbols with different information densities. For instance, groups promoting a distinct, cohesive Slovenia propose sparse national symbols. Conversely, groups promoting a Slovene confederation—an autonomous state existing within Yugoslavia—propose symbols with greater density.

14. Data were verified against United Nations statistics.

15. This source references data for the modern era. Sources documenting cultural configuration *during* the years of symbol adoption (i.e., *Statesman's Yearbook;* Banks 1971; or Mitchell 1975, 1982) provided data on only half of the cases in my sample. Because the historical and modern data were so highly correlated (correlations ranged from .94 to .98), I felt comfortable using the modern data, thus maximizing the cases analyzed here.

16. Correlations ranged from .63 to .76.

17. The formula is as follows: .53 (Total Ethnic Groups) + .59 (Total Linguistic Groups) + .53 (Total Religious Groups). These loadings were derived from the first factor which accounted for 63 percent of the variance.

18. These were Banks (1971); *Chronicle of the World* (1989); *Encyclopedia Britannica Macropedia* (1985), vols. 13–28; *Encyclopedia Britannica Micropedia* (1989), vols. 1–12; Mitchell (1975, 1982); and *Statesman's Yearbook.* Multiple sources were used to insure the necessary information on all nations. Correlations for data from the various sources ranged from .89 to .97.

19. In both this model and the model addressing flag design there were statistically significant associations between the variables representing political arrangement and world-systems location. Therefore, I followed a conservative analytic strategy, running models exploring the effects of political arrangement with and without the world-systems variable. In both conditions, however, political arrangement remained statistically significant and increased explained variance.

20. I used multiple sources to insure full information on all nations: Banks (1971); *Chronicle of the World* (1989); *Chronology of World History* (1975); *Encyclopedia Britannica Macropedia* (1985), vols. 13–28; *Encyclopedia Britannica Micropedia* (1989), vols. 1–12; Kurian (1979); Mitchell (1975, 1982); *Statesman's Yearbook, Worldmark Encyclopedia* (1984), and Wright (1965). Data from these sources were highly correlated (r = .89–.97). Also note that a number of nations were randomly selected for more in depth study. The specific sources used in these cases are cited in the text.

21. When I compared the syntax scores for those nations defined as moderate in focus versus nations labeled as mixed in focus (see Appendix A), I found no significant differences. These group means were .222 and .191, respectively. Therefore, I combined the moderate and mixed categories in all analyses.

22. In both this model and the model addressing flag design, there were significant associations between the event focus variables and the variables representing the syntax of a nation's neighbors, a nation's world-system position, and its political arrangements. Again, I followed a conservative strategy, running models with and

without each of the latter three variables. In every case, however, event triggered focus remained statistically significant and increased explained variance.

23. Because a full set of dummy variables cannot be entered into a regression equation simultaneously, I entered only high and low focus in the first model. I obtained the coefficient for moderate focus via a model including only low and moderate focus. The same procedure was followed in the analysis of flags.

24. No significant difference emerged when comparing means for nations with moderate versus mixed focus. (Group means were .240 and .211, respectively.) Therefore, I combined the moderate and mixed categories in all analyses.

25. I borrow the notion of audience "containment" from Hennion and Meadel (1993), who apply the concept in their study of advertising.

26. This argument compliments those of Beisel (1993), Schudson (1989), and others.

6. "Off Key" Strategy Selections

1. B. Slade, *Same Time Next Year* (London: Samuel French, 1975), 8.

2. Beisel (1993), Blau (1993), DeVault (1990), Griswold (1987), Gusfield (1963, 1981, 1992), Lamont (1987), Schudson (1989), and Sewell (1992) make similar arguments regarding the reinterpretation of symbol meanings.

3. Greenfeld (1992) makes a similar point with regard to national identity construction.

4. See, for example, Berger and Luckmann (1967:41–46), Cherry (1961:chaps. 6–7), Garfinkel (1967:40–45), Marcus and Zajonc (1985:145), McHugh (1968), and Schutz and Luckmann (1973:243–47).

5. Many psychologists argue that all contents of the mind are sorted into schema. Schema serve as information processing units, activated by each message we encounter.

6. Based on Schutz and Luckmann (1973:243).

7. These lyrics are quoted directly from Riding (1992:sec. A, p. 1). Any awkwardness in the text (i.e., the use of *Motherland* rather than *Fatherland*) is a function of that translation.

8. During this period, the Central Art Committee was notorious for the rejection of ornamented designs.

9. Information obtained from correspondence between Dr. Smith and Ms. Dolphin, previously cited.

10. The ultimatums concerned Iraq's withdrawal from Kuwait.

11. Uzbekistan housed the U.S.S.R.'s largest non-Slav population. This Soviet republic ranked third in total population, exceeded only by Russia and the Ukraine.

12. Note that I obtained Uzbekistan's flag design well after compiling my sample. Hence, it is not included in the full sample analysis.

13. For examples in this massive literature, see Barthes (1967); Berman et al. (1983); Blumler (1979); DeFleur and Ball-Rokeach (1982); Erber and Fiske (1984); Espe and Siewert (1986); Garfinkel (1967, esp. pp. 42–44); Goffman (1961); Hendrick (1972); Hovland (1959); Katz et al. (1974); Katz and Gurevitch (1976); Loftus (1980); Loftus and Loftus (1980); Marcus and Zajonc (1985); McQuail (1987); Palmgreen and

Rayburn (1985); Rayburn and Palmgreen (1984); Tajfel (1981); Zerubavel (1991); and Zimbardo et al. (1977). These conclusions are also implied by reception theorists and deconstructionists, for example, Fiske (1984), Griswold (1987), Lamont (1987), Long (1986), and Radway (1984).

14. Note that minimal levels of deviance are thought by some to increase communication effectiveness. See, for example, Barthes (1977); Bower, Black, and Turner (1979); Cerulo (1988, 1995); Fiske et al. (1983); Fiske and Taylor (1984); Gabor (1951); Graesser et al. (1980); Hastie and Kumar (1979); Hastie (1981); Johnson and Judd (1983); Judd and Kulik (1980); Marcus and Zajonc (1985); McLuhan (1965:chaps. 1–2); Meyer (1967); and Srull (1981). However, this chapter addresses symbols whose structures represent extreme deviance. Indeed, as defined here, the deviant symbol is congruent with what elsewhere I have called "noise" (Cerulo 1988).

15. Flags are also assessed with regard to the temporal context.

16. Deviance scores of 0 or 1 equal extreme conformity; scores of 4 or 5 equal extreme deviance. Thirty-six anthems and eighteen flags are extreme conformists; fifteen anthems, and thirty-three flags are extreme deviants. These symbols represent eighty-six different nations.

17. For anthems: Cartledge et al. (1978), Griffith (1952), Mead (1980), Nettl (1967), and Reed and Bristow (1985). For flags: Crampton (1990), Devereux (1992), Smith (1975), Talocci (1977), and more than 150 issues of the *Flag Bulletin*, a journal addressing the design, adoption, and usage of flags and other symbols. I also analyzed informational pamphlets on anthems and flags distributed by the nations in question.

18. Eighty-six nations possessed anthems and/or flags with structures located at the extremes of the normal-deviant continuum (see Appendix B). I interviewed 124 individuals from this group of nations regarding the popular reception of their national anthems and flags. The majority of subjects (99) were cultural attachés and information officers serving at foreign embassies in Washington, D.C. (generally, I interviewed 1 to 2 individuals per embassy). To supplement this group of individuals, I generated a snowball sample of 25 subjects, initiated via graduate and undergraduate exchange students at my university, and extending to foreign visiting scholars, scholars with extensive travel in the pertinent nations, and recent immigrants contacted through community groups. Interviews were open-ended and ranged from twenty-five to fifty-two minutes in length. The sample was not randomly drawn, thus I view the research as exploratory and treat the data as supplemental to the historical data.

19. Note that these categories emerged from the data.

20. The Swedish folk song "Ur Svenska hjertans djup en gang" is translated "From deep in Sweden's heart" (music by Otto Jonas Lindblad; lyrics by Carl Wilhelm August Strandberg); and "Sverige, Sverige, fosterland" is a poem by Werner von Heidenstam, set to music by Wilhelm Stenhammar.

21. Although casual talk of changing the Australian national flag has transpired for nearly forty years.

22. This excerpt, and all letters and reports on this topic, are quoted from Burton (1991).

23. An Australian official speculated that it would take a major change in the identity of the nation—such as the move to a Republic slated for the year 2000—to actually effect a change in the flag.

24. Note that in one area, the commercial use of symbols, the strict dichotomy between the sacred and secular was maintained. Nearly 95 percent of those interviewed would not tolerate the linking of symbols with selling. Indeed, many respondents actually gasped when I posed questions regarding the commercial use of their anthem or flag. (Those discussing the American flag or the Union Jack proved the only exceptions to this rule.) These responses suggest strict boundaries regarding the extent to which symbols can be secularized.

25. In extreme cases, such laws may actually *make* a symbol sacred as opposed to reinforcing its sacredness. Forced worship of totalitarian dictators illustrates this point.

26. Beniger (1986) too maps ways in which certain social settings can generate a need for control.

27. Kuhn (1970) refers to innovation as "revolutionary science."

28. See, for example, Barthes (1977); Bower, Black, and Turner (1979); Cerulo (1988a, 1988b, 1989b, 1995); Fiske et al. (1983); Fiske and Taylor (1984); Gabor (1951); Graesser et al. (1980); Hastie and Kumar (1979); Hastie (1981); Johnson and Judd (1983); Judd and Kulik (1980); McLuhan (1965:chaps. 1–2); Meyer (1967:chaps. 1–2); and Srull (1981).

29. See, for example, Bonnange (1987), Cerulo (1988, 1995), Colley (1961), Dominick (1983:21), Festinger (1957), Greene (1984), Guiraud (1975:14), Haas (1984), Hewes and Planalp (1987:162–63), McGuire (1978), and Moray (1969).

30. Indeed, it is critical to better specify the links that tie certain social conditions to the adoption of deviant expression, and certain audience reactions to the use of deviant expression. Once doing so, we may find that reactions to and regulations of deviant symbols are actions truly targeted at the motivators of deviant expression— that is, factionalism, disruption, etc.

7. Changing Voice

1. I refer to drastic change; minor amendments (e.g., adding stars to the American flag) are not discussed here.

2. I use the terms *symbol* and *referent*, where Saussure and other semioticians adopt *signifier* (or *sign*) and *signified*.

3. Durkheim (1915) also implied this in discussing totems.

4. This includes fantasies, that is, things that we wish had happened or those that we hope will happen.

5. Also see Schutz (1982:33–48) on duration and space-time.

6. This contrast recalls Goffman's distinctions between "dominant involvements" and "subordinate involvements" (1963:44), or Gestalt notions of *figure* and *ground*.

7. Peirce specifies three types of signifier: icon, index, and symbol. Icons actually depict that which they represent; they are direct reflections of their referents. Indexes emerge from that which they represent; they directly suggest their referents. Symbols are abstract and unconnected to their referents; they are neutral objects endowed with meaning.

8. For more detail, see Cerulo (1996); there dangling signifiers are explored with particular attention to changes in the human body and the way in which those changes are perceived.

9. Thanks to an anonymous operator at the Thomson Electronics hot line for sharing this history. Thomson Electronics now owns RCA and has reinstated "Little Nipper" and added a puppy, "Chipper," to the logo as well.

10. Note that concrete national symbols do exist, and often retain their charged character. Indeed, concrete anthems and flags have been cited throughout this book. In some instances, concrete symbols are the product of relatively new nations. As such, their adaptability has not been tested since their referents have yet to undergo significant change.

11. Under certain conditions, a national symbol can become a dangling signifier. Consider the flag of the former Soviet Union. While the flag's referent no longer exists, this symbol lives on. One can spot it sporadically throughout the countries that constitute the new Commonwealth of Nations. Within the spatial plane, the flag can generate memory and emotion among those who recall its referent. In essence, this symbol has taken on an independent empirical life, a life electrified only by temporal energy. The same can be said of the Confederate flag or the anthem of the American South, "Dixie." Both the Confederate flag and "Dixie" retain their ability to stir anger, sadness, and fear. Recall the 1991 scandal created by suspicions that Judge Clarence Thomas, then the Supreme Court nominee, was displaying a Confederate flag in his office.

12. This argument is compatible with those who promote the interaction of social structure and cultural schema in the construction of identity; see, for example, Beisel (1993).

13. The original flag of Vietnam illustrates the rigidity of concrete symbols. During the autonomy negotiations of 1948, the French attempted to redefine the flag's three red stripes, claiming that they represented the main regions of South Vietnam: Tonkin, Annam, and Cochin-China (Smith 1975:297). However, as a hieroglyph, the stripes' meaning could not be manipulated. This inflexibility deemed change inevitable.

14. Haiti's original flag, a blue and red horizontal bicolor, was chosen.

15. Also note that 69 percent of all changing anthems and 50 percent of all changing flags increase in structural normalcy. Only one symbol's structure increased in deviance.

8. Final Notes on Identity Designs

1. For more on this issue, see Cerulo (1994).
2. Cerulo (1995c) addresses the stratification of smells.

Appendix 1. Measurement Information

1. The notes have additive value.

2. Some have suggested alternate formulas for measuring melodic frequency and magnitude. These proposals are discussed and critiqued in Cerulo (1988b, 1989b, 1992).

3. Four musical half-steps equals a major third interval. In general, any interval larger than this is considered disjunct, and thus, capable of disrupting a conjunct melody pattern. Therefore, when melodies are moving in a single direction, $Q = 4.0$; in essence, $Q = $ a major third interval. However, when a melody shifts direction, a smaller interval will be disruptive to listeners. Therefore, I assigned a value of $Q = 3.0$ to the "opposite direction" condition. For more details, see Apel (1974) and Westergaard (1975).

4. Recall, we are dealing with vocal/instrumental music in this research. Slight amendments to the formula are necessary for nonvocal music.

5. In pieces with heavy ornamentation (i.e., one instance per measure or more), ornaments may become the norm, and hence, less startling. Using the square root of r avoids overemphasizing the ornamentation in such pieces. Also note: if $r = 0$, r is dropped from the equation, and calculations are based on N/v.

6. This error could occur if a single ornamentation bore several notes.

7. The behavior of these measures with reference to other musical genres such as symphonies, songs, opera, etc., is, an empirical question for future research.

8. The first factor accounted for 51 percent of the total variance.

9. For these data, Pearson correlations ranged from .01 to .50. Note that the measure for orchestration is not used in this analysis because the anthems were recorded as piano reduction scores.

10. The weights were derived from the first factor of the individual summary measures of syntax; that factor accounts for 41 percent of the variance, Cronbach alpha = .71.

11. Some have suggested that these measures might be better constructed using structural equation models. However, such an approach is not well suited to these data. Consider, for example, the number of variables one would need to include in a model addressing music's overall syntactic structure. In light of my small sample, degrees of freedom issues are simply too serious to make this method viable for my data.

12. The Munsell system is the most frequently used color classification system in the world.

13. Technically, white is defined as the absence of color. In graphic symbols, however, white is perceived as a separate color unit. Therefore, in this study, I treat white as a distinct hue. Because white exists "naturally" and does not result from color combinations, I treat it as a primary color. Black, the combination of all colors, is designated as a secondary color.

14. Of course, the behavior of these measures with reference to other graphic symbols remains an empirical question. This will be true for the measures of graphic stability and distortion as well.

15. All graphic measures were normalized via log transformations before correlations and scale building took place.

16. The weights for this formula were derived from the first factor of the individual measures of density; the factor accounts for 54 percent of the variance. Again, the factors could vary with other samples of graphic symbols.

17. White and black are not included in Munsell's color wheel. Thus in this study, I equated white with the lightest color on the traditional color wheel and black with the darkest color on the wheel.

18. The weights are derived from the first factor of the individual measures of stability; that factor accounts for 67 percent of the variance.

19. Although these variables are not highly correlated, the text illustrates theoretical reason to combine them.

20. The weights are derived from the first factor of the individual measures of distortion; that factor accounts for 53 percent of the variance.

21. These weights are derived from the first factor, which accounts for 63 percent of the variance, Cronbach alpha = .70.

22. Measuring syntactic structure with reference to .25 standard deviations means that 80 percent of all anthems are treated as conformists while 20 percent are defined as truly deviant. Note that when classifying flags, the same criteria are used.

23. Again, choosing this particular cutoff point ensures that only those cases falling at the extremes of the distribution (i.e., 20 percent of all cases) are defined as deviant.

24. When coding flags, deviance is calculated with reference to the interaction between neighboring nations and temporal counterparts.

BIBLIOGRAPHY

Agresti, A., and B. Finlay. 1986. *Statistical Methods for the Social Sciences.* 2d ed. San Francisco: Dellen.

Agulhon, M. 1981. *Marianne into Battle: Republican Imagery and Symbolism in France, 1789–1880.* Cambridge: Cambridge University Press.

Ang, I. 1985. *Watching Dallas: Soap Opera and the Melodramatic Imagination.* New York: Methuen.

Allanbrooke, L. 1959. "The Diary of Lord Allanbrooke." In *Triumph in the West,* edited by A. Bryant, 13–414. New York: Doubleday.

Allport, G. 1961. *Pattern and Growth in Personality.* New York: Holt, Rinehart, and Winston.

Anderson, B. 1983. *Imagined Communities.* London: Verso.

Apel, W. 1974. *Harvard Dictionary of Music.* 2d ed. Cambridge: Belknap Press, Harvard University Press.

Balibar, E. 1988. "The Nation Form: History and Ideology." In *Race, Nation, and Class,* edited by E. Balibar and I. Wallerstein, 86–106. London: Verso.

Banks, A. 1971. *Cross-Polity Time-Series Data.* Boston: MIT Press.

Barey, G. 1965. *Communication and Language: Networks of Thought and Action.* Garden City, N.Y.: Doubleday.

Barraclough, E. 1969. *Flags of the World.* London: Frederich Warke.

Barthes, R. 1967. *Elements of Semiology.* New York: Hill and Wang.

———. 1977. *Image-Music-Text.* Translated by S. Heath. Glasgow: Fontana Collins.

———. 1985. *The Responsibility of Forms.* New York: Hill and Wang.

Baumgartner, M. 1984. "Social Control From Below." In *Toward a General Theory of Social Control,* edited by D. Black, vol. 1, pp. 303–45. New York: Academic Press.

Becker, E. 1973. *Denial of Death.* New York: Free Press.

Becker, H. 1963. *The Outsiders.* New York: Free Press.

Beniger, J. 1986. *The Control Revolution.* Cambridge: Harvard University Press.

———. 1987. "Personalization of Mass Media and the Growth of Pseudo-Community." *Communication Research* 14 (33): 352–71.

Benward, B., and B. G. Jackson. 1975. *Practical Beginning Theory.* 3d ed. Dubuque: W. C. Brown.

Berger, C. R. 1979. "Beyond Initial Interaction: Uncertainty, Understanding, and the

Development of Interpersonal Relationships." In *Recent Advances in Language and Social Psychology*, edited by H. Giles and R. N. St. Clair. Baltimore: University Park Press.

Berger, J. 1972. *Ways of Seeing*. New York: Viking.

Berger, P., and T. Luckmann. 1967. *The Social Construction of Reality*. New York, N.Y.: Anchor Press.

Bergesen, A. 1979. "Spirituals, Jazz, Blues, and Folk Music." In *The Religious Dimension*, edited by R. Wuthnow, 333–50. New York: Academic Press.

———. 1984. "The Semantic Equation: A Theory of the Social Origins of Art Styles." In *Sociological Theory*, edited by R. Collins, 222–37. San Francisco: Jossey Bass.

———. 1987. "The Decline of American Art." In *America's Changing Role in the World System*, edited by T. Boswell and A. Bergesen, 221–34. New York: Praeger.

Bergesen, A., and Jones, A. 1992. "Decoding the Syntax of Modern Dance." In *Vocabularies of Public Life*, edited by R. Wuthnow, 169–84. London: Routledge.

Berman, J. S., S. J. Read, and D. A. Kenny. 1983. "Processing Inconsistent Social Information." *Journal of Personality and Social Psychology* 45:1211–24.

Bernstein, B. 1975. *Class, Codes, and Control*. Vols. 1–3. London: Routledge and Kegan Paul.

Biesanz, R. 1982. *The Costa Ricans*. Englewood Cliffs, N.J.: Prentice-Hall.

Beisel, N. 1993. "Morals Versus Art: Censorship, the Politics of Interpretation, and the Victorian Nude." *American Sociological Review* 58 (2): 145–62.

Biocca, F. 1991. "Viewers' Mental Models of Political Messages: Toward a Theory of Semantic Processing of Television." In *Television and Political Advertising*, edited by F. Biocca, vol. 1, pp. 27–90. Hillsdale: Erlbaum.

Black, C. E. 1966. *The Dynamics of Modernization: A Study in Comparative History*. New York: Harper and Row.

Blau, J. 1980. "A Framework of Meaning in Architecture." In *Signs, Symbols, and Architecture*, edited by G. Broadbent, R. Bunt, and C. Jencks, 333–68. Chichester, England: John Wiley and Sons.

———. 1993. "What Buildings Mean and Architects Say: Economy and Theory of Architecture at a Moment of Crisis." *Current Research on Occupations and Professions* 8:77–99.

Blumler, J. G. 1979. "The Role of Theory in Uses and Gratification Studies." *Communication Research* 6:9–36.

Bogart, L. 1973. "Consumer and Advertising Research." In *Handbook of Communication*, edited by I. Pool, W. Schramm, F. Frey, and W. Maccoby, 706–21. Chicago: Rand McNally.

Boli-Bennett, J. 1979. "The Ideology of Expanding State Authority in National Constitutions, 1870–1970." In *National Development and the World System*, edited by J. Meyer and M. Hannan, 222–37. Chicago: University of Chicago Press.

Bollen, K. 1983. "World-System Position, Dependency, and Democracy: The Cross National Evidence." *American Sociological Review* 48 (4): 468–79.

Bonnange, C., and T. Chantal. 1987. *Don Juan ou Pavlov: Essai sur la Communication Publicitaire*. Paris: Seuil.

Bower, G. H., J. B. Black, and T. J. Turner. 1979. "Scripts in Memory for Text." *Cognitive Psychology* 11:177–220.

Bradac, J. J., and A. Mulac. 1984. "Attributional Consequences of Powerful and Powerless Speech Styles in a Crisis Intervention Context." *Journal of Language and Social Psychology* 3:1–19.

Brinkley, D. 1988. *Washington Goes to War*. New York: Alfred A. Knopf.

Broadbent, G. 1973. *Design in Architecture*. London: Wiley.

Brooks, D. H. 1926. *Our Flag*. New York: Harold Vinal.

Bruner, J. S. 1956. *A Study of Thinking*. New York: John Wiley.

Burk, A., and G. Maier. 1973. *Historical Dictionary of Ecuador*. Metuchen, N.J.: Scarecrow.

Burt, R. 1987. "Social Contagion and Innovation: Cohesion versus Structural Equivalence." *American Journal of Sociology* 92:1287–1335.

Burton, A. C. 1991. "Ausflag Mark 3." *Crux Australis* 7 (29): 17–25.

Calhoun, C. 1991. "Indirect Relationships and Imagined Communities: Large-Scale Social Integration and the Transformation of Everyday Life." In *Social Theory for a Changing Society*, edited by P. Bourdieu and J. S. Coleman, 95–120. Boulder, Colo.: Westview.

———. 1993. "Nationalism and Ethnicity." *Annual Review of Sociology* 19:211–239.

The Cambridge History of the British Empire. 1963. Vol. 8. 2d ed. Cambridge: Cambridge University Press.

The Cambridge History of Poland. 1971. Vols. 1 and 2. Edited by W. F. Reddaway et al. New York: Octagon.

Capella, J. 1987. "Interpersonal Communication: Definitions and Fundamental Questions." In *Handbook of Communication Science*, edited by C. Berger and S. Chaffee, 184–238. Newbury Park, Calif.: Sage.

Cartledge, T., W. L. Reed, M. Shaw, and H. Coleman. 1978. *National Anthems of the World*. New York: Arco.

Cassirer, E. 1955. *The Philosophy of Symbolic Forms*. Vol 2. Translated by R. Manheim. New Haven, Conn.: Yale University Press.

Cassirer, H. R. 1968. "Audience Participation, New Style." *American Sociological Review* 33:529–36.

Cerulo, K. 1984. "Social Disruption and Its Effects on Music: An Empirical Analysis." *Social Forces* 62 (4): 885–904.

———. 1988a. "What's Wrong with This Picture?" *Communication Research* 15 (1): 93–101.

———. 1988b. "Analyzing Cultural Products: A New Method of Measurement." *Social Science Research* 17:317–52.

———. 1989a. "Socio-Political Control and the Structure of National Symbols." *Social Forces* 68 (1): 76–99.

———. 1989b. "Variations in Musical Syntax: Patterns of Usage and Methods of Measurement." *Communication Research* 16 (2): 45–88.

———. 1990. "To Err Is Social: Network Prominence and Its Effects on Self-Estimation." *Sociological Forum* 5 (4): 619–34.

———. 1992. "Putting It Together: Measuring the Syntax of Aural and Visual Symbols." In *Vocabularies of Public Life*, edited by R. Wuthnow, 111–29. London: Routledge.

———. 1993. "Symbols and the World System: National Anthems and Flags." *Sociological Forum* 8 (2): 243–72.

———. 1994. "Re-Orchestrating the Sociology of Music." *Culture* 9 (winter): 1, 5–8.

———. 1995. "Designs on the White House: TV Ads, Message Structure, and Election Outcome." *Research in Political Sociology* 7:63–88.

———. 1995b. "Out of Site, Out of Mind: The Body as Channel to Place and Self." Unpublished manuscript.

———. 1995c. "The Sweet Smell of Success: Mapping the Socioeconomic Code of Smells." Unpublished manuscript.

Cerulo, K., J. Ruane, and M. Chayko. 1992. "Technological Ties That Bind: Media Generated Primary Groups." *Communication Research* 19 (1): 109–29.

Cerulo, K., and J. Ruane. 1996. "Death Comes Alive: Technology and the Reconception of Death." *Science as Culture*. vol. 25.

Cherry, C. 1961. *On Human Communication*. New York: Science Editions.

Chirot, D. 1977. *Social Change in the Twentieth Century*. New York: Harcourt Brace Jovanovich.

Chronicle of the World. 1989. Edited by J. Burne. Mount Kisco, N.Y.: Ecam.

Chronology of World History. 1975. Edited by G. S. P. Freeman-Greenville. London: Rex Collings.

Cicourel, A. 1976. *The Social Organization of Juvenile Justice*. London: Heinemann.

Codrescu, A. 1991. *The Hole in the Flag*. New York: William Morrow.

Cohen, Y. A. 1969. "Social Boundary Systems." *Current Anthropology* 10:103–17.

Coleman, J., E. Katz, and H. Menzel. 1966. *Medical Innovation*. New York: Bobbs-Merrill.

Colley, R. H. 1961. *Defining Advertising Goals for Measured Advertising Results*. New York: Association of National Advertisers.

Collins, D. 1986. *U.S. News and World Report* 100 (May 19): 82–83.

Collins, R. 1988. *Durkheimian Sociology: Cultural Studies*. Cambridge: Cambridge University Press.

Congressional Record. 1930. 72d Cong., 2d sess. Washington, D.C.

Congressional Record. 1931. 73d Cong., 1st sess. Washington, D.C.

Constitutions of African States. 1972. Asian African Legal Consultante Committee. New York: Oceania.

Cooley, C. H. [1909] 1962. *Social Organization*. New York: Schocken.

———. [1902] 1964. *Human Nature and Social Order*. New York: Schocken.

Corner, J. 1986. "Codes and Cultural Analysis." In *Media, Culture, and Society*, edited by R. Collins, J. Curran, N. Garnham, P. Scannell, P. Schlesinger, and C. Sparks, 49–62. London: Sage.

Countries of the World and Their Leaders Yearbook. 1984. New York: Gale Research.

Coser, L. 1956. *The Functions of Social Conflict*. Glencoe, N.Y.: Free Press.

Coser, R. 1991. *In Defense of Modernity*. Stanford, Calif.: Stanford University Press.

Cowen, W., M. Stone, and C. Ware. 1987. *Colour Perception*. Toronto: National Research Council of Canada.

Crampton, W. G. 1985. *Webster's Concise Encyclopedia of Flags and Coats of Arms*. New York: Crescent Books.

———. 1990. *Flags of the World*. New York: Dorsett.

Curti, M. 1946. *The Roots of American Loyalty*. New York: Columbia University Press.

Dahlhaus, C. 1980a. "Harmony." In *The New Grove Dictionary of Music and Musicians,* edited by S. Sadie, vol. 8, pp. 175–88. Macmillan: London.

———. 1980b. "Tonality." In *The New Grove Dictionary of Music and Musicians,* edited by S. Sadie, vol. 19, pp. 51–55. Macmillan: London.

Dallin, L. 1977. *Listener's Guide to Musical Understanding.* 4th ed. Dubuque, Iowa: William C. Brown.

DeFleur, M., and S. Ball-Rokeach. 1982. *Theories of Mass Communication.* 4th ed. New York: Longman.

Delaporte, Yves. 1979. "Communication et Signification dans les Costumes Populaires." *Semiotica* 26 (1/2): 65–79.

Derrida, J. [1967] 1980. *Writing and Difference.* Chicago: University of Chicago Press.

———. [1972] 1981. *Positions.* Chicago: University of Chicago Press.

Deutsch, K. 1953. *Nationalism and Social Communication.* Cambridge: MIT Press.

Deutsch, K., S. Barrell, R. Kann, M. Lee, M. Lichterman, R. Lindgrem, F. Loewenheim, and R. Van Wagenen. 1957. *Political Community and the North Atlantic Area.* Princeton, N.J.: Princeton University Press.

DeVault, M. 1990. "Novel Readings: The Social Organization of Interpretation." *American Journal of Sociology* 95:887–921.

Devereux, E. 1992. *Flags of the World.* New York: Crescent.

Dominick, J. J. 1983. *The Dynamics of Mass Communication.* 3d ed. Boston: Houghton Mifflin.

Douglas, M. 1970. *Natural Symbols.* New York: Pantheon.

———. 1975. *Implicit Meanings.* Boston: Routledge and Kegan Paul.

Dubin, S. 1987. "Symbolic Slavery: Black Representations in Popular Culture." *Social Problems* 34 (2): 122–40.

Duncan, S., Jr. 1972. "Some Signals and Rules for Taking Speaking Turns in Conversation." *Journal of Personality and Social Psychology* 18 (3): 392–402.

Durkheim, E. 1915. *The Elementary Forms of Religious Life.* Translated by J. W. Swain. New York: Free Press.

———. 1933. *The Division of Labor in Society.* New York: Free Press.

Eco, U. 1976. *Theory of Semiotics.* Bloomington: University of Indiana Press.

———. 1985. "How Culture Conditions the Colors We See." In *On Signs,* edited by M. Blonsky, 157–75. Baltimore: Johns Hopkins Press.

Eder, D., and J. L. Enke. 1991. "The Structure of Gossip: Opportunities and Constraints." *American Sociological Review* 56 (4): 494–508.

Eidinger, J. A., and M. L. Patterson. 1983. "Nonverbal Involvement and Social Control." *Psychological Bulletin* 93:30–56.

Elkin, F., and G. Handel. 1984. *The Child in Society: The Process of Socialization.* 4th ed. New York: Random House.

Ellis, W. D. 1950. *The Sourcebook of Gestalt Psychology.* New York: Humanities Press.

Elting, M., and F. Folsom. 1968. *The Flags of All Nations.* New York: Grosset and Dunlap.

Encyclopedia Britannica Macropedia. 1985. Vols. 13–29. Edited by P. Goetz. Chicago: University of Chicago Press.

Encyclopedia Britannica Micropedia. 1985. Vols. 1–12. Edited by P. Goetz. Chicago: University of Chicago Press.

Erber, R., and S. T. Fiske. 1984. "Outcome Dependency and Attention to Inconsistent Information." *Journal of Personality and Social Psychology* 47:709–26.

Erikson, E. [1950] 1963. *Childhood and Society.* New York: W. W. Norton.

———. 1968. *Identity, Youth, and Crisis.* New York: W. W. Norton.

Espe, H., and M. Siewert. 1986. "European Television Viewer Types; A Six Nation Classification by Programme Interests." *European Journal of Communication* 1 (3): 301–25.

Festinger, L. 1957. *A Theory of Cognitive Dissonance.* New York: Harper and Row.

Firth, R. 1973. *Symbols: Public and Private.* London: Allen and Unwin.

Fisher, J. L. 1961. "Art Styles as Cultural Cognitive Maps." *American Anthropologist* 63:79–93.

Fiske, J. 1984. "Popularity and Ideology: A Structural Reading of Dr. Who." In *Interpreting Television: Current Research Perspectives,* edited by W. D. Rowlands and B. Watkins, 165–98. Beverly Hills, Calif.: Sage.

Fiske, S. T., and S. E. Taylor. 1984. *Social Cognition.* Reading, Mass.: Addison-Wesley.

Fiske, S. T., D. R. Kinder, and W. M. Larter. 1983. "The Novice and the Experiment: Knowledge-Based Strategies in Political Cognition." *Journal of Experimental Social Psychology* 19:381–400.

Fitch, J. 1977. *Military Coup d'Etat as a Political Process: Ecuador 1948–1966.* Baltimore: John Hopkins University Press.

Forte, A. 1979. *Tonal Harmony in Concept and Practice.* 3d. ed. New York: Holt, Rinehart, and Winston.

Frank, A. 1969. *Capitalism and Underdevelopment in Latin America.* New York: Monthly Press Review.

Gabor, D. 1951. *Lectures on Communication Theory.* Cambridge: MIT Press.

Gaertner, J. 1955. "Art as a Function of an Audience." *Daedalus* 86:80–93.

Garbus, M. 1989. "The 'Crime' of Flag Burning." *Nation* 248:369–70.

Garfinkel, H. 1967. *Studies in Ethnomethnodology.* Englewood Cliffs, N.J.: Prentice-Hall.

Garraty, J., and P. Gay, eds. 1981. *The Columbia History of the World.* New York: Harper and Row.

Gellner, E. 1983. *Nations and Nationalism.* Ithaca, N.Y.: Cornell University Press.

Giddens, A. 1985. *The Nation-State and Violence.* Berkeley and Los Angeles: University of California Press.

Giles, H., and J. M. Wiemann. 1987. "Language, Social Comparison, and Power." In *Handbook of Communication Science,* edited by C. Berger and S. Chaffee, 350–84. Newbury Park, Calif.: Sage.

Givens, D. 1983. *Love Signals: How to Attract a Mate.* New York: Crown.

Goffman, E. 1959. *The Presentation of Self in Everyday Life.* Garden City, N.Y.: Anchor Press.

———. 1961. *Encounters.* Indianapolis: Bobbs-Merrill.

———. 1963. *Behavior in Public Places.* New York: Free Press.

———. 1981. *Forms of Talk.* Philadelphia: University of Pennsylvania Press.

Goldwasser, T. 1986. *Family Pride.* New York: Dodd, Mead.

Goldwater, R. 1953. *Van Gogh.* New York: Pocket Books.

Gombrich, E. H. 1960. *Art and Illusion: A Study in the Psychology of Pictorial Representation.* New York: Phaidon.

————. 1981. "Image and Code: Scope and Limits of Convention in Pictorial Representation." In *Image and Code,* edited by W. Steiner, 1–36. Ann Arbor: University of Michigan Press.

Gordon, W. J. 1915. *Flags of the World: Past and Present.* London: Frederick Warne.

Gottdiener, M. 1985. Hegemony and Mass Culture: A Semiotic Approach. *American Journal of Sociology* 90 (5): 979–1001.

Graesser, A. C., S. B. Woll, D. J. Kowalski, and D. A. Smith. 1980. "Memory for Typical and Atypical Actions in Scripted Activities." *Journal of Experimental Psychology* 6 (5): 503–15.

Greene, J. O. 1984. "A Cognitive Approach to Human Communication: An Action Assembly Theory." *Communication Monographs* 51:289–306.

Greene, J. P. 1993. *The Intellectual Construction of America: Exceptionalism and Identity from 1492 to 1800.* Chapel Hill: University of North Carolina Press.

Greenfeld, L. 1992. *Nationalism: Five Roads to Modernity.* Cambridge: Harvard University Press.

Gregory, R. W. 1975. *Anniversaries and Holidays.* 3d ed. Chicago: American Library Association.

Griffith, B. 1952. *National Anthems and How They Came to Be Written.* Boston: Christopher.

Griswold, W. 1987. "The Fabrication of Meaning: Literary Interpretation in the United States, Great Britain, and the West Indies." *American Journal of Sociology* 92 (5): 1077–1117.

Guiraud, P. 1975. *Semiology.* Translated by G. Gross. London: Routledge and Kegan Paul.

Gusfield, J. 1963. *Symbolic Crusade: Status Politics and the American Temperance Movement.* Urbana: University of Illinois Press.

————. 1981. *The Culture of Public Problems: Drinking, Driving, and the Symbolic Order.* Chicago: University of Chicago Press.

————. 1992. "Nature's Body and the Metaphors of Food." In *Cultivating Differences,* ed. M. Lamont and M. Fournier, 75–103. Chicago: University of Chicago Press.

Gwendolen, M. 1977. *The Politics of Inequality: South Africa Since 1948.* London: Thames and Hudson.

Haas, Cr. 1984. *Pratique de la Publicité* Paris: Dunod.

Hall, E. 1966. *The Hidden Dimension.* New York: Doubleday.

Hammond, P. E., and K. R. Williams. 1979. "Moral Climates of Nations: Measurement and Classification." In *The Religious Dimension,* edited by R. Wuthnow, 311–32. New York: Academic Press.

Hastie, R. 1981. "Schematic Principles in Human Memory." In *Social Cognition: The Ontario Symposium,* vol. 1, edited by E. T. Higgins, C. P. Herman, and M. P. Zanna, 155–77. Hillside: Erlbaum.

Hastie, R., and P. Kumar. 1979. "Person Memory: Personality Traits as Organizing Principles in Memory for Behavior." *Journal of Personality and Social Psychology* 37:25–38.

Hearings of the Committee on Military Affairs of the United States Senate. 1937. 76th Cong., 1st sess. S. 947. Washington, D.C.

Helman, J. A. 1978. *Mexico in Crisis.* New York: Academic Press.

Hendrick, C. 1972. "Effects of Saliency and Inconsistency on Impression Formation." *Journal of Personality and Social Psychology* 22:219–22.

Hennion, A., and C. Meadel. 1993. "The Artisans of Desire: The Mediators of Advertising between Product and Consumer." *Sociological Theory* 11 (1): 191–209.

Henrotte, G. 1985. "Music and Linguistics: The Semiotic Connection." In *Semiotics*, edited by J. Deely, 659–70. New York: Lanham.

Hervey, S. 1982. *Semiotic Perspectives.* Boston: Allen and Unwin.

Hewes, D. E., and S. Planalp. 1987. "The Individual's Place in Communication Science." In *Handbook of Communication Science*, edited by C. Berger and S. Chafee, 146–83. Newbury Park, Calif.: Sage.

Hirschi, T. 1969. *Causes of Delinquency.* Berkeley and Los Angeles: University of California Press.

Hodge, D., and R. Gandy. 1979. *Mexico, 1910–1976: Reform or Revolution.* New York: Oxford University Press.

Hodge, R., and G. Kress. 1988. *Social Semiotics.* Ithaca, N.Y.: Cornell University Press.

Holt, E. 1970. *Risorgimento.* London: Macmillan.

Hovland, C. I., I. L. Janis, and H. H. Kelley. 1953. *Communication and Persuasion.* New Haven, Conn.: Yale University Press.

Hovland, C. 1959. "Reconciling Conflicting Results Derived from Experimental and Survey Study of Attitude Change." *American Psychiatrist* 14:8–7.

Hunt, S. A., R. D. Benford, and D. A. Snow. 1994. "Identity Fields: Framing Processes and the Social Construction of Movement Identities." In *New Social Movements: From Ideology to Identity*, ed. E. Larana, H. Johnston, and J. R. Gusfield, 185–208. Philadelphia: Temple University Press.

Isaacs, H. 1975. *Idols of the Tribe.* Cambridge: Harvard University Press.

Iser, W. 1978. *The Act of Reading: A Theory of Aesthetic Response.* Baltimore: Johns Hopkins University Press.

Jakobson, R. 1968. *Child Language, Aphasia and Phonological Universals.* The Hague: Mouton.

Jakobson, R., and L. Waugh. 1979. *The Sound Shape of Language.* Brighton, England: Harvester Press.

Janson, H. W., and J. Kerman. 1968. *A History of Art and Music.* Englewood Cliffs, N.J.: Prentice-Hall.

Jencks, C. 1973. *Modern Movements in Architecture.* Garden City, N.Y.: Anchor Press.

Johnson, S. C. 1967. "Hierarchical Clustering Systems." *Psychometrika* 32:241–54.

Johnson, J. T., and C. M. Judd. 1983. "Overlooking the Incongruent and Categorization Biases in the Identification of Political Statements." *Journal of Personality and Social Psychology* 45 (5): 978–96.

Jowett, G. S., and V. O'Donnell. 1986. *Propaganda and Persuasion.* Newbury Park, Calif.: Sage.

Judd, C. M., and J. A. Kulick. 1980. "Schematic Effects of Social Attitudes in Information Processing and Recall." *Journal of Personality and Social Psychology* 38 (4): 569–78.

Kaiser, R. G. 1976. *Russia: The People and the Power.* New York: Pocket.

Kant, I. 1929. *Kant Selections.* Edited by T. M. Greene. New York: Scribner.

Katz, E., J. G. Blumler, and M. Gurevitch. 1974. "Utilization of Mass Communication by the Individual." In *The Uses of Mass Communication,* edited by J. G. Blumler and E. Katz, 19–32. London: Faber.

Katz, E., and M. Gurevitch. 1976. *The Secularization of Leisure: Culture and Communication in Israel.* Cambridge: Harvard University Press.

Katz, R. 1986. *Divining the Powers of Music.* New York: Pendragon Press.

Kecskemeti, P. 1973. "Propaganda." In *Handbook of Communication,* edited by I. Pool, W. Schramm, F. Frey, and W. Maccoby, 844–70. Chicago: Rand McNally.

Kennedy, P. 1987. *The Rise and Fall of the Great Powers.* New York: Vintage.

Kerman, J., and V. Kerman. 1970. *Listen.* 3d ed. New York: Worth.

Knapp, M. L., M. J. Cody, and K. K. Reardon. 1987. "Nonverbal Signals." In *Handbook of Communication Science,* edited by C. Berger and S. Chafee, 385–418. Newbury Park, Calif.: Sage.

Koffka, K. 1935. *Principles of Gestalt Psychology.* New York: Harcourt, Brace.

Kohler, W. 1947. *Gestalt Psychology.* New York: Liverright.

Kollack, P., P. Blumstein, and P. Schwartz. 1985. "Sex and Power in Interaction: Conversational Privileges and Duties." *American Sociological Review* 50:34–46.

Kriznar, N. 1992. "Visual Symbols of National Identity." Paper presented at the Annual Conference of Visual Sociology, Amsterdam.

Kuhn, T. 1970. *The Structure of Scientific Revolutions.* Chicago: University of Chicago Press.

Kumon, S. 1987. "The Theory of Long Cycles." In *Exploring Long Cycles,* edited by G. Modelski, 56–84. Boulder, Colo.: Lynne Rienner.

Kurian, G. T. 1979. *The Book of World Ratings.* New York: Facts on File.

Kurzweil, E. 1980. *The Age of Structuralism: Lévi-Strauss to Foucault.* New York: Columbia University Press.

Labov, W. 1966. *The Social Stratification of English in New York City.* Washington, D.C.: Center for Applied Linguistics.

Lamont, M. 1987. "How to Become a Dominant French Philosopher: The Case of Jaques Derrida." *American Journal of Sociology* 93 (3): 584–622.

Lane, C. 1981. *The Rites of Rulers.* Cambridge: Cambridge University Press.

Lang, A. 1990. "Involuntary Attention and Physiological Arousal Evoked by Structural Features and Emotion Content in TV Commercials." *Communication Research* 17 (3): 275–99.

Langer, E. 1978. "Rethinking the Role of Thought in Social Interaction." In *New Directions in Attribution Research,* edited by J. Harvey, W. Ickes, and R. Kidd, 35–58. Hillsdale: Erlbaum.

Laqueur, W. 1985. *Germany Today.* London: Weidenfeld and Nicolson.

Latner, J. 1973. *The Gestalt Therapy Book.* New York: Bantam.

Lauderdale, P. 1976. "Deviance and Moral Bounderies." *American Sociological Review* 41 (4): 660–76.

Leach, E. 1976. *Culture and Communication.* Cambridge: Cambridge University Press.

Ledrut, R. 1973. *Les Images de la Ville.* Paris: Editions Anthropos.

Leffler, A., D. L. Gillespie, and J. C. Conaty. 1982. "The Effects of Status Differentiation on Non-verbal Behavior." *Social Psychology Quarterly* 45:153–61.

Lemert, E. 1953. "An Isolation and Closure Theory of Naive Check Forgery." *Journal of Criminal Law, Criminology, and Police Science* 44:296–307.

Leukel, F. 1972. *Physiological Psychology.* St. Louis: C. V. Mosby.

Lévi-Strauss, C. 1963. *Structural Anthropology.* Translated by C. Jakobson and C. Schoepf. New York: Basic.

———. 1969. *The Raw and the Cooked.* Translated by J. and D. Weightman. New York: Harper and Row.

Leys, S. 1978. *Chinese Shadows.* New York: Penguin.

Lichtenwanger, N. A. 1970. "National Anthems." *Colliers Encyclopedia* 17:153. New York: Cromwell-Collier Education.

Liebes, T. 1988. "Cultural Differences in the Retelling of Television Fiction." *Critical Studies in Mass Communication* 5:277–92.

Lindley, M. 1980. "Composition." In *The New Grove Dictionary of Music and Musicians,* edited by S. Sadie, vol. 4, pp. 599–602. Macmillan: London.

Littlejohn, S. W. 1983. *Theories of Human Communication.* 2d ed. Belmont, Calif.: Wadsworth.

Loftus, E. F. 1980. *Memories Are Made of This: New Insights into the Workings of Human Memory.* Reading, Mass.: Addison-Wesley.

Loftus, E. F., and E. R. Loftus. 1980. "On the Permanence of Stored Information in the Human Brain." *American Psychologist* 35:409–20.

Lomax, A., ed. 1968. *Folk Song Style and Culture.* Washington, D.C.: AAAS.

Long, E. 1986. "Women, Reading, and Central Authority: Some Implications of the Audience Perspective in Cultural Studies." *American Quarterly* 38:591–612.

Lotman, J. 1977. *The Structure of the Artistic Text.* Ann Arbor: University of Michigan Press.

Lott, A. J., and B. E. Lott. 1961. "Group Cohesiveness, Communication Level, and Conformity." *Journal of Abnormal and Social Psychology* 62:408–12.

Louda, J. 1992. "New Symbols in Czechoslovakia." *Flag Bulletin* 30 (3): 73–77.

McCall, G. J., and J. L. Simmons. 1966. *Identities and Interaction.* New York: Free Press.

McCracken, J. 1958. *Representative Government in Ireland: 1918–1946.* London: Oxford University Press.

McFadden, R. 1986. *New York Times,* July 3, sec. 1, p. 1.

McGuire, W. J. 1985. "The Nature of Attitudes and Attitude Change." In *Handbook of Social Psychology,* 3d ed., edited by G. Lindzey and E. Aronson, 233–46. New York: Random House.

———. 1978. "An Information Processing Model of Advertising Effectiveness." In *Behavior and Management Sciences in Marketing,* edited by H. Davis and A. Silk, 156–80. New York: John Wiley.

McHugh, P. 1968. *Defining the Situation.* Indianapolis: Bobbs-Merrill.

McLeod, J. M., L. B. Becker, and J. E. Byrnes. 1974. "Another Look at the Agenda-Setting Function of the Press." *Communication Research* 1:134–65.

McLuhan, M. 1965. *Understanding Media: The Extensions of Man.* New York: McGraw-Hill.

McQuail, D. 1987. *Mass Communication Theory: An Introduction.* 2d ed. London: Sage.

McQuail, D., J. G. Blumler, and J. Brown. 1972. "The Television Audience: A Revised Perspective." In *Sociology of Mass Communication,* edited by D. McQuail, 135–65. Harmondsworth: Penguin.

Malefakis, E. 1985. "The Republic." In *Encyclopedia Americana* 22:444. Danbury, Conn.: Groller.

Mann, M. 1980. "Review Article: The Pre-Industrial State." *Political Studies* 28:297–304.

Mansfield, M. W., and K. Hale. 1986. "Uses and Perceptions of Political Television." In *New Perspectives on Political Advertising,* edited by L. L. Kaid, D. Nimmo, and K. R. Sanders, 268–92. Carbondale: Southern Illinois University Press.

Marcus, H., and R. B. Zajonc. 1985. "The Cognitive Perspective in Social Psychology." In *The Handbook of Social Psychology.* 3d ed., edited by G. Lindzey and E. Aronson, 137–230. New York: Random House.

Marr, Phoebe. 1985. *The Modern History of Iraq.* Boulder, Colo.: Westview.

Martorella, R. 1982. *The Sociology of Opera.* South Hadley, Mass.: J. R. Bergin.

———. 1989. *Corporate Art.* New Brunswick, N.J.: Rutgers University Press.

Martz, L., M. Kasindorf, and P. McKillop. 1986. *Newsweek* 100 (July 7): 14–18.

Marx, K. 1904. *A Contribution to the Critique of Political Economy.* Translated by N. I. Stone. Chicago: Charles H. Kerr.

———. 1910. *The Poverty of Philosophy.* Chicago: Charles H. Kerr.

———. 1978. "The German Ideology." In *The Marx-Engels Reader.* 2d ed., edited by R. C. Tucker, 146–202. New York: W. W. Norton.

Mascarenhas, A. 1986. *Bangladesh: A Legacy of Blood.* London: Hodder and Stiughton.

Mead, G. H. 1925. "The Genesis of the Self and Social Control." *International Journal of Ethics* 35:251–77.

———. 1934. *Mind, Self, and Society.* Chicago: University of Chicago Press.

Mead, R. 1980. "National Anthems." In *The New Grove Dictionary of Music and Musicians,* edited by S. Sadie, vol. 13, pp. 46–75. Macmillan: London.

Meltzer, L., G. H. Morris, and D. P. Hayes. 1971. "Interruption Outcomes and Vocal Amplification." *Journal of Personality and Social Psychology* 23 (2): 283–92.

Merritt, R. L. 1966. *Symbols of American Community: 1735–1775.* New Haven, Conn.: Yale University Press.

Metz, C. 1971. *Langage et Cinema.* Paris: Larousse.

Meyer, L. 1956. *Emotion and Meaning in Music.* Chicago: University of Chicago Press.

———. 1967. *Music, Emotion, and Meaning.* Chicago: University of Chicago Press.

Meyer, M., and W. L. Sherman. 1987. *The Course of Mexican History.* New York: Oxford University Press.

Mitchell, B. R. 1975. *European Historical Statistics 1750–1970.* London: Macmillan.

———. 1982. *International Historical Statistics for Africa and Asia.* New York: New York University Press.

Modell, Arnold H. 1969. *Object, Love, and Reality.* London: Hogarth Press.

Modelski, G. 1978. "The Long Cycle of Politics and the Nation-State." *Comparative Studies in Society and History* 20:14–35.

Moles, A. A. 1966. *Information Theory and Aesthetic Perception.* Translated by J. E. Cohen. Urbana: University of Illinois Press.

Molino, J. 1975. "Fait Musical et Semiologie de la Musique." *Musique en Jeu* 17:37–62.

Moore, S. F. 1975. "Epilogue: Uncertainties in Situations, Indeterminacies in Cultures." In *Symbol and Politics in Communal Ideologies,* edited by S. F. Moore and B. Myerhoff. Ithaca, N.Y.: Cornell University Press.

Moray, N. 1969. *Attention: Selective Processes in Vision and Hearing.* London: Hutchinson Educational.

Morgan, J., and P. Welton. 1992. *See What I Mean?* London: Edward Arnold.

Mosse, G. L. 1975. *The Nationalization of the Masses*. New York: Howard Fertig.

Mucha, L. 1985. *Webster's Concise Encyclopedia of Flags and Coats of Arms*. New York: Crescent Books.

Munsell, A. H. 1946. *A Color Notation*. Baltimore: Macbeth.

Nattiez, J. J. 1990. *Music and Discourse: Toward a Semiology of Music*. Translated by C. Abbate. Princeton, N.J.: Princeton University Press.

Needler, M. 1967. *Latin America in Perspective*. Princeton, N.J.: Princeton University Press.

Nettl, P. 1967. *National Anthems*. 2d ed. Translated by A. Gode. New York: Frederich Ungar.

Norman, D. A., and D. G. Bobrow. 1975. "On the Role of Active Memory Processes in Perception and Cognition." In *The Structure of Human Memory*, edited by Cofer, 114–32. San Francisco: Freeman.

O'Connor, J. J. 1991. "By Any Name, Roseanne Is Roseanne Is Roseanne." *New York Times*, August 18, Arts and Leisure sec., p. 27.

Palmer, L. F., Jr. 1970. "Black America's Other National Anthem." *Chicago Daily News*, August 4, 1970, pp. 26–27.

Palmgreen, P., and J. D. Rayburn. 1985. "An Expectancy-Value Approach to Media Gratifications." In *Media Gratification Research*, edited by K. E. Rosengren, 61–72. Beverly Hills, Calif.: Sage.

Peaslee, A. J. 1965. *Constitutions of Nations*. 3d. ed. The Hague: M. Nijhoff.

Pedersen, C. 1971. *The International Flag Book in Color*. New York: William Morrow.

Peirce, C. S. 1931–35. *The Collected Papers of Charles Sanders Peirce*. Vols. 1–6, edited by C. Hartshorne and P. Weiss. Cambridge: Harvard University Press.

Peterson, R. A. 1979. "Revitalizing the Culture Concept." *Annual Review of Sociology* 5:137–66.

Petrie, C. 1971. *King Charles III of Spain*. New York: Day.

Piggott, H. E. 1937. *Songs That Made History*. London: Oxford University Press.

Plascov, A. 1982. *Modernization, Political Development, and Stability*. Aldershot: Gower.

Prieto, L. 1975. *Etudes de Linguistique et de Semiologie Generales*. Geneva: Librarie Droz.

Quindlen, A. 1986. *New York Times*, May 18, vol. 1, pt. 2, p. 58.

Radway, J. 1984. *Reading the Romance: Women, Patriarchy, and Popular Culture*. Chapel Hill: University of North Carolina Press.

Ramirez, F. 1987. "Global Changes, World Myths, and the Demise of Cultural Gender: Implications for the United States." In *America's Changing Role in the World System*, edited by T. Boswell and A. Bergesen, 257–74. New York: Praeger.

Ray, J. 1983. "The 'World System' and the Global Political System: A Crucial Relationship?" In *Foreign Policy in the Modern World-System*, edited by P. McGowen and C. Kegley, 13–34. Beverly Hills, Calif.: Sage.

Rayburn, J. D., and P. Palmgreen. 1984. "Merging Uses and Gratification and Expectancy-Value Theory." *Communication Research* 11:537–62.

Reed, W. L., and M. J. Bristow. 1987. *National Anthems of the World*. 3d ed. New York: Arco.

Riding, A. 1992. "Aux Barricades! La Marseillaise Is Besieged," *New York Times*, March 5, sec. A, p. 1.

Riffaterre, M. 1978. *Semiotics of Poetry*. Bloomington: Indiana University Press.

Rimmer, T. 1986. "Visual Form Complexity and TV News." *Communication Research* 13 (2): 221–38.

Ringer, A. 1980. "Melody." In *The New Grove Dictionary of Music and Musicians,* edited by S. Sadie, vol. 12, pp. 118–27. Macmillan: London.

Roberts, A. 1976. *A History of Zambia.* New York: Africana.

Rogers, D. B., and A. Schumacher. 1983. "Effects of Individual Differences on Dyadic Conversational Strategies." *Journal of Personality and Social Psychology* 45:700–705.

Rogers, E. 1972. *Diffusion of Innovations.* New York: Free Press.

Rosa, E., and A. Mazur. 1979. "Incipient Status in Small Groups." *Social Forces* 58:18–37.

Ross, L. 1977. "The Intuitive Psychologist and His Shortcomings: Distortions in the Attribution Process." In *Advances in Experimental Social Psychology,* edited by L. Berkowitz, vol. 10, pp. 173–220. New York: Academic Press.

Rothschild, M. L., E. Thorson, B. Reeves, J. E. Hirsch, and R. Goldstein. 1986. "EEG Activity and the Processing of Television Commercials." *Communication Research* 13:2:182–220.

Ruggie, J. G. 1983. "Continuity and Transformation in the World Polity: Toward a Neo-realist Synthesis." *World Politics* 36:261–85.

Sachs, C. 1963. *World History of Dance.* New York: Norton.

de Saussure, F. [1915] 1959. *Course in General Linguistics.* Translated by W. Baskin. New York: Philosophical Library.

Schegloff, E. 1968. "Sequencing in Conversational Openings." *American Anthropologist* 70:1075–95.

Schlesinger, P. 1993. "Wishful Thinking: Culture, Politics, Media, and Collective Identities in Europe." *Journal of Communication* 43 (2): 6–17.

———. 1994. "Europe Through a Glass Darkly." *Daedalus* 123 (2): 25–52.

Schudson, M. 1989. "How Culture Works: Perspectives from Media Studies on the Efficacy of Symbols." *Theory and Society* 18:153–80.

Schutz, A. 1951. "Making Music Together: A Study in Social Relationship." *Social Research* 18:76–97.

Schutz, A., and T. Luckmann. 1973. *The Structures of the Life-World.* Evanston, Ill.: Northwestern University Press.

———. 1982. *Life Forms and Meaning Structure.* Translated by H. Wagner. London: Routledge.

Schwartz, B. 1987. *George Washington: The Making of an American Symbol.* Ithaca, N.Y.: Cornell University Press.

Sebeok, T. 1974. "Semiotics: A Survey of the State of the Art." In *Current Trends in Linguistics,* edited by T. Sebeok, vol. 12, pp. 211–64. The Hague: Mouton.

Sewell, W. H., Jr. 1992. "A Theory of Structure: Duality, Agency, and Transformation." *American Journal of Sociology* 98 (1): 1–29.

Shannon, C. E. 1951. "Prediction and Entropy of Printed English." *Bell System Technical Journal* 30:50–64.

Shannon, T. R. 1989. *An Introduction to the World-System Perspective.* Boulder, Colo.: Westview.

Shaw, D. L., and M. E. McCombs. 1977. *The Emergence of American Political Issues: The Agenda Setting Function of the Press.* St. Paul: West.

Siegmeister, E. 1965. *Harmony and Melody.* Vols. 1 and 2. Belmont, Calif.: Wadsworth.

Simmel, G. 1955. *Conflict.* Translated by Kurt H. Wolff. Glencoe, N.Y.: Free Press.

Skocpol T. 1977. "Wallerstein's World Capitalist System: A Theoretical and Historical Critique." *American Journal of Sociology* 82:1075–90.

Slade, B. 1975. *Same Time Next Year.* London: Samuel French.

Sless, D. 1986. *In Search of Semiotics.* Totowa, N.J.: Barnes and Noble.

Smelser, N. 1966. "The Modernization of Social Relations." In *Modernization: The Dynamics of Growth,* edited by M. Weiner, 110–21. New York: Basic.

Smith, A. D. 1986. *The Ethnic Origins of Nations.* London: Basil Blackwell.

Smith, E. E., and D. L. Medin. 1981. *Categories and Concepts.* Cambridge: Harvard University Press.

Smith, W. 1975. *Flags Through the Ages and Across the World.* New York: McGraw-Hill.

———. 1988. "New Flags: Ethiopia." *Flag Bulletin* 27 (1): 3–13.

———. 1990. "Recent Flags: Haiti." *Flag Bulletin* 29 (4): 127–48.

———. 1991. "New Flags: Iraq." *Flag Bulletin* 30 (2): 42–49.

———. 1992. "Uzbekistan." *Flag Bulletin* 31 (6): 242–47.

Snyder, D., and E. L. Kick. 1979. "Structural Position in the World-System and Economic Growth: 1955–1970." *American Journal of Sociology* 84 (5): 1109–26.

Sousa, J. P. 1890. *National Patriotic and Typical Airs of All Lands.* New York: Da Capo Press.

Sokal, R. R. 1977. "Clustering and Classification: Background and Current Directions." In *Classification and Clustering,* edited by J. Van Ryzin, 1–15. New York: Academic Press.

Spillman, L. 1994. "Imagining Community and Hoping for Recognition: Bicentennial Celebrations in 1976 and 1988." *Qualitative Sociology* 17 (1): 3–28.

Srull, T. K. 1981. "Person Memory: Some Tests of Associative Storage and Retrieval Models." *Journal of Experimental Psychology* 7 (6): 440–63.

Stanner, W. E. H. 1967. "Reflections on Durkheim and Aboriginal Religion." In *Social Organization,* edited by M. Freedman, 217–40. London: Frank Cass.

The Statesman's Yearbook. Vols. 1–130. New York: St. Martin's Press.

Statistical Abstracts of the United States. 1988. 108th ed. Washington, D.C.: U.S. Dept. of Commerce.

Stein, H. F. 1987. *Developmental Time, Cultural Space.* Norman: University of Oklahoma Press.

Steinfatt, T. M. 1989. "Linguistic Relativity: Toward a Broader View." In *Language, Communication, and Culture,* edited by S. Ting-Toomey and F. Korzenny, 35–78. Newbury Park, Calif.: Sage.

Stockton, J. 1983. *Designer's Guide to Color.* San Francisco: Chronicle Books.

Stryker, S. 1980. *Symbolic Interactionism: A Social Structural Version.* Palo Alto, Calif.: Benjamin/Cummings.

———. 1987. "Identity Theory: Developments and Extensions." In *Self and Identity,* edited by K. Yardley and T Honess, 89–103. New York: John Wiley and Sons.

Swanson, G. 1960. *The Birth of the Gods.* Ann Arbor: University of Michigan Press.

———. 1967. *Religion and Regime.* Ann Arbor: University of Michigan Press.

Swidler, A. 1986. "Culture in Action: Symbols and Strategies." *American Sociological Review* 51 (2): 273–86.

Tajfel, H. 1981. *Human Groups and Social Categories.* Cambridge: Cambridge University Press.

Talocci, M. 1977. *Guide to the Flags of the World.* New York: Quill.

Tambiah, S. J. 1986. *Sri Lanka: Ethnic Fratricide and the Dismantling of Democracy.* Chicago: University of Chicago Press.

Tannen, D. 1990. *You Just Don't Understand: Women and Men in Conversation.* Boston: William Morrow.

Templer, Sir W. 1972. *Observations Upon the United Province of the Netherlands.* Oxford: Clarendon Press.

Thomas, G. M., and J. Meyer. 1984. "The Expansion of the State." *Annual Review of Sociology* 10:461–82.

Thompson, W. 1983. "Introduction: World System with and Without the Hyphen." In *Contending Approaches to World-System Analysis,* edited by W. Thompson, 7–26. Beverly Hills, Calif.: Sage.

Toffler, A. 1964. *The Culture Consumers.* New York: St. Martin's Press.

Toland, J. 1976. *Adolf Hitler.* New York: Ballantine.

Tonnies, F. [1887] 1957. *Community and Society.* Translated by Charles A. Loomis. East Lansing: Michigan State University Press.

Traetteberg, H. 1978. "The History of the Flags of Norway." *Flag Bulletin* 17 (3): 73–82.

Trimboli, C., and Walker, M. B. 1982. "Smooth Transitions in Conversational Turn-taking: Implication for Theory." *Journal of Personality and Social Psychology* 117:305–6.

Tromel-plotz, S. 1981. "Review Article: The Languages of Oppression." *Journal of Pragmatics* 5:67–80.

Vygotsky, L. 1962. *Thought and Language.* Cambridge: MIT Press.

Wagner-Pacifici, R., and B. Schwartz. 1991. "The Vietnam Veterans Memorial: Commemorating a Difficult Past." *American Journal of Sociology* 97 (2): 376–420.

Wallerstein, I. 1974. *The Modern World-System.* Vol. 2. New York: Academic Press.

———. 1975. "The Present State of the Debate on World Inequality." In *World Inequality,* edited by I. Wallerstein, 9–29. Quebec: Black Rose Books.

———. 1979. *The Capitalist World Economy.* Cambridge: Cambridge University Press.

———. 1980. *The Modern World-System.* Vol. 3. New York: Academic Press.

———. 1983. "An Agenda for World-Systems Analysis." In *Contending Approaches to World-System Analysis,* edited by W. Thompson, 299–308. Beverly Hills, Calif.: Sage.

———. 1984. "Patterns and Prospectives of the Capitalist World Economy." *Contemporary Marxism* 9:59–70.

Walzer, M. 1967. "The Facsimile Fallacy." *American Review of Canadian Studies* 12 (2): 82–86.

Ward, R. 1977. *The History of Australia.* New York: Harper and Row.

Watkins, S. 1991. *From Provinces into Nations.* Princeton, N.J.: Princeton University Press.

Weaver, W. 1928. "Attention and Clearness in the perception of Figure and Ground." *American Journal of Psychology* 40:51–74.

Weimann, J. M. 1985. "Interpersonal Control and Regulation in Conversation." In *Sequence and Pattern in Communication Behavior,* edited by R. L. Street Jr. and J. N. Cappella, 85–102. London: Edward Arnold.

Weitman, S. 1973. "National Flags." *Semiotica* 8 (4): 328–67.

Wellman, B. 1983. "Network Analysis: Some Basic Principles." In *Sociological Theory,* edited by R. Collins, 155–200.

Westergaard, P. 1975. *An Introduction to Tonal Theory.* New York: W. W. Norton.

Wheeler, D. 1978. *Republican Portugal: A Political History, 1910–1926.* Madison: University of Wisconsin Press.

White, H. C. 1992. *Identity and Control.* Princeton, N.J.: Princeton University Press.

White, H. C., and C. A. White. 1965. *Canvases and Careers.* New York: John Wiley and Sons.

Wiley, N. 1979. "Notes on Self-Genesis: From Me to We to I." *Studies in Symbolic Interaction* 2:87–105.

Williams, R. 1990. *Hierarchical Structures and Social Value: The Creation of Black and Irish Identities in the United States.* Cambridge: Cambridge University Press.

Wiltz, J. E. 1973. *The Search for Identity: Modern American History.* Philadelphia: J. B. Lippincott.

Worldmark Encyclopedia. 1984. 6th ed. Vols. 2–5. New York: Worldmark Press.

Wright, Q. 1965. *A Study of War.* 2d ed. Chicago: University of Chicago Press.

Wuthnow, R. 1980a. "The World Economy and the Institutionalization of Science in Seventeenth-Century Europe." In *Studies of the Modern World-System,* edited by A. Bergesen, 25–56. New York: Academic Press.

———. 1980b. "World Order and Religious Movements." In *Studies of the Modern World-System,* edited by A. Bergesen, 57–76. New York: Academic Press.

———. 1987. "America's Legitimating Myths: Continuity and Crisis." In *America's Changing Role in the World System,* edited by T. Boswell and A. Bergesen, 235–56. New York: Praeger.

Yeoman, R. S. 1974. *Current Coins of the World.* Racine, Wisc.: Western Publishing.

Youngblood, J. 1958. "Style As Information." *Journal of Music Theory* 2 (1): 23–35.

Zelinsky, W. 1988. *Nation into State.* Chapel Hill: University of North Carolina Press.

Zerubavel, E. 1985. *The Seven Day Circle: The History and Meaning of the Week.* New York: Free Press.

———. 1987. "The Language of Time: Toward a Semiotics of Temporality." *Sociological Quarterly* 28 (3): 343–56.

———. 1991. *The Fine Line.* New York: Free Press.

Zikmund, Joseph, II. 1969. "National Anthems As Political Symbols." *Australian Journal of Politics and History* 15 (3): 73–80.

Zimbardo, P. G., and M. R. Leippre. 1991. *Attitude Change and Social Influence.* Philadelphia: Temple University Press.

Zimbardo, P. G., E. Ebbesen, and Maslach, C. 1977. *Influencing Attitudes and Changing Behavior.* Reading, Mass.: Addison Wesley.

Zolberg, A. 1983. "'World' and 'System': A Misalliance." In *Contending Approaches to World-System Analysis,* edited by W. Thompson, 269–90. Beverly Hills, Calif.: Sage.

INDEX

ABOUT THE AUTHOR

Karen A. Cerulo is an assistant professor of sociology at Rutgers University. Her research explores the social foundations of symbolic communication systems, with a special emphasis on nonverbal systems and their use in the projection of identity. She has published many articles in such journals as the *American Sociological Review, Social Forces, Sociological Forum, Research in Political Sociology, Social Science Research, Law and Policy,* and *Communication Research.* Currently, she is writing a book on informational structure and its effects on the perception of violence.